Marek J. Murawski
Asen Atanasov

Messerschmitt Bf 109
Early Versions

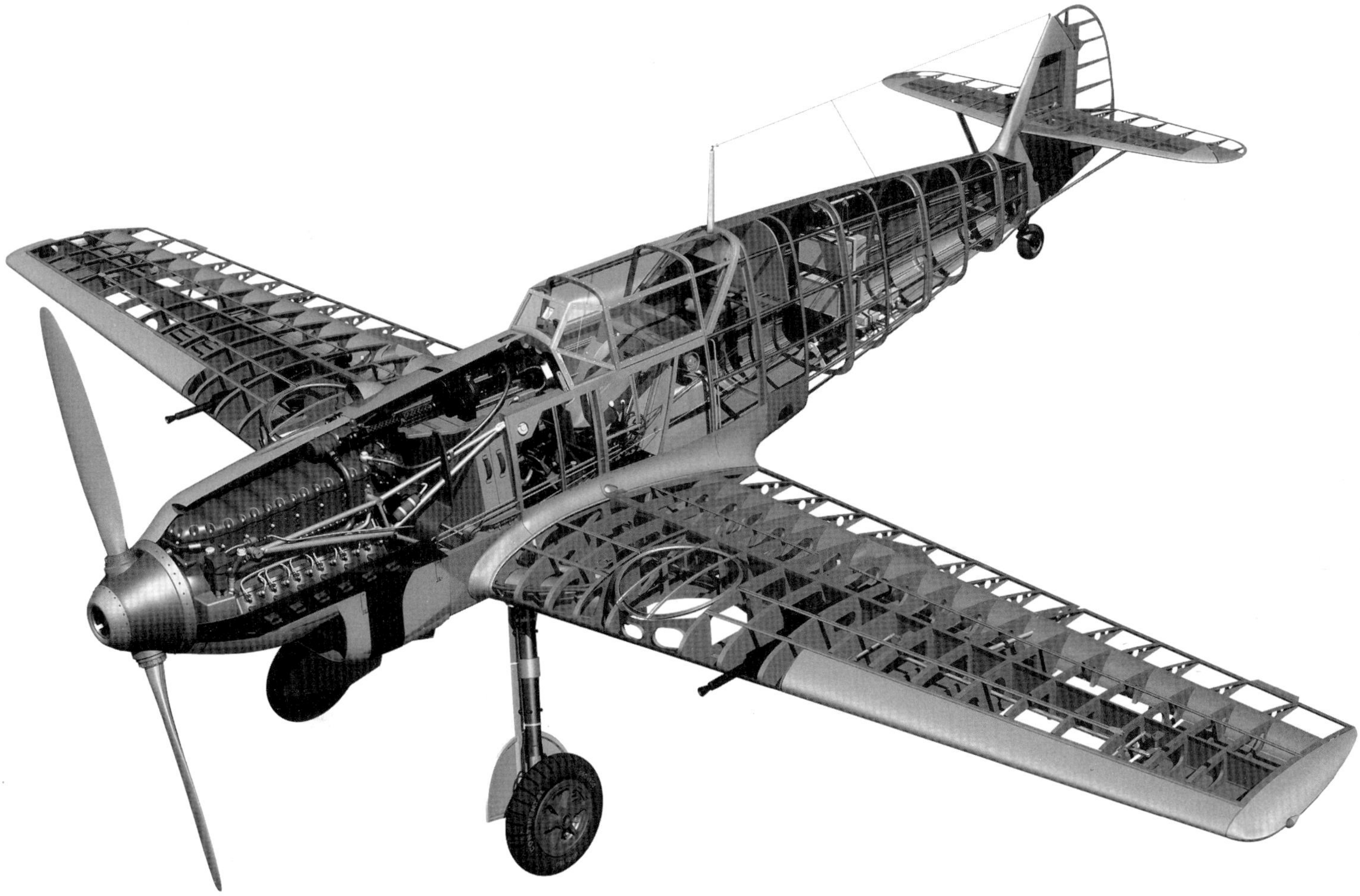

MORE FROM KAGERO

www.shop.kagero.pl • phone + 4881 5012105

The authors want to thank Mr. Mariusz Łukasik for help given during preparing the publication.

Messerschmitt Bf 109 Early Versions • Marek J. Murawski, Asen Atanasov • First edition • LUBLIN 2015

© All rights reserved. With the exception of quoting brief passages for the purposes of review, no part of this publication may be reproduced without prior written permission from the Publisher. Nazwa serii zastrzeżona w UP RP • **ISBN 978-83-64596-38-4**

Editing: **Marek J. Murawski** • Translation: **Piotr Kolasa** • Visualisation 3D: **Asen Atanasov, Bolek Rykowski** • Scale drawings: **Mariusz Łukasik**
• Photos: **Marek J. Murawski's archive** • Color profiles: **Janusz Światłoń** • Design: **KAGERO STUDIO, Łukasz Maj**

Oficyna Wydawnicza KAGERO
Akacjowa 100, Turka, os. Borek, 20-258 Lublin 62, Poland, phone/fax: (+48) 81 501 21 05
www.kagero.pl • e-mail: kagero@kagero.pl, marketing@kagero.pl
w w w . k a g e r o . p l
Distribution: Oficyna Wydawnicza KAGERO

Messerschmitt Bf 109 B-1 featuring a metal VDM propeller and equipped with the FuG VII radio. The antenna consisted of three wires running from the antenna mast to the tips of the vertical fin and horizontal stabilizers.

Messerschmitt Bf 109 A-D

The enemy aircraft were growing ever bigger, almost filling my windshield. I could now clearly see the wide, red fuselage bands. I attacked from above slicing through the formation at the highest possible speed before pulling up sharply to target the second flight of the bomber stream. Within seconds my presence was detected and I was greeted with a wild volley of bullets. Hang on now, don't panic, hold your fire until you're really close! The aircraft on the right is growing in my sights. When its starboard engine completely fills the gun sight I move my fingers to the gun triggers. At just 20 meters the three guns begin to rattle. There is a bright flash of fire as I haul on the stick and stand my aircraft on the tail. In the corner of my eye I catch a glimpse of the enemy bomber exploding in mid-air and falling to the ground in hundreds of pieces. I am completely calm and composed, which clearly cannot be said of the flight leader: having lost his cool he drops the nose and runs for the deck in a mad dash. I quickly catch up with his flight and position myself behind his left wingman. As the white trails of tracer rounds are streaking past my aircraft, I again put my machine guns to work. There is a flash of fire followed by a loud explosion and within seconds I'm flying through the spot where the enemy bomber used to be just moments ago: now it's just a cloud of smoke and burning debris. It's just me and the flight leader then. Within seconds his machine too is engulfed in a ball of fire and disintegrates in the air. The remaining bombers are bogging out in a loose formation. I decide to give chase targeting the lead flight. Taking a quick look around I spot Rata fighters setting up for an attack, hell-bent on knocking me out of the sky. I also notice three 109s whose pilots have already detected the threat and are on their way to join the fight. "The leader has to go down" – the thought replays itself in my head like a mantra. I can now clearly see the lead flight at my 12 o'clock, still maintaining a fairly tight formation. The only way to get to the leader is to squeeze right between his two wingmen. As I hurl my aircraft between the two enemy machines, just barely clearing their wingtips, the gunners open up on me. I can see the blue muzzle flashes and hear the ominous rattling sound of bullets hitting the fuselage of my fighter. It is too little, too late, though: my machine guns also begin to talk and seconds later the enemy bomber is falling out of the sky like a comet trailing a tail of fire and thick smoke. There goes number four of the day.

Then, out of the blue, my aircraft is violently jolted by a tremendous impact. The rudder is stuck and the cockpit is quickly filling with thick smoke. Looks like it is me now who is about to go down like a falling comet. It was not to be, though: I needed that little bit of luck and my prayers were answered. The Messerschmitt was still controllable. I calmed down and took another look around to take stock of the situation. The mad air battle was still raging be-

Origins and history of the design

Messerschmitt Bf 109 B-1, 6•52 from 2.J/88 flying a combat air patrol over the frontlines.

hind me. Taking a glance at the engine instruments I noticed the oil temperature was rapidly rising. The engine's oil system was clearly damaged. I set course for the home plate when suddenly there was a flash of fire just behind the cockpit and I heard a loud bang. I immediately went into a steep climb followed by a wingover and a run for the deck. As I leveled off just meters above the ground and looked back to check my six. There was nothing there except a trail of thick, black smoke. I stayed as low as I could skimming over the ground at just ten meters. Then, right in front of me, there was the Teruel church tower. I knew I was crossing the frontline when small arms fire erupted on the ground. I made it! Now it was just a matter of finding a suitable place for a forced landing. I soon spotted a fairly large field and put the Messerschmitt down. The rollout was uneventful and soon the machine came to a halt. Now the stress of combat finally got me – I was frozen in my seat, completely unable to climb out of the cockpit. I looked around: high above I could still see trails of black smoke crisscrossing the sky: one, two, five, nine. Feeling extremely exhausted, with my hands shaking wildly, I finally managed to extract myself from the cockpit. When I looked at my aircraft I couldn't believe my eyes: it was riddled with bullet holes! The rudder control cables were severed, oil and fuel tanks completely shot up. So were the wings and the canopy. Theoretically, I was a dead man[1].

Origins and history of the design

The Messerschmitt Bf 109, also known as the Me 109, is without a doubt one of the most remarkable fighter designs in the history of military aviation. Built in the record-breaking numbers (over 32 000 examples) it was one of the iconic symbols of the Luftwaffe's might. The Bf 109 produced not only German top-scoring aces of the war, including Erich Hartmann (352 kills), Gerhard Barkhorn (301 victories), Günther Rall (275 kills), Hans-Joachim Marseille (158 kills), Werner Mölders (114 victories) or Adolf Galland with 104 confirmed kills, but also fighter aces from other nations: Finland's Ilmari Juutilainen (94 kills, including 58 in Bf 109s), Hans Wind (75 victories, 36 in Bf 109s) and Eino Luukkanen (56 air-to-air kills, of which 39 were scored at the controls of the Bf 109); Hungarians - Dezsö Szentgyörgyi (31 kills) and György Debrödy (26 victories); Croatians - Mato Dukovac with 44 kills and Cvitan Galic (38 air-to-air victories); Slovaks - Ján Režnák (32 kills) and Izidor Kovárik (28 victories); Romanians - Alexandru Serbanescu (49 kills) and Constantin Cantacuzino (43 air-to-air victories); Bulgarians - Stojan Iliev Stojanov (5 kills) and Petar Angelov Bochev (5 victories), or Italian aces Adriano Visconti di

Messerschmitt Bf 109 B-1, 6•53 from 2.J/88 of the Condor Legion.

Origins and history of the design

Lampugnano (26 kills) and Teresio Martinoli with 23 aerial victories.

The Messerschmitt Bf 109, similarly to its nemesis the Supermarine Spitfire, was the aircraft that already at its inception set new trends in the development of fighter designs. It was one of the first mass produced single-seat, all-metal monoplanes with retractable landing gear and fully enclosed cockpit. For ten years, from the start of production in 1935 until the war's end in 1945, it remained one of the world's most potent fighter aircraft.

The Bf 109 will always be associated with its chief designer Wilhelm Emil Messerschmitt (better known as Willy). Born in Frankfurt am Main on June 28, 1898 Willy moved with his family to Bamberg in 1906 where his father was to take over his brother's wine merchant's business. Willy began to build his first rubber-powered models when he was only 12 years old. A year later he met the pioneer of German glider design, Friedrich Harth, who recognized the young Messerschmitt's talents and invited him to join his design team. Shortly before the outbreak of World War I they finished work on the S 4 glider.

Soon thereafter Friedrich Harth was drafted into the army, while the S 4 glider, stored in a shed on Heidelstein mountain near Bischofsheim, was vandalized. The 16 year-old Messerschmitt used the materials from Harth's workshop to build his first full-fledged flying machine – the Harth-Messerschmitt S 5 glider. Friedrich Harth flight tested the glider in early September 1915 during his short leave from the service. Harth made several flights ranging from 80 to 300 meters, but was not overly impressed with the machine's performance. Shortly thereafter he designed and built its successor, the S 6.

In the meantime Messerschmitt passed his final high school exams in 1917 at Oberrealschule Nürnberg and was promptly drafted into active military service. Between June 5 and November 8 he underwent basic training at Fliegerpionierabteilung Milbertshofen. Willy continued working closely with Harth, who by that time had finished work on the S 7 glider, followed by the S 8 design that was ready soon after the war's end.

Between 1918 and 1923 Willy Messerschmitt studied engineering at Technische Hochschule München. It was during that time that he set up his first company: *Later on, in 1923, 25 year-old Messerschmitt enlisted his brother's help to set up the 'Flugzeugbau Messerschmitt Bamberg', a company specializing in aeronautical design and engineering. It was in a primitive shed at 41 Lange Straße that Willy built the first Messerschmitt gliders. Originally the business was underwritten by Willy's brother Ferdinand. Among the first original Messerschmitt's designs were the S 14 glider (which was also Willy's engineering degree project) and the S 15 powered glider*[2].

The S 14 design enjoyed some success at the Rhön glider competition held on August 20, 1923. Messerschmitt's glider came in first in the maximum flight ceiling category and second in the flight endurance event. The S 15 was a high wing, all plywood design powered by the 10 HP Victoria engine. The machine was ready in the early spring of 1924. Within the next few months Messerschmitt designed and built two more powered gliders – the S 16a and S 16b. The machines also took part in the Rhön competition, but did not fare well due to a series of engine malfunctions. The man who stole the show and took virtually all prizes was Ernst Udet at the controls of his famous "Kolibri".

Discouraged by the lackluster performance of his powered gliders, Messerschmitt turned his attention to the design of light aircraft. His first machine, designated M 17[3], was a two-seat, all-wood light aircraft that featured cantilevered high wing and a conventional puller propeller. Messerschmitt built seven examples of the aircraft powered by various types of powerplants ranging from 24 to 28 HP.

Condor Legion ground crews posing in front of one of their Bf 109s at León airfield. Notice seven victory bars on the fighter's fin.

Origins and history of the design

Prof. Willy Messerschmitt and Hubert Bauer photographed in Augsburg in 1938.

One of the M 17s, W.Nr. 24, D-612, was flown by Carl Croneiß during the *Internationaler Flugwettbewerb* held in Schleißheim between September 12 and 14, 1925. The aircraft won the maximum flight ceiling and speed events and came in fifth in the relay race, which earned Messerschmitt 6 750 marks in prize money.

Messerschmitt scored another success when his M 17 W Nr. 26, D-612 was entered in the light aircraft competition held from May 31 to June 14, 1925. Flown by E. von Cont the aircraft came in first in the overall flight performance category.

The success of Messerschmitt's designs did not go unnoticed. Among those who took interest in the work of the young engineer was Theo Croneiß, the founder of Nordbayerischer Verkehrsflug GmbH Fürth, who was looking for a light passenger aircraft for his company. The four-seat machine was to be based on the M 17 design. With the maximum unit price set at 25 000 marks the aircraft would cost a third of similar planes in use at that time.

The new aircraft, designated M 18a, would be an all-metal design powered by a seven cylinder Siemens-Halske Sh 11 engine developing 80 HP. The first prototype was flight tested by Theo Croneiß himself on June 15, 1926. Following the completion of the flight test program the machine received its registration – D-947. Soon to follow was the M 18b - a modified version of the aircraft designed to carry five passengers.

At around that time the assets of the bankrupt Udet-Flugzeugbau GmbH were taken over by the newly established Bayerische Flugzeugwerke (BFW). Soon the new company would expand and acquire grounds and production buildings of the former Rumpler-Werke AG in Augsburg. Since the Reich's Ministry of Economy (*Reichswirtschaftsministerium*) regulations did not allow subsidizing two aviation companies based in Bavaria, the concerns were merged. The new entity, Flugzeugwerke AG Augsburg, would soon launch the production of aircraft designed by none other than Willy Messerschmitt. The official contract was signed by Messerschmitt on September 8, 1927.

The first aircraft to be built by the new company was an all-metal BFW M 20, which was designed to carry ten passengers and two crew. Deutsche Luft Hansa Berlin ordered two prototypes of the new aircraft. The first one, M 20 W.Nr. 371, was ready by February 26, 1928 and took off for its first flight on the same day. The flight went well until a skin panel separated from one of the wings, just aft of the leading edge section. Hans Hackmack, who was at the controls during the ill-fated flight, misjudged the situation, panicked and tried to bail out of the aircraft that flew at just eighty meters above the ground. Hackmack was killed on impact with the ground and the aircraft was completely destroyed.

Following the crash of the first prototype the Deutsche Luft Hansa order was cancelled. Nonetheless, the BFW finished work on the second machine and flight tested it on August 3, 1928. Flown by Theo Croneiß himself the aircraft performed so well that Deutsche Luft Hansa decided to order two BFW M 20as powered by 700 HP BMW VI powerplants. A year later the company submitted an order for two more aircraft, this time the modified M 20b version.

Origins and history of the design

In 1928 the BFW Augsburg was to be floated. Willy Messerschmitt feared that he might lose his independence as a designer should an external investor become a majority shareholder. He therefore began to look for a potential business partner. Messerschmitt eventually managed to convince the Stromeyer-Raulino family from Bramberg to invest 330 000 marks in the company's stock, while he himself came up with 70 000 marks, the proceeds from the sale of his old company's assets to the BFW AG.

In the late 1920s the BFW built a number of prototype designs, including the M 21 trainer, twin engine M 22 and a light sports trainer M 23. The 1930s began on a sour note: on October 6, 1930 one of the M 20bs, W.Nr. 443, D-1930, crashed on approach to Dresden during a scheduled Berlin –Vienna flight. Eight people perished in the crash. Several months later, on April 4, 1931, another M 20b (W.Nr. 442, D-1928) crashed during a Muskau – Görlitz flight, killing the pilot and radio operator. Four of the eight Reichswehr officers traveling onboard the ill-fated plane suffered minor injuries.

The incidents resulted in the cancellation of Deutsche Luft Hansa order for two more M 20b2 aircraft and brought about an open conflict between Willy Messerschmitt and Luft Hansa's director general, Erhard Milch. After Milch had become the secretary of state at the Reich's Aviation Ministry, the animosity between the two men flared up again and would continue until the war's end in 1945.

In the meantime the BFW lost ten more aircraft orders, which sealed the struggling company's fate. On June 1, 1931 the BFW management officially filed for bankruptcy at Augsburg court.

In those dire circumstances Willy Messerschmitt decided to return to his old company Messerschmitt-Flugzeugbau GmbH and continue the design work.

Not long thereafter several German aeronautical companies (including Messerschmitt-Flugzeugbau GmbH) received invitations to deliver six aircraft that would represent the country[4] during the 1932 edition of an international aviation event, known in Germany as Europa-Rundflug[5]. Messerschmitt's contribution was a super modern design designated M 29 – a low-wing aircraft with a fully enclosed cockpit, whose graceful lines resembled those of a modern fighter. On April 13, 1932

An advertisement of the M 23 light trainer aircraft.

The M 17 was Willy Messerschmitt's first design. Seven examples of this all-wooden two-seater were built.

Origins and history of the design

The first Bf 109 prototype – V1. Notice the civilian registration on the wings and national markings on the vertical stabilizer.

Messerschmitt Bf 109 V1, W.Nr. 758, D-IABI, at Haunstetten airfield.

the machine was test flown by Erwin Aichele. The tests revealed superb flight characteristics of Messerschmitt's new design: it had a top speed of 250 kph, a time to climb to 1 000 m of just 3 minutes and the operating ceiling of 6 000 m. Unfortunately, the aircraft suffered two accidents on August 8 and 9, 1932, which effectively ended its chances of entering the competition. The event's top prize went to a Polish pilot Franciszek Żwirko flying the RWD-6 aircraft.

Messerschmitt continued work on other designs, although several of them (M 30, M 31, M 32, M 33 and M 34) did not proceed beyond the drawing board[6]. In the meantime Peter Rakan Kokothaki took over as the president of the BFW AG, which was still under bankruptcy protection. Kokothaki worked closely with the company's administrator to find ways of ending the concern's financial problems. As a result an agreement was reached with the company's key creditors, which was officially sanctioned by the ruling of Augsburg district court dated April 27, 1933. Based on the court's decision the company was cleared to re-start its operations on May 1, 1933. During the same period of time

Messerschmitt designed another light trainer/aerobatic aircraft, the M 35. Fifteen examples of this low-wing, cantilevered design were built. The aircraft was a two-seater of mixed construction and featured a tapered wing.

After the Nazi's rise to power in 1933 Germany saw a gradual process of restoration of its independence, which until then had been severely curtailed by the Treaty of Versailles. One of the first priorities of the newly established government was the rebuilding of Germany's armed forces, which had been previously limited to 100 000 members of the Reichswehr. The air force, armored units and the submarine fleet were abolished altogether. In September 1933 the Reich's Aviation Ministry (*Reichsluftfahrtministerium* – RLM) submitted a requirement for six prototypes of a four-seat "liaison" aircraft (known in the German nomenclature as *Reiseflugzeug*. The order was placed with Bayerischen Flugzeugwerke and the new aircraft was to be ready for the 1934 edition of the Challenge event. Similar orders went to Fieseler (Fi 97) and Klemm (Kl 36). The companies were given only nine months to design, build and flight test the new aircraft.

Origins and history of the design

Willy Messerschmitt personally coordinated the work on the new design, supported by Robert Luser as the project director, Richard Bauer as the design office chief and the head of flight test department, Hubert Bauer. The new aircraft was a cantilevered low-wing design with retractable landing gear. The single-spar wing featured all-metal skin, automatic leading edge slats and fowler flaps. The wing sections could be folded by removing a bolt in the wing's center box. The gear retracted outwards into the wing bays, activated by a manual worm drive gearbox. The aircraft featured a conventional, fixed tail wheel.

The first prototype of the Bf 108 A V-1 (D-IBUM) was flight tested in June 1934 (at that time the aircraft was equipped with a wooden wing). Within the next month the remaining five aircraft were ready, with the last example making its first flight on July 28, 1934. Shortly after the German pilots had begun their workups in preparation for the upcoming competition, a tragedy struck. One of the Bf 108 A V-1s hit a tree during a slow flight practice and crashed, killing its pilot Freiherr Wolf von Dungern[7]. In the aftermath of the accident manager of the German team, Theo Osterkamp, demanded that the Bf 108 be withdrawn from the competition. The RLM representative Maj. Fritz Loeb ignored Osterkamp's pleas and four Bf 108s did took part in the event (Bf 108 A V-3, W.Nr. 697, D-IZAN, Bf 108 A V-4, W.Nr. 698, D-IGAK, Bf 108 A V-5, W.Nr. 699, D-IMUT and Bf 108 A V-6, W.Nr. 700, D-IJES[8]).

Because the rules of the Challenge favored the aircraft capable of performing various slow-speed maneuvers, the winner of the event was a Polish flyer Jerzy Bajan at the controls of the RWD-9. Theo Osterkamp flying the Bf 108 A V-5 (W.Nr. 699, D-IMUT) did win the top speed event hands down (291 kph over a 300 km course), but that was not enough to reach for the competition's top prize. Eventually Osterkamp came in fifth overall, with Werner Junck just behind him in the sixth place. Another German pilot, Carl Francke, finished sixteenth, while Otto Brindlinger was disqualified after committing an error on one of the rally's legs. Nonetheless, the Messerschmitt's design was enthusiastically received by aeronautical experts from all over Europe. The aircraft's excellent flight performance caught attention of the RLM officials, who promptly placed an order for 45 examples of the modified Bf 108 B version. The machine was to enter service with the German air force as a liaison aircraft.

The RLM's interest in his design was unquestionably a personal victory for Messerschmitt, especially that the RLM's secretary of state in charge of all aeronautical production in Germany, was Willy's archenemy Erhard Milch. Initially Milch tried to marginalize Messerschmitt's ambitions by planning to use the BFW facilities for license production of other manufacturers' designs, including 30 examples of the Dornier Do 11, 70 Heinkel He 45s, 35 He 50s, 90 Arado Ar 66s and 115 examples of the Gotha Go 145[9]. The successful debut of

Messerschmitt Bf 109 V1 undergoing static tests. The aircraft is yet to receive its registration and national markings.

Development of the Bf 109 design

Messerschmitt Bf 108 A, D-IJES powered by the Hirth HM-8U engine.

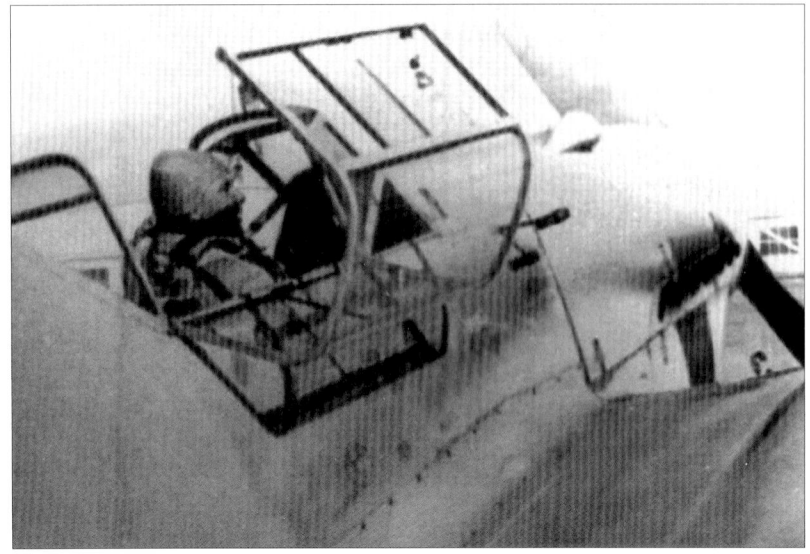

Ernst Udet pictured in January 1936 at the controls of the Messerschmitt Bf 109 V2, W.Nr. 759, D-IILU.

the Bf 108 in a coveted international competition resulted in the RLM orders for 7 version 0 examples of the aircraft, followed by 45 serial production machines. Additionally, 10 version 0 Messerschmitt Bf 109 fighters were ordered, supplemented by 8 version 0 examples of the Bf 110 "destroyer" aircraft.

Development of the Bf 109 design

The first fighter aircraft to go into service with the now officially established Luftwaffe were biplane designs, including the Arado Ar 65 and Ar 68 and Heinkel He 51 - the types that were already obsolete at the time when their first examples rolled off the production lines. Hermann Göring, who served in Hitler's government as the Reich's Commissar for Aviation (Reichskommissar für Luftfahrt), was very much aware of the urgent need for new aircraft designs, especially bombers and fast, single-seat fighters. In the fall of 1933 Göring wrote a confidential letter to Theo Croneiß, who at that time served as the BFW's Chairman of the Board and was also in charge of the development of aircraft production in Bavaria:

Dear Mr. Croneiß,

I am writing to you in strict confidence to assure you that I view your efforts to energize the aeronautical industry in Bavaria as critically important. I have no doubt that your passion for work will soon bear fruit in the shape of an aeronautical company capable of delivering a first class transport aircraft!!!

Of equal importance, however, is the development of an extremely fast liaison aircraft, a single-seater of course!!! If you feel you do not have sufficient expertise in the design of such aircraft, we can certainly discuss the matter further and perhaps start license production in your facilities. This way the company could gradually reach the necessary level of experience and recruit skilled work force to undertake design and production of the new types. I do insist that you look into the matter closely and offer your opinion at the earliest opportunity. It is in our best interest to establish in Augsburg a strong aeronautical company[10].

What Göring meant by a "first class transport aircraft" was in fact a bomber, while the "extremely fast liaison aircraft" was a reference to a single-seat fighter.

By the end of 1933 the RLM published the technical requirements for a new fighter for the German air force. The document entitled *Taktische Forderungen für den Jagdeinsitzer G.Kdos.*

Nr.L.A. 1432/33 quotes the following tactical specs:
1. Tactical application: single-seat day fighter
2. Number of engines: 1
3. Crew: 1
4. Armament: two machine guns with a supply of 1 000 rounds of ammunition, or a single 20 mm cannon with 100 rounds
5. Communications suite: air-to-ground and air-to-air radio telephony equipment
6. Safety and life support: seat harness, parachute, oxygen system, cockpit heating
7. Airspeed: 400 kph at 6 000 m
8. Range or flight endurance: $1\frac{1}{2}$ hours at maximum speed at 6 000 m.
9. Rate of climb: 17 minutes to 6 000 m
10. Operational ceiling: 9 000 m. Max ceiling: 10 000 m
11. Operational airfield requirements (German standard): 400x400 m airfield dimensions, landing distance from 20 m: 400 m
12. Safety measures: fire protection capabilities
13. Storage (in field conditions): open air
14. Other: flight in low visibility and in overcast conditions must be considered as a possibility; aircraft in land transport configuration must have overall dimensions adhering to railroad standards
15. General remarks: ad. 3: provide the best possible cockpit visibility for air-to-air combat; ad. 4: fixed armament should provide the widest possible field of fire and ease of maintenance; ad. 7 – 11: in terms of flight characteristics the aircraft should be easy to operate by a pilot of average skills. The required flight endurance is to be understood as the total flight time at 6 000 m, including take-off roll and a glide during the approach phase. The maximum airspeed at the operational ceiling of 6 000 m must be maintained up to 20 minutes. Aircraft must be fully controllable in dives. Aircraft must be easily recoverable from spins. Turns at operational ceiling must not result in a loss of height.

Flight characteristics will be assessed in the following order:
1. Airspeed in level flight
2. Rate of climb
3. Maneuverability

In February 1934 the RLM forwarded the tactical specifications of a light fighter aircraft to three companies: Arado, BFW and Heinkel. Focke-Wulf did not receive the documentation package until seven months later, i.e. September 1934[11].

In early March 1934 head of BFW's design bureau, Robert Lusser, began a series of meetings at the RLM to clarify some of the particulars of the proposed fighter's technical specs. Among the subjects discussed in those meetings were issues concerning the choice of powerplant and details of the aircraft's armament.

The future fighter was to be powered by a twelve-cylinder, inverted V engine: the 610 HP Junkers Jumo 210 A (to be installed in prototypes) and the 750 HP BMW 116 in production examples. At least three different configurations of fixed armament were considered: one MG C30 20 mm cannon firing through the hollow drive shaft, two MG 17 7.92 mm machine guns firing through the propeller arc, or two fuselage mounted MG 17s and a single MG FF 20 mm cannon installed between the cylinder blocks.

The BFW team began work on the new aircraft as soon as all issues arising from the RLM's requirements had been resolved. German aviation historian Rüdiger Kosin offers the following: *The lessons learned during the design and construction of the BFW Me 108 undoubtedly facilitated the company's work on the Bf 109 project. Many of the key issues, such as the placement of the main landing gear struts in front of the wing's spar and the proper distribution of forces acting on the gear wells, or the flight control surfaces arrangement, had already been tried and tested during the development of the Me*

The engine cowling of the Messerschmitt Bf 109 V1. The aircraft was powered by the Rolls-Royce "Kestrel" II S inline engine developing 583 HP.

Development of the Bf 109 design

Messerschmitt Bf 109 V3, W.Nr. 760, D-IOQY, in flight over Lech on June 26, 1936. At the controls is Dr. Hermann Wurster.

108. In fact, the Me 108 looked almost identical to the Bf 109's proof-of-concept aircraft, or, to look at it from the opposite angle, the Bf 109 was the Me 108 design adapted to a fighter role[12].

The new aircraft emerged as a cantilevered, low-wing, single-seat fighter, featuring a retractable landing gear and a fully enclosed cockpit. The fuselage had an elliptical cross section and a semi-monocoque duralumin structure covered with stressed, flush-riveted skins. To simplify the manufacturing process, both fuselage halves featured integral frames. Five duralumin longerons installed in each fuselage section provided longitudinal rigidity. The aft part of the fuselage featured an oval, bolted section supporting the aircraft's tailplane assembly. The fixed tail wheel was attached to its lower surface. The fuselage mid section housed the cockpit covered by a three-piece transparency, which was mounted flush with the aircraft's spine. The sideways-opening mid section provided access to the cockpit. Under the cockpit floor, and partly underneath he the pilot's seat, was the L-shaped main fuel tank.

The cantilevered, tapered wing was of a full-metal construction and consisted of two sections. It featured automatic slats along the leading edge, as well as conventional ailerons and trailing edge, fabric-covered flaps. Each wing section was mated to the fuselage via three attachment points: at the upper and lower main spar points and at the main landing gear pivot point, which was at the same time the lower part of the engine mount. The wing's internal ribs were press-formed, which simplified the manufacturing process.

Another photograph of the same aircraft. Shown to the advantage is the prop spinner adapted to accommodate the barrel of an MG C/30 L cannon.

Development of the Bf 109 design

The all-metal tailplane featured horizontal stabilizers supported by tubular steel struts covered by aluminum fairings. The horizontal stabilizers angle of incidence could be adjusted from the cockpit from –8° to +3°. A single vertical stabilizer had an asymmetrical profile to compensate for strong propeller slipstream. Flight control surfaces were mass balanced. The rudder actuation mechanism featured steel cables and pulleys, while the elevator was operated by pushrods and steel cables.

The aircraft's landing gear was of a conventional design with a fixed tail wheel. The single-strut main landing gear assemblies were attached to pivot points on each side of the fuselage lower section. The main wheels retracted outwards, into the wing wells. The landing gear legs featured metal fairings extending to about half of the wheel's diameter. Hydraulic system was provided for the landing gear extension and retraction. The fixed tail wheel assembly included a standard wheel fork attached to a single strut.

Bf 109 V1, W.Nr. 758, D-IABI[13]

The work on the prototype of the new fighter (designated P.1034) began just three weeks after the contract had been officially awarded. The mockup of the machine was revealed during a ceremony held in Augsburg on May 11, 1934. During the event the most hotly debated topics were issues concerning the mounting of powerplant and various armament arrangements. In the latter case, the favored solution was the installation of two MG 17 machine guns on top of the engine and a single MG C/30 20 mm cannon firing through the engine shaft. Also considered was the addition of a third MG 17 gun in place of the 20 mm cannon. On July 1, 1934 the mockup of the BMW 116 engine arrived at the BFW plant. At the same time Richard Bauer and his team at the BFW's design bureau had just began work on the final version of the project. By December 10, 1934 Moritz Asam, head of experimental and prototype aircraft department, had received the first technical drawings of the Bf 109 V1. On January 16 and 17, 1935 the final version of the aircraft's wooden mockup was submitted for inspection, which was duly recorded in a detailed protocol.

Unavailability of the adequate powerplant remained one of the major problems facing the design team. The RLM decided to stop the development of the BMW 116 engine, making room for the manufacturing of license-built Prat & Whitney radial engines. The BMW 116's successor was to be the Junkers Motorenwerke AG Jumo 210. However, the Junkers engine still suffered from some serious teething problems and as such was unsuitable to power Messerschmitt's new fighter. In this situation the RLM capitalized on Heinkel's business contacts with Rolls-Royce (the latter acquired the rights to the HE 70 design) and acquired several Rolls-Royce Kestrel engines rated at 583 HP. Two of those powerplants were delivered to BFW, while the remaining units went to Arado and Heinkel.

Equipped with the British-made Kestrel engine the Bf 109 V1 (D-IABI) flew for the first time on May 28, 1935. At the controls was BFW's rookie test pilot Dietrich Knoetzsch. The first flight, with the landing gear in the extended position, went without any major problems. Prior to the commencement of the flight test program the engineering team performed numerous gear extension and retraction tests. It soon turned out that part of the main landing gear legs would not fully retract into the wing wells. It was soon established that the culprit was the main landing gear tires which kept getting wedged against the wing's upper surface

The blisters on the upper wing surfaces of the Bf 109 V3 allowed the full retraction of the main landing gear into the wing wells.

Development of the Bf 109 design

Focke-Wulf Fw 159 V1, D-IUPY.

skin panels. The quick fix was to cut out a section of aluminum skins on the upper surface of the wing and replace them with bulged panels.

The aircraft had a wingspan of 9.89 m, overall length of 8.884 m and the wing area of 16 m². The engine drove a wooden, two-bladed Schwartz propeller with the diameter of 3 m. The coolant radiator had a capacity of 11 liters and was placed in a housing under the engine's cowling. Oil cooler was placed in the leading edge section and the upper wing root of the port wing. The oil tank was placed in the starboard wing, close to the fuselage.

The Bf 109 V1's test program continued in Augsburg throughout the summer of 1935. On October 15, 1935 Knoetzsch ferried the aircraft to the flight test center at Rechlin. Since the distance to Rechlin was over 550 km, the aircraft, with the range of only 400 km, would have to make a refueling stop at Jüterbog-Damm, home to JG 132 "Richthofen". One of the unit's pilots at that time was Adolf Galland, future General der Jagdflieger[14].

Having landed at Rechlin Knoetzsch had to make one more test flight, one of the requirement prior to handing the aircraft over to the *Erprobungsstelle*[15]. The young test pilot performed all the required flight maneuvers and set up for the approach to land which ended in a crash. One of the engineers who witnessed the incident later filed an eight-page report detailing the mishap. In all likelihood the report was submitted at the request of Heinkel design team: *The aircraft was flown at Rechlin by a factory test pilot. The accident sequence began with a very hard touchdown, followed by a bounce and a subsequent drop from about 1 to 1 $\frac{1}{2}$ m. The left main landing gear and the tail wheel contacted the ground first. Upon impact the tail wheel separated and the fuselage cracked in three places. The left main landing gear strut was bent inwards. moment later the left wingtip hit the ground, which was followed by a quick swing to the right. The aircraft came to rest in an inverted position. After the accident the aircraft was taken apart, which gave me an opportunity to take a close look at various subassemblies*[16].

In the aftermath of the crash Messerschmitt immediately fired Knoetzsch, while the fighter was transported back to Augsburg and repaired. The prototype was the ferried to a flight test center at Travemünde, where the test program

Arado Ar 80 V2, D-ILOH featuring a characteristic gull wing design.

began in earnest and continued through July 1936 (in June 1936 alone the aircraft made no fewer than 54 flights accumulating 9 h 39 min of flight time). The first flight took place on February 26, 1936 with Dipl.-Ing. Gerhard Geicke at the controls. On July 17, 1936 BFW's newly appointed chief test pilot, Dr. Ing. Hermann Wurster, brought the Bf 109 V1 back to Augsburg, where the flight test program would continue. Different aircraft configurations were tested, including the shortened leading edge slats which could potentially allow the installation of fixed armament in the fighter's wings. Trials at Augsburg began on August 24, 1936 and continued until January 13, 1937. The last officially recorded flight of the Bf 109 V1 took place on February 11, 1938. According to one of the former Messerschmitt employers the aircraft was stored for several months in the back of one of the hangars before it was finally scrapped.

Messerschmitt Bf 109 V2, W.Nr. 759, D-IILU[17]

The Bf 109 V2 took to the skies for the first time on December 12, 1935 powered by an in-line Junkers Jumo 210 A engine rated at 610 HP. The installation of the new powerplant necessitated redesign of the aircraft's cowling. A new TZ-3 engine coolant radiator was placed under the engine, while a small oil cooler was added underneath the port wing. The aircraft was fitted with a wooden, two-bladed constant pitch propeller manufactured by Schwartz.

On February 21, 1936 BFW's chief test pilot, Dr. Ing. Hermann Wurster, flew the aircraft to the flight test center at Travemünde where the competitors in the light fighter program would face off in a series of "comparative" trials. The tests were scheduled to begin in March 1936.

Competing with the Messerschmitt design were submissions by Arado, Focke-Wulf and Heinkel. The work on the Arado prototype, initially designated Projekt-Nummer E 200, began on April 23, 1934. It was Arado's first attempt at an all-metal aircraft design, which eventually emerged as the Arado Ar 80 V1. Although Arado's design bureau was headed by Walter Blume, most of the initial work was done by Walter Rethel. It was not until Rethel's resignation that Blume took over as the chief designer. The wooden mock up was ready by June 9, 1934 and the final version of the design drawings went to the production department on June 15, 1934. The prototype made its maiden flight at Warnemünde on July 26.1935.

The Arado Ar 80 V1 was a single-seat, single engine, low-wing monoplane. The all-metal design featured a flattened "W" wing, whose internal structure included welded steal tubes covered by removable aluminum skin panels. The main landing gear, attached to the lowermost part of the wing, was designed to retract rearwards into the wing, with the simultaneous 90° rotation of the landing gear legs. The system never worked as advertised, which forced Blume and his design team to provide the aircraft with fixed landing gear equipped with wheel spats. The aircraft featured a tailplane characteristic of other Arado designs, which included a vertical stabilizer mounted slightly forward of the fuselage tail section and a cantilevered horizontal stabilizer. The cockpit was equipped with a windshield only, with no additional glazing above or on the sides. Similarly to

The modern lines of the Messerschmitt Bf 109 V3 made it a favorite subject of photographs published in the industry press.

The first prototype of the Heinkel design, He 112 V1, D-IADO.

Development of the Bf 109 design

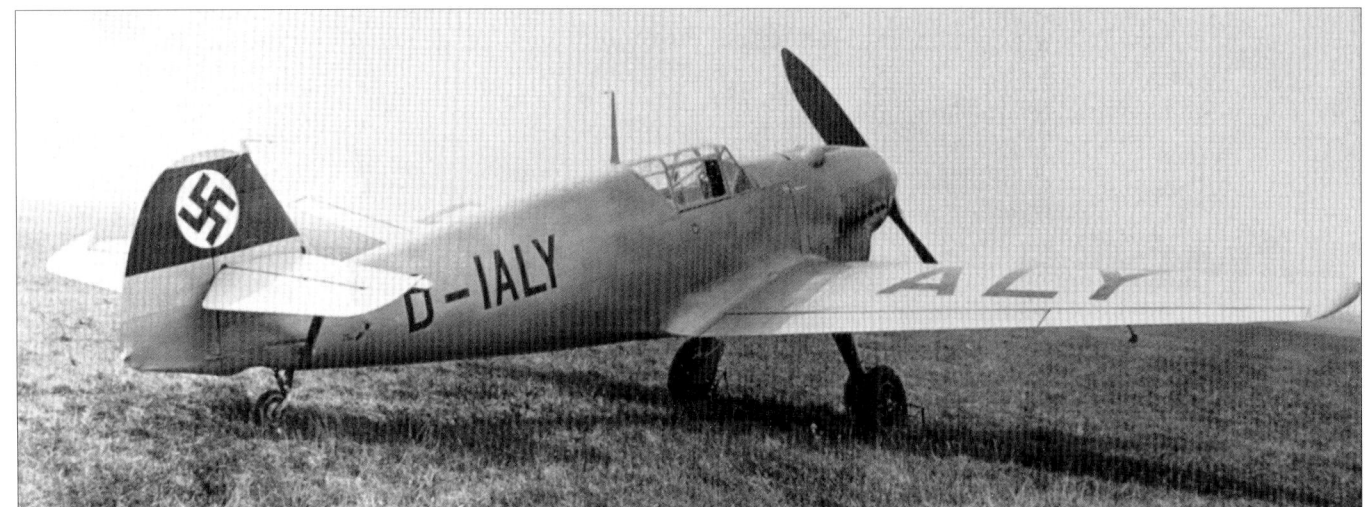

Messerschmitt Bf 109 V4, W.Nr. 878, D-IALY, made its first flight on September 26, 1936 with Dr. Hermann Wurster at the controls.

Messerschmitt Bf 109 V4 was equipped with the Junkers Jumo 210 B engine driving a wooden Schwarz propeller.

the Bf 109 V1, the Arado prototype was power by the Rolls-Royce Kestrel II S engine developing 583 HP. The engine drove a wooden, two-bladed propeller. The aircraft proved to be too heavy and, therefore, underpowered. Additional drawbacks were the fixed landing gear arrangement and the open cockpit.

Focke-Wulf AG from Bremen was the last company to receive the invitation to participate in the Luftwaffe's new fighter competition. The company received the relevant documents seven months later than the other competitors. It is therefore even more surprising why the Focke-Wulf team should choose to base their entry on the design principles that had already been considered "passé" at the time the new project was first taking shape. Focke-Wulf's prototype was designed as an "umbrella" type high-wing monoplane. The most likely explanation is that the RLM officials wanted to have a more conservative option available should the revolutionary and untested low wing monoplanes fail to deliver on their promises. The new aircraft was designated Focke-Wulf Fw 159 and was in fact a development of a highly successful light fighter, Focke-Wulf Fw 56 "Stößer". The machine's chief designer, Ob.Ing. Robert Blaser, delivered an all-metal, single-seat, single engine fighter with a fully enclosed cockpit and retractable landing gear. The Focke-Wulf high-wing prototype was ready in the spring of 1935. Flugkapitän Wolfgang Stein took the new aircraft for its first flight, which went very well until the landing phase: the landing gear extension mechanism failed and the aircraft crashed. Focke-Wulf sent the second prototype (Fw 159 V2, D-INGA) to take part in the Travemünde fly-off. During the trials it quickly became clear that the machine's performance was well below its rivals. Complex and unreliable gear extension mechanism in addition to the aircraft's outdated design, eliminated the Focke-Wulf entry almost at the start of the trials.

Thus the only design that could successfully compete with the Bf 109 V2 was the Heinkel He 112 V2. The Heinkel team began work on their fighter prototype soon after the RLM documentation arrived in February 1934. Leading the design team was a duo of extremely talented siblings, Walter and Siegfried Günther. The first prototype of the Heinkel He 112 V1 (W.Nr. 1290) was ready by August 28, 1935. The machine was powered by Rolls-Royce Kastrel II S engine and featured a two-bladed, wooden propeller made by Heidenheimer Kupferwerke. The Heinkel prototype was an all-metal, low wing monoplane. Its elliptical wing had a span of 12.6 m and the wide-track main landing gear was fully retractable into the wing wells. The aircraft featured a fixed tail wheel. The second prototype of the Heinkel fighter (He 112 V2, W.Nr. 1291, D-IHGE) was rolled out on November 10, 1935. It was fitted with a new powerplant – a Junkers Jumo 210 C engine. Rated at 640 HP the Jumo drove a three-bladed, variable pitch propeller. To improve high speed performance the second prototype had its wingspan reduced to 11.5 m. It also carried fixed armament, which included a single MG C/30L 20 mm cannon mounted between the cylinder blocks and firing through a port in the propeller's hub. The aircraft was delivered to the E-Stelle at Travemünde in late January 1936.

Most of the trials at Travemünde were carried out by factory test pilots and the E-Stelle personnel, but some of the senior RLM officials, including Ernst Udet and Robert Ritter von Greim were also involved in the flight test program. The Heinkel design was marred by bad luck almost from the start. On February 2, 1936 the He 112 V2 crashed during a forced landing attempt, injuring the pilot, Friedrich Ritz. The cause of the accident was traced back to a malfunction in the fuel cut-off valve assembly. The aircraft suffered only minor damage in the mishap, so by February 16 it was ready to fly again. Bad luck struck again on April 15, 1936. While displaying the He 112 V2 for a group of the RLM officials Gerhard Nitschke maneuvered the aircraft into a spin from which he was unable to recover. Nitschke managed to bail out before the Heinkel impacted the ground.

In the end the Bf 109 emerged as the winning design, although the He 112 was a worthy competitor. The Heinkel fighter featured strong and aerodynamically advanced design and wide-track landing gear which resulted in very good ground handling characteristics. Where the He 112 was inferior to the Messerschmitt was quite simply economics. The Heinkel's elegant, elliptical wing was more expensive to build than a simple, trapezoid wing on the Bf 109. In terms of ease of production, as well as the unit cost, the Bf 109 beat the Heinkel entry hands down.

An insider's view into the Heinkel – Messerschmitt face-off during the final stage of the Luftwaffe fighter competition is offered by Messerschmitt factory test pilot, Dr.-Ing. Hermann Wurster: *The RLM's fighter design competition followed the Luftwaffe's requirements for a single-seat fighter aircraft of excellent level flight performance, coupled with exceptional vertical and horizontal maneuverability, dive performance and good spin recovery qualities.*

At that time pressurized cockpits were still a thing of the future and the standard issue Dräger oxygen masks were not designed to feed oxygen under high pressure. There was, therefore, a risk that pilots transiting to the patrol area at high altitudes

Messerschmitt Bf 109 V7, W.Nr. 881, D-IJHA after arrival at Zürich-Dübendorf airfield for an international air meet held in July 1937.

An interesting shot of the Messerschmitt Bf 109 V4, W.Nr. 878. The civilian registration D-IALY is painted on the wing's lower surface.

Development of the Bf 109 design

Major Hans Seidemann and Dipl. Ing. Carl Francke at the Zurich air meet.

Messerschmitt Bf 109 V7 pictured at Zürich-Dübendorf wearing its official air meet number.

(above 10 000 m) could suffer from hypoxia and lose consciousness.

It was in such situations, when the airplane was cruising close to its maximum ceiling, that inadvertent spins were a real danger. Having spun through several thousand meters of altitude the aircraft would eventually reach more oxygen-saturated air and the pilot, having regained consciousness, would have to be able to recover from the spin. It was therefore very important for fighter aircraft designs to demonstrate the ability to perform at least ten full spin rotations to the left and to the right to ensure that they would not enter the flat spin, which was usually completely unrecoverable.

During the trials at E-Stelle Travemünde I performed all the usual flight maneuvers, but in addition I demonstrated very difficult spins consisting of 21 rotations to the right and 17 rotations to the left. I also put the aircraft into a vertical dive from the altitude of 7 500 m and recovered safely close to the ground (...)

The display made a lasting impression on the officials on the ground and built their confidence in the Bf 109 design, especially that some of them witnessed Nitschke's bailout from the Heinkel after he had failed to regain control of the spinning aircraft.

While at the E-Stelle the test pilots had many opportunities to fly their competitors' aircraft and thus had good basis for direct comparisons of the designs. As I was getting ready to climb into the He 112 cockpit, the chief of flight test department, Dipl.-Ing. Francke came up to me and said: 'Herr Wurster, just remember that you cannot do the same crazy things in the He 112 that you had shown us in your Me 109...'

I had a feeling that the He 112 was not as easy to handle during aerobatics as the Bf 109. It was especially evident while turning around the longitudinal axis, which is the basis of most air-to-air combat maneuvering. In addition, the He 112 would drop the wing much quicker in tight turns, which was not the case in the '109" with its leading edge slats. In the case of accelerated stalls in inverted position lateral stability was much worse in the He 112 than in the Bf 109. This, again, was due to the lack of high lift devices.

The Bf 109's superior maneuvering characteristics were confirmed by other military and civilian test pilots. Among them was General Udet, one of the leading fighter aces of the Great War, as well as an accomplished aerobatic pilot. If anyone was qualified to express opinion about flight characteristics of a fighter aircraft, it was certainly General Udet. The same can be said about General Robert Ritter von Greim, who was also impressed with the Bf 109's performance. Both Udet and von Greim performed a number of flights not just for fun and because of their seniority, but because they wanted to test the new designs in conditions closely simulat-

Development of the Bf 109 design

Messerschmitt Bf 109 V13, W.Nr. 1050, D-IPKY during a successful attempt to break the world speed record on November 11, 1937.

ing actual air combat. I could attest to the Bf 109's superiority having flown numerous mock dog fights against the other two competing fighters..

The Me 109 had a smaller wing area than the He 112, so it also benefited from less induced drag. Besides, although it had a very sturdy design – the fact confirmed through many flight trials – it was also lighter than the Heinkel, which gave it better acceleration in level flight with the use of less power. That is why the Messerschmitt fighter was faster than the He 112 in level flight. Both aircraft had practically identical climb performance.

The landing gear on the Bf 109 was very reliable. The main landing gear legs were spliced outwards, which gave good ground handling performance even during landings or take-offs in adverse conditions. In the case of the landing gear malfunction (not a rare occurrence in field or combat conditions) the Bf 109 could be landed on just one wheel without causing significant damage to the wing or the airframe.

Although I never had an opportunity to land the He 112 with just one landing gear leg extended, I believe that because of the gear's wide track holding wings level during the landing rollout would not be possible for too long. At high landing speeds that would surely lead to a ground loop and pose the risk of the aircraft's nosing over. The same was true in asymmetric brake application: aircraft with wide landing gear track are more prone to ground loops than narrow tracked machines.

The fact that the Bf 109's landing gear legs were attached directly to the fuselage meant that the engine or wing could be removed and replaced without the need for any extra equipment, such as cranes or lifts. That was a definite advantage, both at the assembly line and during field maintenance. That particular landing gear arrangement also allowed the forces induced at touchdown to be dissipated evenly by the wing's spar in its static center, and not transferred to the fuselage as was the case in the He 112.

Finally, the Me 109 had obvious manufacturing advantages. It was a simple design and inexpensive to mass produce. The wing's simple trapezoid profile and easily shaped skin panels made them easy to manufacture. Also the fuselage sections were designed to be cost and labor effective: they were pressed from a single sheet of metal, complete with internal frames. The manufacturing process of the Me 109 required less riveting than the He 112 and fewer specialized jigs and tools had to be used.

When compared to the He 112, the Bf 109 was quite simply a better aircraft, with its superb flight characteristics being the most important advantage.

The Messerschmitt fighter did not win the RLM competition as a result of political lobbying or because Messrs Milch and Lucht favored the design. It was truly a matter of informed opinions of the aircrews testing the new designs. The decision to mass produce the Me 109 instead of the He 112 or He 113 was clearly the right one, because the Messerschmitt was simply a better single-seat fighter[18].

The Bf 109 V2 continued the flight test program at -Stelle Travemünde. On April 1, 1936 the aircraft was destroyed during a forced landing near Ivendorf after the cockpit canopy's front section separated shortly after take-off. The fighter was transported back to the Mess-

Messerschmitt V13 powered by the DB 601 Rennmotor III engine ready for the record breaking flight.

Development of the Bf 109 design

A highly airbrushed propaganda photograph featuring the Messerschmitt Bf 109 A, W.Nr. 809, D-IUDE. The aircraft, which first flew on January 8, 1937, featured the FuG VII radio installation.

erschmitt's plant in Augsburg were it was later scrapped.

Messerschmitt Bf 109 V3, W.Nr. 760, D-IOQY

Dr.-Ing. Hermann Wurster made the first flight at the controls of the Bf 109 V3 on April 8, 1936. The aircraft was powered by the 640 HP Junkers Jumo 210 C engine, which drove a wooden, fixed pitch propeller. The aircraft was a base model for the Bf 109's A variant – a fact often overlooked by many authors. It was also the first Bf 109 prototype that was fitted with internal weapons consisting of two MG 17 machine guns mounted on top of the engine and firing through the propeller arc. The ammunition was stored in two 500-round magazines. Both machine guns had mechanically actuated trigger mechanisms. Since the MG C/30 L cannon was still not cleared for operational use at that time, it was not fitted to the Messerschmitt prototype.

The aircraft could also carry additional weapons under common designation So-3. Those included Elvemag 5 C X bomb ejectors and 5 S.C. 10 bombs, which were placed in vertical magazines behind the pilot's seat. Since the work on the bombs' electric fuses was still in progress, the weapons were never used.

The aircraft was also fitted with the FuG VII radio and an antenna mast positioned on the fuselage spine, just aft of the canopy. The antenna wires ran from the mast to the tip of the vertical stabilizer and both horizontal stabilizers. The characteristic "blisters" on the upper wing surfaces were reshaped to accommodate low pressure tires used on the landing gear wheels. Another characteristic feature of the V3 prototype was a cannon port in the propeller spinner (the aircraft was originally designed to carry an internally mounted 20 mm cannon).

On July 1, 1936 the Bf 109 V3 arrived at the E-Stelle Travemünde for a series of flight trials. According to the preserved flight test documentation the aircraft made no fewer than 36 flights in September 1936 alone, which translated into a total flight time of 16 hours and 54 minutes. In October 1936 the fighter was disassembled, crated and shipped to Spain where it was to be taken on charge by the VJ/88 of the "Condor Legion". It flew in Spain with the fuselage codes 6•2 and, later, 6•1.

Dr.-Ing. Hermann Wurster was at the controls of the Bf 109, in which he achieved the speed of 610.95 kph.

Development of the Bf 109 design

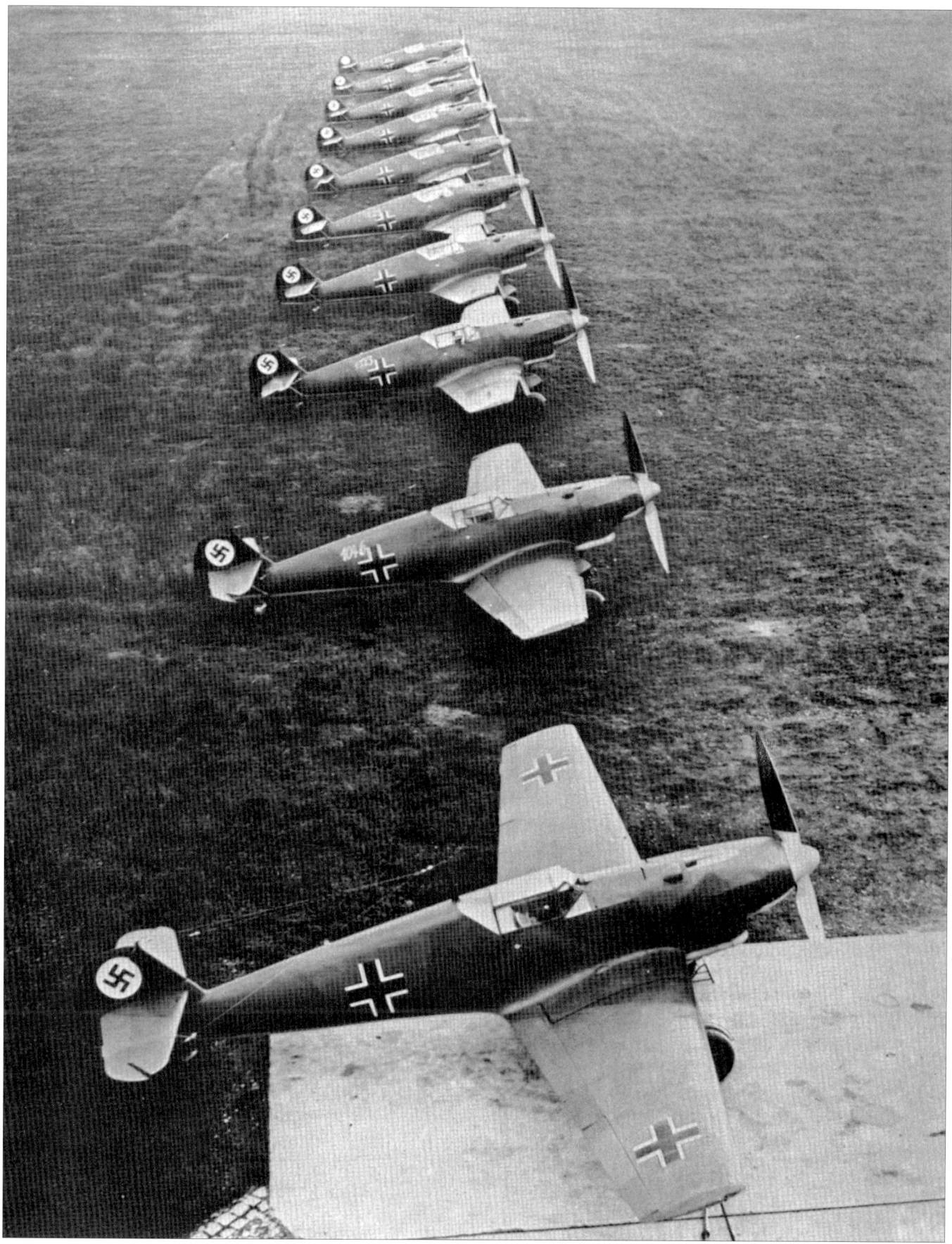

Messerschmitt Bf 109 A

The first production variant of the Messerschmitt fighter was the Bf 109 A. What is interesting, the aircraft was fully compatible with the later B version standards, which is perhaps why many sources ignore the existence of the variant claiming that it was really the B model. However, according to the document dated August 25, 1937 ("Abgelieferte Bf 109 A und B-1" – delivered Bf 109 A and B-1 aircraft) the fol-

Messerschmitt Bf 109 B-1s from the first production batch parked at Augsburg airfield. The fighters featured two-bladed Schwartz propellers.

Messerschmitt Bf 109 Early Versions 21

Development of the Bf 109 design

lowing examples of the A version were manufactured:

W.Nr.	Civilian registration	Powerplant	First flight	Delivery date
760, V3	D-IOQY	Jumo 210 C	08.04.1936	30.06.1936
808	D-IIBA	Jumo 210 D	31.12.1936	21.01.1937
809	D-IUDE	Jumo 210 D	08.01.1937	19.02.1937
810	D-IHNY	Jumo 210 D	08.01.1937	21.01.1937
883	D-ITGE	Jumo 210 D	31.12.1937	14.01.1937
884	D-IXZA	Jumo 210 D	30.12.1936	19.01.1937
994	D-IMRY	Jumo 210 B	06.01.1937	01.02.1937
995	D-IPLA	Jumo 210 B	09.01.1937	19.02.1937
996	D-IVSE	Jumo 210 B	08.01.1937	19.02.1937
997	D-IZQE	Jumo 210 D	12.01.1937	14.01.1937
1000	D-IMTY	Jumo 210 D	22.01.1937	19.02.1937
1001	D-IPSA	Jumo 210 B	?	?
1002	D-IQMU	Jumo 210 B	28.01.1937	18.02.1937
1003	D-IVTO	Jumo 210 B	28.01.1937	20.02.1937
1004	D-ILZY	Jumo 210 B	02.02.1937	19.02.1937
1005	D-IJFY	Jumo 210 D	05.02.1937	20.02.1937
1006	D-IBLE	Jumo 210 D	04.02.1937	20.02.1937
1007	D-IHDU	Jumo 210 D	10.02.1937	20.02.1937
1008	D-IYTY	Jumo 210 D	12.02.1937	20.02.1937
1009	D-IOMY	Jumo 210 D	16.02.1937	20.02.1937

Similarly to the Bf 109 V3 the aircraft were fitted with two Mg 17 guns and the So-3 weapons suite, which allowed 5 S.C. 10 bombs to be carried internally. Most of the Bf 109 As flew in Spain with the Condor Legion. The A models used by VJ/88 most likely carried fuselage codes from 6•3 to 6•18 (16 aircraft in total).

Messerschmitt Bf 109 V4, W.Nr. 878, D-IALY

The fourth prototype of the Bf 109 was to become the base model for the B version of the fighter. It was powered by the Junkers Jumo 210 B engine and featured a wooden, constant pitch Schwarz propeller. The armament fit used on the V4 was the So-1 standard, i.e. two MG 17 7.92 mm guns mounted above the engine. The aircraft flew for the first time on September 23, 1936 with Dr.-Ing. Hermann Wurster at the controls. After a few test sorties at Augsburg the aircraft was ferried to the E-Stelle Travemünde with a short stopover at Gotha. Because the fighter was being prepped for combat in the skies over Spain, it returned to Augsburg as early as November 6, 1936. In early December the fighter was crated and shipped to Spain, where it received its fuselage code 6•1. The V4 was destroyed on December 10, 1936 during a take-off accident at Tablada. The mishap pilot was Uffz. Erich Kley.

Messerschmitt Bf 109 B-1

The V4 prototype was the base model for the B-1 version of the Messerschmitt fighter. 341 examples of the variant were built in different locations: BFW plant manufactured 76 aircraft (W.Nr. 998-1064 and 1701-1719), the Erla Maschinenwerk GmbH Leipzig delivered 175 aircraft (W.Nr. 272-416 and 540-617), while Gerhard Fieseler Werke GmbH Kassel produced 90 Bf 109 B-1 fighters (W.Nr. 3000-3089). All aircraft featured the Junkers Jumo 210 D powerplant driving a VDM variable pitch propeller.

Initially the B-1 fighters were armed with two or three (aircraft with the VDM propeller) MG 17 guns. Two machine guns were mounted above the engine and fired through the propeller arc. The aircraft carried 500 rounds of ammunition per gun. The third MG 17 was placed between the engine cylinder blocks and fired through a port in the spinner. The engine-mounted gun was fed from an ammo box containing 600 rounds. However, squeezed between the engine blocks the gun was prone to overheating and frequent jams. It was therefore often removed in the field, which saved some weight, but at the same time reduced the fighter's firepower. A pneumatic/electric system was used for the guns operation (three 1 liter compressed air tanks and a pressure reduction device). The reflector gun sight (Revi C/12B or C/12C) was placed behind the windshield. The B-1 underwent minor modification during its production run: the length of the leading edge slats was reduced, while three antenna wires were replaced with a single wire running from the mast to the tip of the vertical stabilizer.

According to the original factory documentation the only B version of the fighter in existence was the B-1 model. However, most sources differentiate between the B-1 version (using a fixed pitch Schwartz propeller) and the B-2 variant equipped with the variable pitch VDM prop. This appears to be an incorrect interpretation of the facts.

The table below presents basic technical specifications of the B-1 version

Dimensions	Wingspan	9.90 m
	Length	8.70 m
	Height	2.45 m
	Landing gear track	2.00 m
	Wing area	16.00 m²
	Airfoil	NACA 2 R
Weights	Empty	1 432 kg
	Take-off	1 955 kg
Other	Fuel load	235 l
	Engine oil	24.5 l
Performance	Max airspeed (MSL)	430 kph
	Cruising speed (MSL)	371 kph
	Max airspeed at 2 700 m	460 kph
	Cruising speed at 2 700 m	395 kph
	Max speed at 6 000 m	428 kph
	Max dive speed	800 kph
	Landing speed	105 kph
	Time to climb to 1 000 m	1.25 min
	Time to climb to 6 000 m	9.80 min
	Max ceiling	8 750 m

Development of the Bf 109 design

Messerschmitt Bf 109 V14, W.Nr. 1029, D-ISLU, which crashed near Thun during the Zurich air meet. The mishap pilot was Ernst Udet.

Messerschmitt Bf 109 B-1 with a metal VDM prop pictured at the factory airfield.

Messerschmitt Bf 109 A, W.Nr. 808, D-IIBA after a landing accident.

Development of the Bf 109 design

Another fine example of the Messerschmitt publicity photos showing the Bf 109 B-1.

One of the characteristic features of the Bf 109 B-1 was a massive engine coolant radiator under the cowl. The aircraft were armed with two or three MG 17 7.92 mm machine guns.

Messerschmitt Bf 109 V5, W.Nr. 879, D-IIGO

The aircraft was first flight tested by Dr.-Ing. Hermann Wurster on November 5, 1936. The prototype was used in the trials of the pneumatic/electric gun operation system, designated EPAD 17 (*elt.-pneumatische Abzugs- und Durchladevorrichtung 17*). The fighter was powered by the Junkers Jumo 210 B engine. In January 1937 the aircraft was handed over to the E-Stelle Travemünde for further testing of the EPAD 17 system. In late 1937 the machine arrived at the E-Stelle Rechlin from where it was ferried to the E-Stelle Tarnewitz in early 1938.

Messerschmitt Bf 109 V6, W.Nr. 880, D-IHHB

The V6 prototype first flew on November 11, 1936. At the controls was the BFW test pilot Dr.-Ing. Hermann Wurster. The aircraft was equipped with the Junkers Jumo 210 D powerplant. In December 1936 the fighter was shipped to Spain where it received its fuselage code 6•3. After the loss of the Bf 109 V4 on December 10, 1936 the V6's code was changed to 6•2. The aircraft crashed near Cáceres on February 11, 1937 killing the pilot, Lt. Paul Rehahn.

Messerschmitt Bf 109 V7, W.Nr. 881, D-IJHA

The V7 was equipped with the Junkers Jumo 210 G engine featuring direct fuel injection system and rated at 730 HP. Dr.-Ing. Hermann Wurster took the fighter for its maiden flight on November 5, 1936. The aircraft was unarmed, since it was being prepared for participation in the international air meet to be held in Zurich from July 23 to August 1, 1937. After the event the aircraft returned to Augsburg where it continued to be used as a test bed in various test programs.

Messerschmitt Bf 109 V8, W.Nr. 882, D-IMQE

The V8 first flew on December 29, 1936 with Dr.-Ing. Hermann Wurster at the controls. The fighter's Junkers Jumo 210 D engine drove a two-bladed, variable pitch VDM propeller. The V8 was armed with two MG 17 guns featuring mechanical trigger control. The prototype was initially used for flight endurance tests at Augsburg, but later on flew to Rechlin, where it was flight tested with a number of different engine types, including the only example of the Daimler-Benz DB 600 ever mounted in the Bf 109.

Messerschmitt Bf 109 V9, W.Nr. 1056, D-IPLU

The aircraft was first flown on July 23, 1937 by a Messerschmitt factory test pilot Fritz Wendel. The V9 was fitted with the Junkers Jumo 210 G engine in preparation for the Zurich air meet. After the event the fighter was handed

Development of the Bf 109 design

A standard splinter camouflage pattern of RLM 70/71 applied to the upper and side surfaces of the Messerschmitt Bf 109 B-1.

The basic paint scheme on the wing and fuselage surfaces of the Bf 109 B-1s remained unchanged until 1939/1940 when the RLM 02 paint was introduced in place of the RLM 70.

Development of the Bf 109 design

Impressive image of the Bf 109 B-1 published in a German weekly.

A propaganda shot of the Messerschmitt Bf 109 B-1 published in one of German popular magazines.

The Messerschmitt Bf 109 B-1 awaiting delivery to the Luftwaffe at factory airfield. Notice the WL-IPGK markings on the wing's lower surfaces.

Development of the Bf 109 design

One of the very few Messerschmitt Bf 109 C-3s armed with wing-mounted MG FF 20 mm cannons.

over to the flight test center at Rechlin, where it arrived on October 28, 1938.

Messerschmitt Bf 109 V10, W.Nr. 1010, D-IAKO[19]

The most likely time of the aircraft's first flight is October 1937. The V10 was powered by the Junkers Jumo 210 D powerplant. Its first recorded test flight (a 30 minute sortie) took place on November 1, 1937. The fighter remained in Augsburg to be used as an experimental airframe.

Messerschmitt Bf 109 V11, W.Nr. 1012, D-IFMO

The fighter was powered by the Junkers Jumo 210 D engine driving a two-bladed VDM propeller with variable pitch. The V11 featured a new wing design, known as *Waffenflügel* (armed wing). Two MG 17 guns with 500 rounds of ammunition per gun were mounted internally, just outboard of the main landing gear wells. The ammunition was fed from ammo belts that ran along the wing spar. Access to the ammunition belts was provided via access panels on the wing's upper surface and through detachable wingtips. The gun barrels were placed inside steal tubes that were attached to gun ports in the leading edge of the wing. Both guns were air cooled. The internal gun installation necessitated the use of shorter leading edge slats and modified mass balance of the ailerons.

The aircraft's armament was complemented by a pair of MG 17s mounted in their usual place on top of the engine. Two magazines mounted inside the fuselage provided 1 000 rounds of ammunition per gun. Spent casings

Messerschmitt Bf 109 C-1 sporting four MG 17 machine guns.

Messerschmitt Bf 109 Early Versions

Development of the Bf 109 design

Only 58 examples of the Messerschmitt Bf 109 C-1 were produced. The fighter was powered by the Junkers Jumo 210 G engine.

were ejected into a common box which could be emptied via an access panel in the lower section of the engine cowling. The guns were set to converge at 400 m.

The prototype made its maiden flight on March 1, 1937 before being handed over to the E-Stelle Travemünde on May 14, 1937. At Travemünde the prototype's new armament arrangement went through a series of tests, which were successfully concluded in late June 1937. More testing followed between July and October 7, 1937 when the aircraft finally returned to Augsburg.

Messerschmitt Bf 109 V12, W.Nr. 1016, D-IVRU

Flugkapitän Fritz Wendel performed the first flight in the V12 on March 13, 1937. The fighter was equipped with the Junkers Jumo 210 D engine and a two-bladed, variable pitch VDM propeller. The aircraft was to be used in testing different configurations of the *Waffenflügel*. The left

One of the ten Messerschmitt Bf 109 D-1s that were exported to Switzerland. Pictured here is J-310, W.Nr. 2305 in service with Fliegerkompanie 15 which was shot down on June 4, 1940 over Boécourt by a Bf 110 from II./ZG 1.

Development of the Bf 109 design

Messerschmitt Bf 109 D-1s parked at Bernburg airfield.

wing section was modified to accept either the MG 17 gun, or the MG FF 20 mm cannon. The right wing housed a single MG FF weapon. After a lengthy period of tests and trials performed at Augsburg, the aircraft was formally handed over to the E-Stelle w Travemünde on September 14, 1937. When the fighter finally landed at Travemünde on October 6, 1937 the test program could begin in earnest. During the first live firing trials it became evident that internal mounting of the MG FF cannon lacked the necessary strength: some of the rivets holding the front section of the cannons mount gave way when the weapon was in operation. The faulty mount was quickly fixed and the testing continued. During twelve live firing runs in horizontal flight the guns per-

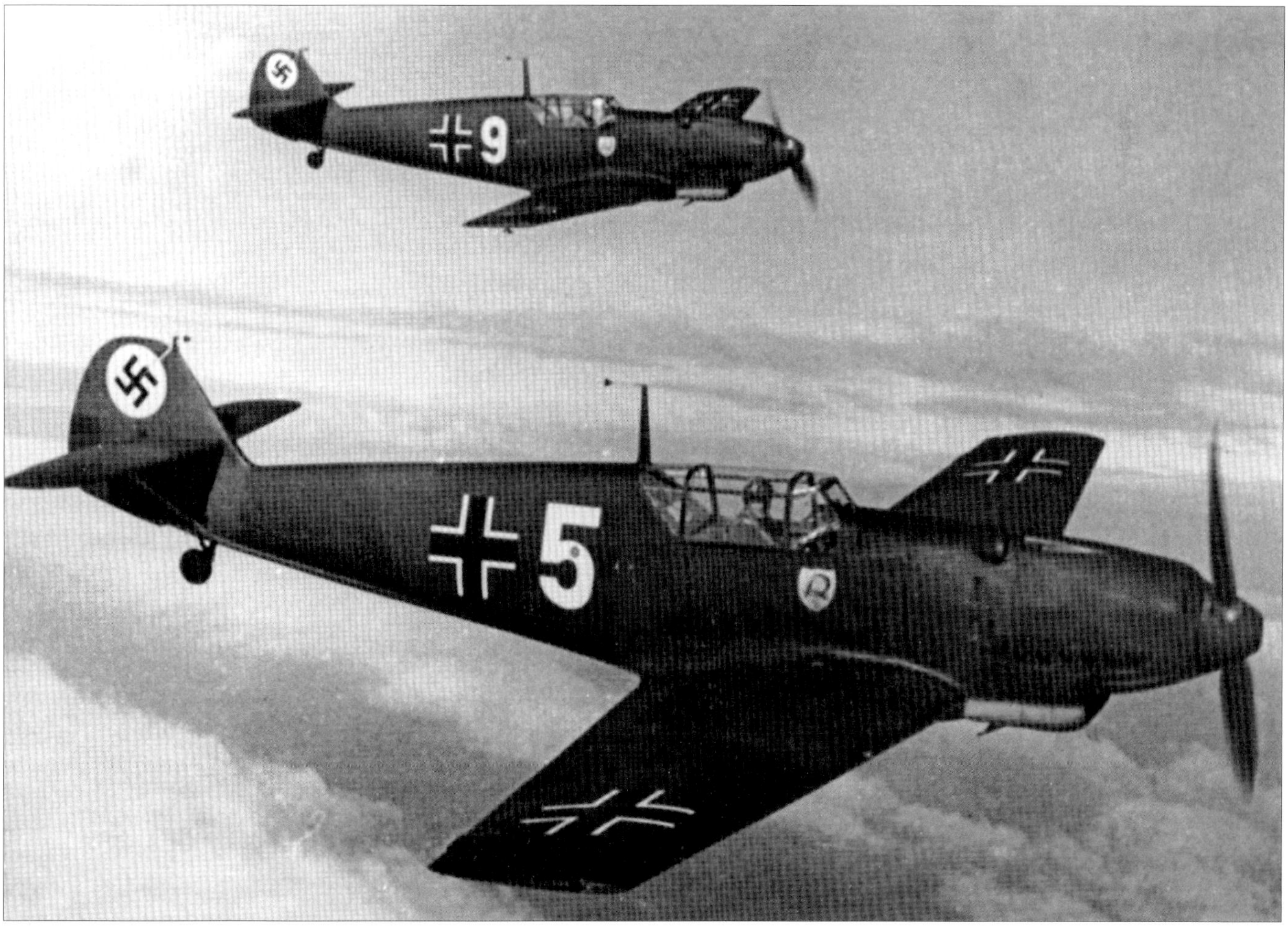

A pair of Messerschmitt Bf 109 D-1s from 10./JG 132 en-route to Karslbad on October 5, 1938. The fighters were flown by Ofw. Fritz Beeck and Uffz. Kröschmann. Notice the early type of national markings on the vertical fins and unit badges under the windshields.

Messerschmitt Bf 109 Early Versions 29

Development of the Bf 109 design

Cranking up the Junkers Jumo 210 powering the Bf 109 D-1 took a lot of muscle. Pictured here is the "yellow 7" from 3./ZG 2.

formed flawlessly, without jams or other malfunctions. However, the cannon mount riveted to the wing's ribs did not perform as advertised. It was clear that the entire mounting assembly would have to be completely redesigned. In the meantime, in order to continue the tests, rivets were replaced with bolts. In late November 1937 the aircraft returned to Augsburg on a railway flatbed. Based on the results of the test program the Messerschmitt team decided to equip the future Bf 109 C and D models with the *Waffenflügel* carrying two MG 17 machine guns. The work on the wing mounted MG FF cannon continued and later on several Bf 109 C-3 were built in this configuration.

Messerschmitt Bf 109 V13, W.Nr. 1050, D-IPKY

The first flight of the V13 took place on July 10, 1937. At the controls was Messerschmitt factory test pilot Dr.-Ing. Hermann Wurster. The aircraft was build to compete at the VI international air meet in Zurich and to attempt to set the new speed world record. At that time the world speed record over a 3 km course in the C class category (land aircraft) belonged to Howard Hughes and stood at 567.115 kph. According to the FAI (Fédération Aéronautique Internationale) rules the new record would be recognized only if it exceeded the current record speed by at least 8 kph.

The V13 was a standard B model airframe stripped of the armament and with modified nose section. It was powered by the Daimler-Benz 601/III "Renmotor" (racing engine), which was a modified version of the DB 601 A. The powerplant drove a three-bladed, variable pitch VDM propeller.

After its appearance at the Zurich air meet the aircraft returned to Augsburg where the preparations for the record-breaking flight would begin. All the fuselage skin panel lines were filled in and sanded to obtain the smoothest possible surfaces. The fuselage was then painted and highly polished to minimize drag. The aircraft also received a new, streamlined canopy and engine cowling. The engine cowl lines smoothly converged towards the pointy propeller spinner. The aircraft also featured flat oil and engine coolant radiators.

The FAI regulations dictated that the 3 km course had to be overflown four times at the height below 75 m. The course was set along the Augsburg-Buchloe railroad line, near the town of Bobingen. Dr.-Ing. Hermann Wurster made the record-breaking flight in the early afternoon (between 1409 and 1431) on November 11, 1937. The officially recorded speed was 610.950 kph. Official documents submitted to the FAI by the Germans claimed that the aircraft was the "B.F. 113R" powered by a Daimler-Benz DB 600 engine rated at 950 HP.

Between December 11, 1937 and January 19, 1938 Hermann Wurster made eight attempts to better the speed record set by the Bf 109 V13, but failed each time.

In the spring of 1938 the V13 was modified again, this time to test the revolutionary surface cooling system which was to be used on the Me 209 design. Wurster flew the modified aircraft for the first time on April 19, 1938. One of the test flights (July 20, 1938) ended with an emergency landing at Lechfeld when the fighter lost all of its engine coolant. The aircraft was undamaged in the mishap and Wurster flew it twice more before handing the machine over to another Messerschmitt test pilot, Fritz Wendel. It was Wendel who made the last test flight in the V13 on November 5, 1938. On November 30, 1938 he delivered the fighter to the *Flieger-Technischen-Schule München* (Aviation Technical School at Munich).

Messerschmitt Bf 109 V14, W.Nr. 1029, D-ISLU

The V14 prototype was first flown by Dr.-Ing. Hermann Wurster on April 28, 1937. Similarly to the V13, the machine was scheduled to appear at the Zurich air meet. The airframe was a standard Bf 109 B model, sans the armament and re-engined with the new Daimler-Benz DB 601 "Renmotor II" powerplant developing 1 565 HP at 2 620 rpm. Prior to its departure to Switzerland the aircraft was inspected on July 14 and 15 by Obstlt. Werner Junck and Fl.-Haupting. Spies. Generalmajor Enst Udet was scheduled to fly the V14 during the event.

A truly impressive array of various aircraft types represented Germany at the IV international air meet taking place in Zurich between

The ground crews replenish 7.92 mm ammunition for the MG 17s mounted on a Messerschmitt Bf 109 D-1 from 3./JG 21.

Development of the Bf 109 design

Lt. Hannes Trautloft posing with ground crew members. The aircraft in the background is the Bf 109 V3, 6•1.

Lt. Hannes Trautloft's Messerschmitt Bf 109 V3, 6•1. Painted under the cockpit is the green heart, the symbol of Thuringia.

July 23 and August 1, 1937. Among them were Dornier Do 17 M V1, Henschel Hs 123 V5, Heinkel He 112 A-03 and as many as five Messerschmitt Bf 109 examples (Bf 109 V7, Bf 109 V9, Bf 109 V13, Bf 109 V14 and Bf 109 B-1, W.Nr. 1062).

The first event in which the Bf 109s took part was an air race over a 202 km rectangular track. Because the French had withdrawn their two aircraft from the race, the event was to be a face-off between the Messerschmitt Bf 109 V14 with Ernst Udet at the controls and the Percival "Mew Gull" flown by an English pilot Gardner. To make things a bit more interesting the Germans proposed to enter another Bf 109 in the competition – the V7 flown by Dipl.-Ing. Carl Francke from the E-Stelle Rechlin. The English pilot accepted the challenge and Francke was allowed to take part in the race.

Shortly after take-off Udet's aircraft developed throttle problems, which forced the German pilot to return to the Dübendorf airfield immediately. Francke won the race with the time of 29 min 35.2 sec and the average speed of 409.64 kph. Gardner needed 34 min 33.8 sec to cover the same distance, which translated

into the average speed of 350.66 kph. During the decoration ceremony Francke gave up his trophy and handed it over to Gardner as a way of expressing his gratitude for allowing him to race.

The next event, scheduled for July 27, 1937, was a climb and dive competition. The goal was to climb to 3 000 m and then descent in a steep dive and on a prescribed heading to cross the finish line at the height of 100 to 400 m. It took Dipl.-Ing. Carl Francke just 1 min 45 sec to reach 3 200 m in the Bf 109 V13. He then entered a 75° dive, reaching the speed of over 600 kph. Within the next 20 seconds Francke crossed the finish lines with a total time of 2 min 5.7 sec, which gave him the first place.

On July 27 and 29 the crews competed in a navigational event over the Alps in three different aircraft categories. The event was set over a triangular route leading from Dübendorf to Thun (105 km), from Thun to Bellinoza (125 km) and from Bellinoza back to Dübendorf (137 km), a total distance of 367 km. The Bf 109s were entered in the race in two categories: A – single-seat aircraft and C – a flight in a three-ship formation[20]. The aircraft taking part in the A category race included the Bf 109 V9 (flown by Seidemann), the Bf 109 V14 with Udet at the controls, a French Dewoitine D.510 and four Czechoslovakian Avia B-534s. One of the Czech pilots, Capt. Engler, had to return to Dübendorf shortly after take-off. Just minutes later an oil line broke in Udet's Messerschmitt, which forced the pilot to make an emergency wheels-up landing near Thun airfield. On short final the aircraft hit power lines and crashed into the ground. The rear fuselage section separated on impact, just aft of the pilot's seat. Miraculously, Udet walked away from the crash with nothing more than a bruised shoulder. The winner of the race was Maj. Seidemann flying the Bf 109 V9. Seidemann's time over the 367 km route was 56 min 47.1 sec, which translated into the average speed of 387.4 kph. The second place (average speed 347 kph) went to a Czech pilot, Lt. Hlado.

The C category race began on July 29, 1937. Germany was represented by Hptm Restemeier, Oblt. Trautloft and Oblt. Schleif flying the Bf 109 V7, V9 and B-1. Although the German team was considered to be the strongest of the field, the beginning of the race did not go well for the Messerschmitt flyers: soon after take-off one of the fighters began to lose engine oil, which forced the pilot to throttle back in order to keep the engine from overheating. The remaining two aircraft also had to slow down to stay in formation. After a nerve-wrecking fight against the Czech formation, the Germans did manage to finish first with the time of 58 min 52.9 sec, narrowly beating the Czechs whose total flight time was 60 min 54.4 sec.

Messerschmitt Bf 109 C-1/3

The prototypes of the C-1 version were Bf 109 V11 and V12, which sported the new *Waffenflügel*. The C-1s were manufactured at the Messerschmitt plant at Augsburg, which delivered 58 examples of the type (W.Nr. 1720-1777). The Bf 109 C-1 was an all-metal, single-seat low wing monoplane with retractable landing gear and fully enclosed cockpit. The fighter was powered by the Junkers Jumo 210 G engine. The aircraft's technical details and specifications are presented in the following table:

Dimensions	Wingspan	9.90 m
	Length	8.70 m
	Height	2.50 m
	Landing gear track	2.00 m
	Wing area	16.40 m²
Weights	Max take-off weight	2 160 kg
Performance	Max airspeed (MSL)	410 kph
	Max airspeed at 4 500 m	465 kph
	Max dive speed	800 kph
	Landing speed	111 kph
	Time to climb to 1 000 m	1.0 min
	Time to climb to 5 000 m	7.5 min
	Ceiling	9 000 m
	Flight endurance	2 h

The aircraft carried four MG 17 7.92 mm machine guns. Two were placed on top of the engine block and had a supply of 500 rounds of ammunition per gun. The other two MG 17s were mounted in the wing with a supply of 1 000 rounds per barrel. The reflector gun sight (Revi C/12B or C/12C) was mounted in the cockpit, on top of the instrument panel. One of the features of the C-1 version and the subsequent models was a different location of the external power receptacle and the oxygen charging port: both were placed on the starboard side of the fuselage, just below the cockpit.

Several Messerschmitt Bf 109 C-1s were upgraded to the C-3 standard, which featured the

The Messerschmitt Bf 109 V6 in service with the Condor Legion as 6•2. Of notice is the characteristic prop spinner.

Development of the Bf 109 design

Messerschmitt Bf 109. As from 2.J/88 shortly after arrival in Spain.

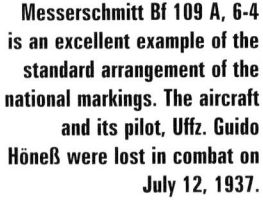

This picture of the Messerschmitt Bf 109 A, 6-4 is an excellent example of the standard arrangement of the national markings. The aircraft and its pilot, Uffz. Guido Höneß were lost in combat on July 12, 1937.

"armed wing" with two MG FF 20 mm cannons. Sixty rounds of ammunition per cannon were stored in drum magazines placed next to the weapons (on the right side of the left wing cannon and on the left side of the cannon mounted in the right wing section). Special fairing were added to the wing's lower surface to accommodate the ammunition drums, which otherwise would not have fitted inside the wing structure. Spent casings were ejected into a container placed between wing ribs 3b and 4, which could be accessed via a panel on the wing's lower surface.

There were plans to develop versions C-2 and C-4 of the fighter, which were to carry a heavier armament fit. The C-2 variant was to be equipped with an additional MG 17 mounted between the cylinder blocks. An MG FF 20 mm cannon was to be placed in the same location on the C-4 variant.

Messerschmitt Bf 109 D-1

The new version of the Bf 109 was to be powered by the Daimler-Benz DB 601 engine. However, the development of the new poweplant suffered some delays, which forced the RLM to give a go-ahead for the production of an interim model equipped with the Junkers Jumo 210 D.

Designated Bf 109 D-1, the new fighter was an all-metal, cantilevered monoplane with retractable landing gear and fully enclosed cockpit. It was powered by the inline Junkers Jumo 210 D carbureted engine. The aircraft's armament fit was identical to the arrangement used on the C-1 model (four MG 17 machine guns). The fighter was fitted with the Revi C/12D reflector gun sight.

Based on available documents, several W.Nr. batches cannot be traced back to any of the existing manufacturing facilities (W.Nr. 2110-2150, 2365-2370, 2440-2476, 2513-2625, 2650-2730 and 2812-2940). It is quite possible that some of the serials were not used in production at all.

Externally the Bf 109 D-1 was practically identical to the C-1 version, the only significant difference being a redesigned tailwheel assembly. Some of the D-1s featured a port for a flare gun mounted on the right side of the windshield. Beginning in 1940 some of the "Doras" in service with combat units were retrofitted with exhaust stacks identical to the ones used on the Bf 109 E.

The Bf 109 D-1 in service with foreign air arms

In addition to the Luftwaffe, the D-1 model was offered to foreign customers as well. The first nation to receive Bf 109 D-1s was Switzerland, which placed an order for five D-1s and a single Bücker Bü 180 in 1938. Under the 731 000 RM contract Switzerland received the first fighter in December 1938. The Swiss liked their new fighter so much that they immediately placed an order for additional five aircraft, which were delivered along with the original batch in January 1939.

In Switzerland the Bf 109 D-1s served with 15. Fliegerkompanie, where they were operated alongside E-3s, also acquired from Germany. In May and June 1940 there were several incidents involving the 15. Fliegerkompanie fighters and the Luftwaffe machines, which wandered into Swiss airspace. On June 4, 1940 a pair of Bf 109 D-1s belonging to Fl. Kp. 15 launched for a routine patrol from their base at Olten. The aircraft flown by Oblt. Suter and Lt. Rickenbacher had no radios. Rickenbacher took off first and set course for Saignelegier. After about five minutes he was joined by Suter and both fighters continued to climb to 3 500 m. Over La Caux-de-Fonds Suter spotted a formation of three unidentified aircraft flying on a north-easterly heading along the Swiss border. Being unable to positively identify the country's border, Suter continued to shadow the unidentified formation. Minutes later he lost visual contact with his lead.

Shortly the three Bf 110s (which Suter initially thought were bomber types) were joined by one more aircraft. After a while the new arrival performed a split S and disappeared in the cloud deck. The other three aircraft quickly followed and soon Suter lost contact with the German flight.

It is very likely that the lone aircraft that Suter saw was the Bf 109 D-1, J-310, piloted by Lt. Rickenbacher. The Swiss fighter crashed into the ground after a near vertical dive, its engine still running at full power. Rickebacher's body was later found some 400 m from the wreckage. The Swiss pilot was most likely shot down by Uffz. Kutschera from 5./ZG 1 flying a Bf 110. After the incident the D-1s were withdrawn from combat patrol duties. The Messerschmitt fighters soldiered on in Swiss service until 1949. A pair of Bf 109 D-1s was also delivered to Hungary, where the aircraft served with tactical codes V.601 and V.602.

The table below presents details of the D-1 production run:

Manufacturer	Quantity	W.Nr.
Bayerische Flugzeugwerke, Augsburg	4	?
Erla Maschinenwerk, Leipzig	168	417-539 618-665
Fieseler-Werke, Kassel	80	3090-3170
Focke-Wulf Flugzeugbau, Bremen	123	?
AGO Werke, Oschersleben	128	?
Arado Werke, Warnemünde	144	2066-2080 2201-2325
Total:	647	

The table below summarizes technical specs and performance figures of the D-1 model:

Dimensions	Wingspan	9.90 m
	Length	8.70 m
	Height	2.50 m
	Landing gear track	2.00 m
	Wing area	16.40 m^2
Weights	Max take-off	2 160 kg
Performance	Max airspeed at MSL	410 kph
	Max airspeed at 3 000 m	450 kph
	Max dive speed	800 kph
	Landing speed	111 kph
	Time to climb to 1 000 m	1.35 min
	Time to climb to 5 000 m	8.51 min
	Operational ceiling	8 100 m
	Flight endurance	2 h

The table below presents details of all Bf 109 D-1s in Swiss service:

W.Nr.	Swiss serial	In service from:	Stricken from inventory:	Remarks
2297	J-301	19.01.1939	28.12.1949	–
2299	J-302	19.01.1939	28.12.1949	–
2295	J-303	17.12.1938	09.02.1948	Destroyed in an emergency landing mishap. Pilot: H. Bachofner
2298	J-304	10.01.1939	28.12.1949	–
2300	J-305	05.01.1939	28.12.1949	–
2301	J-306	10.01.1939	28.12.1949	–
2302	J-307	07.01.1939	28.12.1949	–
2303	J-308	10.01.1939	02.09.1947	–
2304	J-309	19.01.1939	28.12.1949	–
2305	J-310	05.01.1939	04.06.1940	Shot down by a Bf 110 from ZG 1. Pilot R. Rickenbacher from Fl. Kp. 15 was killed.

Development of the Bf 109 design

Messerschmitt Bf 109 A, 6•15, which made a forced landing behind the Republican lines on December 4, 1937. The aircraft's pilot, Fw. Otto Polenz from 1. J/88, became a POW.

This Bf 109 A, 6•15 was shipped via France to the Soviet Union, were it was disassembled and thoroughly studied.

Fw. Norbert Flegel's Messerschmitt Bf 109 A, 6-7.

Messerschmitt Bf 109 A/B/C/D in service with the Condor Legion

Messerschmitt Bf 109 A, 6-16 wearing the 2.J/88 badge on the fuselage.

Messerschmitt Bf 109 A/B/C/D in service with the Condor Legion

The rule of the socialist government in Spain led to the outbreak of a nationalist uprising on July 17, 1936. The nationalist forces under General Franco seized Morocco and a small part of the Iberian Peninsula. To maintain momentum Franco needed to find a way to transport the colonial troops from Morocco to Spain. Since the Republican navy controlled the shipping lines, the only available option was airlift. The Reich's Chancellor, Adolf Hitler, came to Franco's aid and agreed to provide any necessary support in the fight against the Popular Front.

On July 26, 1936 Hitler established *Sonderstab W* (Special Staff W) to coordinate German efforts to provide military assistance to the Spanish nationalists. On the following day a German Junkers Ju 52/3m (D-APOK) began to airlift nationalist troops from Tetuan to Jerez

This Bf 109 A, 6•16 received a metal VDM propeller during an overhaul. Later on the aircraft was flown by Oblt. Mölders during his time with 3.J/88.

Messerschmitt Bf 109 D-1, 6•51, flown by the CO of 1.J/88, Hptm. Wolfgang Schellmann.

Messerschmitt Bf 109 A/B/C/D in service with the Condor Legion

Messerschmitt Bf 109 B-1, 6•30 destroyed in a landing accident in August 1937. The pilot, Uffz. Wilhelm Staege, walked away from the crash with only minor injuries.

Lt. Walter Adoph crashed this Messerschmitt Bf 109 during a botched landing attempt on September 5, 1937.

de la Frontera in Spain. The single Junkers was joined by ten more Ju 52s on August 9, 1936. By October 11, 1936 German crews had airlifted 13 528 troops and 270 000 kg of cargo.

The Condor Legion was officially established on November 7, 1936. The organization consisted of 4 500 volunteers under the command of Generalmajor Hugo Sperrle. The establishment of the Legion was a direct response to the International Brigades created to support the Republicans. The Legion included two fighter outfits: J/88 – Jagdgruppe 88 (88. Fighter Group) and VJ/88 – Versuchsjagdstaffel 88 (88. Experimental Fighter Squadron).

In early December 1936 VJ/88 received three Bf 109 prototypes: V3, V4 and V6. The Bf 109 V4 did not last very long in Spain. The aircraft, wearing its 6•1 code on the fuselage, crashed on take-off from Tablada airfield on December 10, 1936. The mishap pilot was Uffz. Erich Kley. One of the aircrews tasked with combat testing of the Luftwaffe's new fighter was Lt. Hannes Trautloft. Here is how he remembers his first impressions of the Messerschmitt[21]: *December*

12 – the Bf 109[22] is absolutely gorgeous. Next to her the good old He 51 looks like an aging beauty, although saying good bye to this old friend still breaks my heart.

Unfortunately, the Bf 109 won't be ready until tomorrow – her engine is still making some funny noises. (...)

December 13 – the Bf 109 is still not ready to go flying. There are still some issues with the engine. Somebody said: 'She's like a real thoroughbred, you almost expect her to have serious attitude problems at first.' In addition to the engine, the starboard machine gun isn't working. And she's not wearing the proper military paint scheme. I give up the top hat[23], but insist on the green heart: Thuringia, the green heart of Germany, just has to be there. (...)

Lt. Josef Fözö from 3.J/88 pictured at Figueroas airfield shortly after the return from another combat sortie.

Messerschmitt Bf 109 from J/88 during one of the escort sorties.

A flight of Bf 109 D-1s from 3.J/88 during a routine patrol over the frontlines.

December 14 – at last the 109 is ready. The take-off feels a bit awkward, but once airborne I feel totally at home. The machine is just wonderful. I spot an Italian Fiat overflying the field. Up till now it has been Franco's fastest fighter. Not anymore: I catch up with the Italian aircraft in seconds and seconds later it is just a speck in the sky, far behind me. Oh, how badly we needed aircraft like this one, at least ten of them, right from the start. Things would look so much different now - Eberhard and Henrici would still be alive...

December 14 – 23 – I've been in Seville for almost two weeks now. The Bf 109 is still suffering from some teething problems. Nothing serious, sometimes it's the tail wheel, some other time it might be the coolant pump, carburetor or landing gear fairings. Whatever the case, repairs always take forever. Once when I was in the pattern over the

Messerschmitt Bf 109 A/B/C/D in service with the Condor Legion

The badge of 3.J/88 painted on the fuselage of one of the unit's Bf 109s.

Hptm. Werner Mölders, the CO of 3.J/88 photographed next to his Messerschmitt Bf 109 D-1, 6•79, "Luchs".

field the engine quit and I had to dead-stick the airplane. It all went well and I landed in one piece.(...)

December 24 – at around noon the alarm sounded. All aircraft got airborne immediately, even non-fighter types. If the Reds were to show up they would find an empty airfield. Flying my Bf 109 I quickly passed everybody else on the way to 4 500 m. Once there I was joined by other Nationalist aircraft – Spanish, Italian and German – and we began to orbit the airfield. The Reds would be in for a nice surprise! Well, in the end they never showed up – another false alarm. (...)

January 14 – my Bf 109 is ready. The weather isn't especially good, but I'm still going to go to Villa del Prado, near Escalona, just 40 km south-west of Madrid. Flying the Bf 109 is sheer joy. I've never had that feeling before: time and space, except for a patch of ground down below my wings, just cease to exist. The weather deteriorated and I had to land at Caceres. Even then the people who came up to my aircraft looked like extraterrestrials to me – they were moving so slowly! It took a while before I got used to walking on the ground again...

A gaggle of Spanish mechanics gathered around my Messerschmitt admiring this technological marvel. (...)

January 20 – it's 1000 hours and I'm hanging 5 000 m above Madrid. From above the Spanish capital looks small and very quiet. I've been flying up and down the frontline for over an hour, but my prayers have not been answered: there's not one Red in sight. The fuel's getting low, time to go home. On the way back I head for Torijos to show the Italians what my Bf 109 can do. Two Fiats are airborne over the field and I zoom by them so fast that they seem to be standing still. (...)

On landing the tail wheel fails to extend from the fuselage – that's already the second time. The vertical stabilizer is damaged, and although the work to fix it begins immediately, the aircraft won't be ready until the next day. After much deliberation I tell the mechanics to block the tail wheel in the extended position. It'll be much better to just leave it like that in flight, than to waste more time on repairs. (...)

February 10 – the airfield is still very muddy, but I decide to take a chance anyway. During the take-off roll the aircraft swerves to the left. When I finally get airborne my left wingtip is almost touching the ground. I depart the field feeling great relief that there were no obstacles on the ground.

It feels so great to go flying again after such a long break. I'm playing in the air like a stallion let

Messerschmitt Bf 109 B-1 from the early production batch. The II./JG 132 machine is pictured here during an exercise conducted in the summer of 1937.

An early example of the Messerschmitt Bf 109 B-1 featuring a wooden Schwartz propeller. This aircraft belonged to II./JG 132 and was photographed at Jüterbog-Damm airfield in the summer of 1937.

Messerschmitt Bf 109 A/B/C/D in service with the Condor Legion

This Messerschmitt Bf 109 B-1 was flown by Lt. Walter Oesau from Stab J/88.

loose from a stuffy stable. The rains have brought a fresh feeling into the air, the first sign of spring. Down below everything is greening. The fields and meadows now have a richer shade of green, the kind of color I have not seen in a long time.

Having made sure that my guns are in order, I decide to go for a little bit of a sweep over the frontlines. Just want to see if the Reds are also enjoying the coming of spring.

4 000 meters below me is Cerro de los Angeles; I'm sure the infantry down below are waving at me while the Reds are pounding their bunkers. I circle over Madrid trying to keep the sun behind my back. I might get lucky only if I manage to catch the Reds by surprise. They still don't want to come out to play, although I've been flying in circles right above their heads for over an hour. Finally I've had enough of this and leave.

It was to be my first landing at Almoror. As soon as wheels touch the ground I can feel that the field is completely rain-soaked. The main wheels sink deeper and deeper and the tail begins to rise dangerously high. God, have mercy! Just a few more centimeters and I will definitely nose over! The good old Bf 109 hesitates for a split second, then drops the tail and sinks into the muddy ground.

I enlist the help of ground personnel to pull the aircraft from the muddy trap. All in vain – no amount of human strength will do. 'I'll get the oxen', says one of the mechanics and is off to the nearby field ,where a farmer is using the animals to plough his lot. The mechanic is a smart cookie from Saxony: in no time at all he explains to the farmer why we need to borrow his beasts. Then it's only a matter of minutes before my Bf 109 is finally freed from the mud. After the work is done I approach the mechanic and ask him how he managed to explain our plight to the farmer. 'In Saxon, of course!' is the reply. (...)

February 11 – when I took Neumann, our staff doctor, back to Villa del Prado in a Klemm the weather was perfect. The timing of our arrival couldn't be better: the crews of three Junkers and three Romeos were just getting ready to fly a bombing sortie against the Reds' positions near Madrid. I quickly jumped into the Bf 109 and joined three He 51s from Roth's squadron [3.J/88 – author's note] and a few Italians. On the way out I stayed some 1 000 meters above the Junkers. On approach to Madrid I spotted five Red fighters, which stayed well clear of our formation. The Junkers dropped their bombs, while the Reds just looked on and it seemed they really couldn't care less. When I eventually climbed higher to attack them using altitude advantage, they quickly turned east and ran like hell. (...)

February 14 – two full fighter squadrons launch in the afternoon, this time without the bombers. Our aim was to patrol over the frontlines as long as possible, hoping that the Reds might finally want to come out and fight. So far their only activity have been quick, hit and run attacks against our bombers. The CO himself led the formation. Flying with us were Roth's [3.J/88 – author's note] and Winterer's [V.J/88 – author's note] squadrons. I flew alone in my Bf 109, above the main formation to maintain altitude advantage over any potential threat. We stayed up above the frontline for over an hour and the Reds again refused to fight. Well, we thought the world of those guys, but they disappointed us yet again. (...)

February 16 – a new offensive is to be launched just east of Pinto. To support the ground troops ten Junkers got airborne tasked with bombing the known Reds' positions. Their top cover was provided by 18 He 51 and yours truly. The Junkers and Heinkels cruised at 4 000 m, while I again stayed 1 000 m above them to have a better picture of the situation.

Throughout the flight I had to keep the throttle in check and fly a zigzag pattern, or else I would leave the rest of the formation far behind. Just south of Madrid I spotted a loose formation of five aircraft flying north some 800 m above me. It appeared that they haven't detected me. I pulled up into a climb and soon realized that the aircraft were Italian Fiats. Then I spotted a large number of aircraft some 1 000 m below that were also heading towards Madrid. When I returned to the Junkers flight I noticed that one of the He 51 squadrons was flying in a very loose formation. The gaps between aircraft were irregular – a type of formation you would assume every time there was an imminent threat of a Red attack. Although I kept a very careful lookout, I couldn't see any Red aircraft in the area. The only traffic I could see were five small specks to the north that must have been those Italian Fiats that I had stumbled upon a few minutes before.

In the meantime the Junkers crews released their bomb loads. The results of the bombing were hard to assess from altitude – all I could see was plumes of smoke shooting up from the ground.

Our bombers and fighter squadrons set course for home and I turned with them, staying well above the main force. Somewhere behind us were those five Italians cruising even higher than me. I looked around to see if I can make them out. There they are: behind me and to the right. I couldn't see them clearly because the canopy framing was getting in the way. Besides, the sun was shining right in my face. To get a better look I slightly altered my course to head east. Suddenly one of the five aircraft launched into a mad attack against me. Now I could see that the attacking aircraft had no fixed landing gear. Neither did another one that was just setting up for attack. What the hell is going on? Those must be five Red Ratas![24] By the time I realized what was happening, the entire five-ship formation was in a wild dive to get me. I had only one option: run straight down! I did a quick half roll and stood the aircraft on its nose. Ratas were just above me, soon the bullets from their guns would start hitting my 109. I instinctively curled myself into a ball to make myself as small a target as possible. I screamed towards the deck at absolutely amazing speed. I could see nothing behind me, so I concentrated on looking to the left and right of the cockpit. I could not believe that there were still no tracer trails zooming by my aircraft, I heard no tell-tale rattling sound of bullets hitting the fuselage skins. I began to recover from the dive at about 1 000 m. God, that must have been the fastest ride down from 5 000 m in my life! My head was humming and I felt like I was about to black out. I finally leveled out and made a few shallow turns that made me feel much better (a medical explanation of this anyone?). The Reds had disappeared. It looked like I got lucky yet again. I was still very angry with myself for mistaking the Ratas for Italian Fiats. I should've recognized them a lot sooner. Only God knew why those guys gave up on me and didn't blow me to heavens come.

We returned to base and had a very short lunch break. Right after the meal we launched again: 19 Heinkels and I – an escort force for 11 Junkers bombers crewed by Spaniards. This time the Italians didn't fly with us.

I am again 1 000 meters above the bombers and both He 51 units. We reached the frontlines without contact with enemy fighters. Again the bombs were released, very close to the targets we had bombed earlier in the day.

I was extremely vigilant on the way back home: I just wouldn't have the Ratas take me by surprise again. But, ironically, when you've got all your ducks in the row the Reds never show up. When I descended slightly towards the Junkers formation I noticed

This Bf 109 B-1 "yellow 12" from 3./JG 132 is having her guns' convergence adjusted at Döberitz airfield.

Messerschmitt Bf 109 A/B/C/D in service with the Condor Legion

Pictured in the foreground is the Bf 109 B-1 "yellow 10" from 3./JG 132. The aircraft in the background are Heinkel He 51s and a single Junkers Ju 52/3m transport.

three very fast aircraft approaching our territory. I went into a steep dive passing the Junkers and our fighters on the way down. I wanted to take a closer look at those babies. Suddenly there were tracer rounds flying all around my aircraft. Somebody was shooting at me! I arrested the dive and pulled back sharply on the stick. What I then saw literarily took my breath away: our own He 51s were firing at me with all they had! Those guys were from Strümpell's squadron. They obviously failed to see the markings on my fighter and took me for a Rata. I let loose of a combination of curses and obscenities that no sailor, driver, grunt or common porter would be ashamed of. Strümpell should be glad he couldn't hear that.

When I passed by along the entire formation they finally recognized me and ceased firing. I could now resume on the way down. The three aircraft were still down there, but when I got closer I just cursed myself: 'You dumbass, those are Italian Romeos on their way back from a recon sortie!'[25]

In March 1937 2.J/88 received sixteen Bf 109 A fighters. The unit's commander was Oblt. Günther Lützow, who on April 6, 1937 was credited with the first air-to-air kill flying the Bf 109: *The first kill: 1745 hours, 2 400 m, north west of Ochandiano, a Curtiss biplane. Three others escaped towards Bilbao chased by myself, Hptm. von Janoson and Heilmayer. We could not get a clear shot as the Curtiss quickly flew into the cloud. The enemy pilot safely bailed out and landed behind our lines. An 18 year-old rookie. During interrogation he claimed that he was flying the Santander-Bilbao-Barcelona-Valencia route*[26]

On April 22, 1937 Lt. Radusch and Fw. Heilmayer from 2.J/88 each downed an I-15 fighter. One of the downed I-15 pilots was Felipe del Rio, a Republican ace with seven kills under his belt. In the north the Republican presence in the air was very weak indeed, which explains why the Bf 109 pilots did not score another victory until May 22, 1937. On that day Oblt. Lützow shot down an I-15 over Bilbao. He bagged another I-15 five days later near Santander.

On July 5, 1937 the Republicans launched a major offensive near Brunette, west of Madrid. Three days later, on July 8, 1937 Lt. Pingel and Uffz. Höneß from 2.J/88 shot down two SB-2 bombers. On July 11, 1937 Uffz. Flegel crashed in his Bf 109 during an emergency landing attempt following a major engine malfunction. The following day saw a flurry of air battles during which the pilots from 2.J/88 scored five air-to-air kills: Lt. Pingel downed

Messerschmitt Bf 109 B-1 from 3./JG 132 sporting a medal VDM propeller.

Hptm. Stormer from Stab Tr.Gr. 186. The unit operated Messerschmitt Bf 109 B-1 fighters.

an SB-2 bomber and an I-16, Uffz. Höneß dispatched two Aero 101s, while Fw. Boddem added a single I-16 to his tally. Fw. Buhl also claimed an I-16, but the kill was not officially confirmed. On the same day the Condor Legion suffered the first Bf 109 combat loss: Uffz. Guido Höneß's Messerschmitt was attacked by an I-16 (flown by an American volunteer Frank Tinker) and impacted the ground after a vertical dive from 2 500 m. The German pilot was killed in action.

On July 13, 1937 Fw. Boddem shot down an I-15 flown by an American volunteer Harold Dahl. The Republican pilot was taken prisoner after he had bailed out from his aircraft. Three days later, on July 16, 1937, Lt. Pingel chalked up another aerial victory when he dispatched an I-16. On the following day Lt. Handrick's Bf 109 suffered an engine failure right after a fight against several Ratas north of Madrid. The German pilot managed to nurse his aircraft across the frontline and made a successful forced landing near Escalon.

On July 18, 1937 Franco's forces began a counter attack near Brunete. There was also heavy fighting in the air: Ofw. Hillmann downed an I-16, while Uffz. Harbach, having been hit by enemy fire, had to bail out of his Bf 109 A, 6•14.

At around that time another batch of 22 Messerschmitt fighters arrived at Leon air base, including two A models and 20 Bf 109 Bs. By the end of the year seven more Bs and five Bf 109 Cs had been delivered to Spain, which allowed 1.J/88 and the squadron's HQ flight to convert to the new fighters. Later on, in the fall of 1937, 3.J/88 also traded their Heinkels for Bf 109s.

On July 21 and 25, 1937 Fw. Boddem scored two more air-to-air kills. By July 28, after the battle of Brunete, the Nationalists re-captured the territories they had previously lost during

Messerschmitt Bf 109 B-1s from I. and II./JG 132 parked at Jüterbog-Damm airfield during an official visit of the Yugoslavian prime minister on January 18, 1938.

Messerschmitt Bf 109 A/B/C/D in service with the Condor Legion

Some of the Messerschmitt Bf 109 C/Ds from I./ZG 144 (later renamed II./ZG 76) featured a stylized shark's mouth motif on the lower front section of the engine cowling and radiator intake.

the Republican offensive. The CO of 2.J/88, Oblt. Lützow, wrote a very interesting report detailing his unit's actions during the battle of Brunete: *On average we would fly three sorties per day, not counting alarm scrambles. Each sortie lasted for about 1½ hours and was flown between 6 000 and 7 000 meters. At that time we still operated without oxygen masks, which we soon learned was not a good idea. High altitude flying without oxygen can be a very grueling experience. We were all exhausted: on top of the physical demands of combat flying we had to make sure all air-to-air kills were properly recorded and confirmed, since there were so precious few of them back then. Time after time we faced the enemy who outnumbered us in every encounter. That meant that we never had enough time to properly engage enemy aircraft. One had to stay close to his comrades and at the same time keep the enemy at bay when friendly bombers or reconnaissance aircraft were working over the frontlines.*

The alarm scrambles were the worst. From dawn to dusk two pilots were always strapped in

Messerschmitt Bf 109 A/B/C/D in service with the Condor Legion

Ground crew members of 11./JG 132 "Richthofen" and one of the unit's "109s" – the Bf 109 D-1 "red 7". Karlsbad airfield, fall of 1938.

and ready to go at a minute's notice. The pair would launch immediately, whenever the artillery observation posts reported enemy aircraft in the air. Given the short distance to the frontline, that was the only way to have a shot at intercepting enemy bombers before they could reach their intended targets. As fighting went on, there was a lot of anxiety on both sides. On many occasions the overzealous observers mistook friendly aircraft for enemy bombers, which resulted in false alarms and frequent scrambles of alert aircraft. Those false alarms made everybody even more jumpy and agitated. Pretty soon we were all in a state of permanent anxiety. Just about anything could spark a major row. People were cursing and barking at one another for no apparent reason at all. Of course, not everybody acted like that, but the overall aura of nervousness could be felt everywhere.

The ground personnel from 2./JG 71 replenish machine gun ammunition in this Messerschmitt Bf 109 D-1. The photograph was taken in August 1939.

Messerschmitt Bf 109 Early Versions — 47

Messerschmitt Bf 109 A/B/C/D in service with the Condor Legion

Messerschmitt Bf 109 C/Ds from I./ZG 2 parked at Groß Stein airfield in late August 1939. The "white 11" is a Bf 109 C-3 equipped with wing-mounted MG FF cannons. The "yellow 12" on the left is the personal mount of the CO of 3./ZG 2, Oblt. Josef Kellner-Steinmetz.

A pair of Messerschmitt Bf 109 D-1s pictured at one of the forward airfields shortly before the outbreak of war.

One day, as we were having a nice, quiet moment sitting in the shade near our aircraft, we heard a rumble of aircraft engines coming from the south. The sound was really intense, so we knew there had to be quite a formation out there. Then we could finally see them: they looked like Italian Savoias on their way back home. I raised the binoculars to take a closer look. They were, indeed, the Savoias. By now we could see their markings quite clearly with a bare eye. They were flying in a perfect formation, some 1 500 above the field. We counted ten aircraft, when somebody yelled: 'They're dropping bombs!' I just froze and couldn't believe what I'd just heard: 'It's impossible', I thought. But then I saw for myself little black specks separating from the aircraft and heading straight for us! I yelled: 'Everybody take cover!' just as the first bombs began to explode. I saw a bunch of ground crews running like mad to their shelters, some of them just dropping flat to the ground half way across the field. I was mad and completely helpless. I just clenched my fists and thought in anger: 'Dear God, just let me get a piece of those guys!'

The bombs were expertly aimed and dropped smack in the middle of the airfield. Thankfully, our aircraft were all parked in dispersal areas, which saved them from certain destruction. Our alert pilots both kept their cool and so did their ground crews. They didn't abandon their posts and used all their strength to crank up those engines. It was all in vain, though. Both pilots managed to get airborne, zigzagging between the bomb craters on their take-off rolls, but it was too late and they had no chance of catching up with the cowardly traitors. The attack was a complete surprise. Nobody could believe that the Reds were capable of such a clever plot. The aircraft were actually French Potez types, which in fact resemble Savoias. We could now understand how those guys managed to sneak through our lines and all the way to our airfield. Everybody, including us, believed those were Nationalist aircraft.

In the aftermath of the attack the observation posts saw every aircraft wearing Nationalist markings as a cleverly camouflaged Red bomber. I have to say that we too had our doubts now. It really was a weird feeling. There were similarities between many of the modern types, so sometimes we weren't sure if we were dealing with a friendly or hostile aircraft. Now things got even more complicated, which led to a tragic mistake:

On a cloudy day, just before dawn, we launched in a five-ship formation for a routine patrol over the frontlines. Over the previous few days the Reds used the pre-dawn twilight to attack our forward positions. I was intent on putting an end to that practice. We slowly climbed to 3 000 on our way to the patrol area. Before long our 'eagle eye' and one of the best pilots in the unit, Fw. Boddem, spotted five black dots approaching slightly above us. He pointed them to me and I immediately gave a signal to attack. If they were friendly aircraft I would've known about it, since our communication lines with other units usually worked very well. Those had to be enemy

Messerschmitt Bf 109 A/B/C/D in service with the Condor Legion

aircraft, probably Red bombers on an early morning stroll. One way or the other, they had to be attacked. My guys quickly took stock of the situation, spread out and charged the five approaching aircraft. I thought we were in for a great hunt! I was already congratulating myself for making a right decision and taking that early morning run over the frontlines. Even the wake-up call at that ungodly hour didn't seem so bad any more. In the meantime the tight bomber formation came very close to us. Being slightly below them we could not get to the bombers right away. I pushed the throttle all the way forward, hoping that my machine would not let me down. That was not enough, though: we didn't mange to get to the bombers before they reached our airfield. They flew over the airfield, made a sharp right turn and headed back towards the frontlines. Now they were flying right into us, there was no way they could escape. I turned towards them setting up for an attack. I was still trying to pick my first target when a I had a startling revelation: 'That type, I've seen it before!'. And then it all became clear to me: 'God, those are Italian bombers that worked with us back over the Northern Front!' I remember flying

Messerschmitt Bf 109 D-1s of I./ZG 2 ready to launch from their base at Groß Stein.

This Messerschmitt Bf 109 D-1 "yellow 1" was flown during the Polish campaign by the CO of 3./JG 21, Oblt. Georg Schneider. Notice the pennant mounted at the tip of the antenna mast.

Messerschmitt Bf 109 Early Versions — 49

Messerschmitt Bf 109 A/B/C/D in service with the Condor Legion

Ground crew members prepare the Bf 109 D-1 "white 2" for another sortie. The machine belonged to 1./ZG 2 and the black-white-black fuselage band identifies it as the personal aircraft of the unit's CO, Oblt. Waldemar von Roon.

on their wings for a while during the return flight from one of the missions. I remember their glazed cockpits bristling with twin machine guns. We even waived to each other. 'Well, I could do just that now', I thought. 'You have time to spare, go on, give them a wave'. I closed up on the bomber formation from the side. Now I could clearly see their national markings. Trying to be funny I flew just two meters over three Savoias leading the formation. At that instant I caught a glimpse of one of the gunners' somber face and noticed twin machine gun barrels pointing right at me. 'Well, here's one trigger happy guy', I thought. In the meantime the gunner wasted no time and began to fire away. I felt my aircraft shudder and at the same time something very hard hit my right shin. I also had a painful, stinging sensation in my right hand. I instinctively pulled up sharply paying no attention to the damage that the

Messerschmitt Bf 109 D-1 from 1./ZG 2 being refueled. The squadron's insignia is painted under the windshield, while the engine cowl wears the flight's badge.

Messerschmitt Bf 109 D-1 flown by the CO of I./ZG 2, Hptm. Johannes Gentzen. The photograph was taken on September 10, 1939 at Groß Stein airfield. Notice two white victory bars painted on the fighter's fin representing Gentzen's kills scored on September 2 and 3, 1939.

hits could have caused. Arming the guns and turning on the gun sight I was determined to return fire, regardless of the consequences. At the last moment, by God's grace, I came to my senses. I took a good look around and saw the airfield just behind me. There were no bomb craters there or any other visible sign of damage. Those guys could not have been the Red bombers then. The gunner most likely mistook me for an enemy fighter ,that's all. I turned off the gun sight and put the guns on safe. The right leg of my pants was torn to pieces, my shin looked like a real mess. The round must have gone right through the muscle tissue, because I felt no pain there anymore. My right glove was riddled with tiny holes and blood was seeping through every one of them. That didn't look too bad either – I could still move my fingers. Just in case I decided to take it easy: I approached to land as if I was coming in from my first solo.

I was really lucky: the bullets penetrated the right wing next to the fuselage and went through the seat. One of the rounds got lodged in the control stick, just below where my right hand had been. There was some minor damage to the wiring, but all in all the aircraft required only small repairs before it was ready to fly again. As I later found out, the rookie Italian gunner did mistake me for a Red fighter wearing Nationalist markings. He thought he had a bead on a bad guy and opened up on me without hesitation.(July 10, 1937)

Fighting at Brunete reached its apex. Despite our efforts in the air the Red bombers continued to harass the Nationalist positions. One day I was heading home after a long patrol over Talavera, Aranjuez, Madrid and Escorial when I saw white puffs of exploding AA shells right over our airfield. I looked around as hard as I could, but couldn't find any enemy aircraft in the area. A quick glance at the clock told me I had been airborne for 70 minutes. I had no time for investigation. Suddenly, to my left and slightly below, I saw four Martin bombers running towards Madrid at full throttle. Now I knew what our AA guys were trying to hit. Should I go after them, or is it a bad idea? The fuel gauge showed little more than fumes, but what red-blooded fighter pilot would waste an opportunity like that? Heading downstairs, I quickly armed the guns and turned on the sight. I fire-walled the throttle and gave chase to the four Martins. Opening up from quite a distance away I was hoping to use all ammunition in the short time that I could stay in the air. Not a smart thing to do, especially that the bombers were flying straight into the sun. To make things even worse, the bulb in my reflector sight burned out, which rendered it completely useless. I had to aim the guns using the engine cowling as the only point of reference.

I assumed from the start that I just wouldn't get any good hits. I kept firing like crazy, but I was still miles away from the last bomber in the formation. The barrels quickly overheated and all three machine guns jammed at exactly the same time. I was cursing and swearing: now I was just thirty meters behind the enemy bomber, frantically trying to get the guns to work. One of the enemy gunners quickly seized the opportunity and started firing at me like crazy. Thankfully, he must have been really nervous since not one round found its mark. I had to make a quick decision: disengage (a smart move if I wanted to make it back home in one piece), or try to get the guns working and take another pass at the bombers. The latter would inevitably lead to an *off-airfield landing (fuel starvation), a difficult task in the mountainous terrain.*

At long last reason prevailed – we had precious few serviceable aircraft at that time, so with a great deal of sadness I bid my adversaries farewell. I didn't exactly feel like a hero back then, but as a squadron commander I was responsible for the unit's aircraft and for the prudent use of the available assets.

When I landed at Avila I noticed that both alert aircraft had been scrambled and went after the Red bombers. One of the pilots returned to base shortly thereafter, having lost contact with the bandits. The other one, Fw. Boddem, chased the Reds all the way to their base and shot one of them down as the bomber was setting up to land. When Boddem came in to report the kill I felt a sting in my heart. Once again I started brooding over the whole affair: Boddem's success was proof positive that the man had made the right decision. But I was right, too, although I didn't score a kill. How can one make any sense of that? I don't know the answer to this day. It may be a matter of luck, or maybe it's just all written in the stars. (July 21, 1937)[27]

During the first ten days of August 1937 the Condor Legion units began to operate in the area around Santander. On August 13 Fw. Boddem shot down a Republican I-16 fighter. By August 25 Santander had fallen into the Nationalist hands with a little help from the Condor Legion fighters: the German Bf 109 pilots shot down no fewer than nine Republican aircraft over the city.

By that time 1.J/88 had also converted to the new Messerschmitt fighter. The CO, Oblt. Harro Harder, scored the unit's first kill flying the Bf 109: *The Martin bomber is a nimble, sturdy and extremely fast aircraft. Sigmund and I split up during the fight. Terry peels back to watch our six. I come in real close to the bomber, my aircraft dancing in its prop wash. Taking careful aim I squeeze off a single burst. That is enough to set the large bomber on fire. Pulling up sharply I watch the Martin crash into a plowed field down below.*[28]

During a period of heavy fighting in Asturia, in September and October 1937, the crews from 1. and 2.J/88 downed fifteen Republican aircraft. Among the most successful pilots were Hptm. Harder (1.J/88) and Fw. Boddem (2.J/88), who scored 10 kills each during the Spanish campaign.

In November 1937 the Bf 109 units operated over Saragossa, where the pilots from 2.J/88

Hptm. Johannes Gentzen, the CO of I./ZG 2 in the cockpit of a Bf 109 D-1.

achieved six air-to-air kills. In early December 1937 General Franco began his drive towards Madrid through the Guadarrama Mountains. On December 4, 1937 Fw. Otto Polenz from 1. J/88 made an emergency landing behind enemy lines. His Bf 109 A (6•15) was captured, repaired and shipped via France to the Soviet Union, where it was thoroughly inspected and studied.

On the following day another pilot from 1.J/88, Ofw. Leo Sigmund, was shot down and taken prisoner. By the end of December 1937 the crews of 1.J/88 had shot down four enemy aircraft. Also in December Hptm. Harder handed over the command of 1.J/88 to Oblt. Wolfgang Schellmann. The new CO scored his first air-to-air victory on January 17, 1938. Prior to that other 1.J/88 pilots also achieved confirmed kills: on January 12 Ofw. Seiler and Uffz. Staege each added an enemy aircraft to their tallies (Staege's victory was at the same time the 100th kill scored by J/88 aircrews). During fighting at Teruel in January 1938 the Bf 109 pilots shot down eight Republican aircraft without a single loss among their own ranks.

The Nationalist forces launched their decisive offensive at Teruel on February 5, 1938. During the first few hours of the operation Uffz. Lohrer from 2.J/88 downed a Rata fighter. On the following day another pilot from the same unit, Uffz. Stange, dispatched an I-16 fighter flown by Luis de Frutos, one of the leading Republican aces. The Spanish pilot was killed in action.

February 7, 1938 was the Condor Legion's most successful day in the entire campaign: German pilots shot down as many as twelve enemy aircraft (ten SB-2 bombers and two I-16s). Four of the bombers fell victim to the guns of Oblt. Balthasar, while Lt. Mayer and Ofw. Seiler both achieved double kills. Four other pilots returned to base with single victories to their credit: Ofw. Prestele, Uffz. Quasinowski, Uffz. Terry and Oblt. Schlichting. This is how Hptm. Handrick remembers those events: *Our bomb squadron was tasked with attacking enemy positions at Teruel. I took off as the leader of two flights of escort fighters. I personally led 1. Staffel, while 2. Staffel flew some distance ahead of us.*

Shortly after arriving over the frontlines I spotted a large formation of heavy aircraft approaching on the reciprocal heading. At first I thought that our bombers must have arrived early and were already heading home having dropped their bombs. However, just minutes later I could clearly see the red Republican markings painted on the bombers' fuselages. Those were definitely Russian machines. The Republicans were immediately engaged by the 2. Staffel flying ahead of us. In the meantime we tried to squeeze every bit of power from our engines to also get a piece of the action. After all 22 Martin

Armorers replenish ammunition magazines feeding two MG 17s of a Bf 109 D-1 from I./ZG 2.

This Messerschmitt Bf 109 D-1 "white 9" from 1./JG 71 was involved in a landing mishap at Fürstenfeldbrück airfield in the fall of 1939.

bombers without fighter escort was a target not to be missed. It is not every day that you see that kind of scene through your gun sight. The Rojos[29] crews turned around and began to run for their lives as soon as they spotted us. They were jumped when still in the turn and within seconds two of them went down trailing thick, black smoke behind them. Both aircraft disintegrated in mid air, just moments after their crews bailed out. The remaining bombers were bogging out at full throttle. By that time, however, they were within range of our guns and in no time at all eight more SB-2s were tumbling to the ground in flames.

I closed in to within 150 meters of one of the Martins. I could clearly see the gunner who was madly firing at me. In my sights the bomber loomed bigger than a barn. I squeezed the trigger, but after only fourteen rounds both machine guns fell silent. I couldn't believe it – they were both jammed! As soon as I disengaged I noticed three or four Rata flights descending upon us like spring rain. The bomber's escorts arrived! During a short and intense fight two Ratas went down in flames. We then had to re-join our bombers to protect them from the Republican fighter threat. However, the enemy fighters didn't seem too keen to keep us company. The Reds disappeared into thin air making a beeline back towards Valencia. Not surprisingly, the bombers reached their targets completely unmolested.[30]

By the end of February 1938 the Bf 109 pilots from 1. and 2.J/88 added ten more Republican aircraft to their tallies, including seven kills scored on February 21 alone. On the following day Franco's troops marched into Teruel.

After the fall of Teruel General Franco revised the priorities of his campaign. Instead of the drive towards Madrid, he chose to launch an offensive across Aragon towards the Mediterranean coast and cut the Republican-held territory in half.

The first two air victories during fighting over Aragon were scored on March 8, 1938 by Oblt. Schellmann and Lt. Awe z 1.J/88. Two days later the Bf 109 pilots launched low level strafing attacks against enemy airfields at Belchite and Jatiel destroying three I-15 fighters parked on the ground. Several I-15s and I-16s took off to defend their bases, but were quickly dealt with by the German fighters: Uffz. Rochel, Oblt. Schlichting, and Ofw. Prestele all scored single kills. On the following day the Bf 109 crews were flying an escort sortie in support of 33 Heinkel He 111 bombers, when the formation was attacked by over 30 Republican fighters. The Germans managed to defend the bombers, although one Messerschmitt pilot was lost in the fight: Oblt. Alexander Graf zu Dohna from 2.J/88 was killed in action during his second combat sortie. Although five He 111s suffered various degrees of damage, the entire formation made it safely back to base.

On March 13, 1938 the 2.J/88 crews avenged the death of their comrade by shoot-

Messerschmitt Bf 109 D-1 flown by the CO of JGr. 152, Hptm. Wilhelm Lessmann. Biblis airfield, September 17, 1939.

Another shot of the Bf 109 D-1 presented on the previous page: the ground crew members are hard at work replacing the fighter's engine.

Messerschmitt Bf 109 A/B/C/D in service with the Condor Legion

Messerschmitt Bf 109 D-1, "yellow 2" from 3./JGr. 152 undergoing gun convergence adjustments at Biblis airfield.

ing down two I-15s near Caspe. The victorious pilots were Lt. Ettling and Uffz. Ihlefeld. More fighting took place on March 24, 1938 over the Ebro River, where Lt. Awe, Oblt. Schellmann and Uffz. Stark both achieved single I-15 kills. Four days later, on March 29, 1938 Lt. Hans-Karl Meyer from 1.J/88 celebrated his fourth air-to-air kill – a Republican I-15 fighter that he downed over Lerida.

On April 4, 1938 two Bf 109s (6•20 and 6•21) collided in mid air during a repositioning flight to Lanaja airfield. Lt. Fritz Awe was killed in the crash, while Uffz. Borchers suffered severe injuries.

On April 23, 1938 Franco's forces began their drive towards Valencia. While heavy fighting continued on the ground, the skies remained relatively quiet until May 11, 1938 when Uffz. Ihlefeld from 2.J/88 shot down a single I-16. Four days later Lt. Priebe dispatched another I-16 over Sagunto, while on May 18 Uffz. Rochel and Hptm. Handrick both scored single aerial victories.

The J/88 base at La Cenia came under attack on June 2, 1938 when a formation of nine SB-2 bombers made their appearance over the field. The enemy bombers were immediately intercepted by the alert aircraft. Within minutes Lt. Heinrich shot down three Red bombers, while Uffz. Meyer and Uffz. Ihlefeld both reported single kills. The Reds returned on June 10, 1938. This time the J/88 alert crews did not manage to make contact with the enemy until the bombers were already on their way back home. After a short pursuit Uffz. Seufert and Uffz. Rochel took care of two escort I-16s, while Lt. Mayer sent one of the SB-2s to the ground. On the following day Lt. Neumann bagged an I-16 fighter during a "free hunt" mission.

On June 13, 1938 a large force of Red fighters jumped a formation of He 111s escorted by Bf 109s from J/88. The Germans claimed six confirmed kills, although six of the Heinkels also suffered damage in the fight. On the following day J/88 suffered two combat losses: flying his 140th combat sortie Lt. Priebe was escorting Stuka bombers when the formation was attacked by Republican fighters. Priebe was hit in the lungs and his Bf 109 B-1 (6•33) was severely damaged. The seriously wounded pilot did manage to safely force land his stricken aircraft. Seeing one of his comrades go down Fw. Kuhlmann quickly got on the tail of one of the I-15s and sent the Republican fighter to the ground. In the meantime a flight of four I-16s jumped another Bf 109, flown by Lt. Henz. The Messerschmitt received a number of hits and its pilot was forced to put the machine down in a hurry. Henz landed on a sandy patch along the Rio Mijares, which was well inside the enemy territory and the German pilot promptly became a POW. In the meantime six other Messerschmitts swooped low over Henz's fighter and set it on fire in a couple of strafing passes to prevent the Republicans from getting their hands on the machine.

Combat losses and hectic tempo of operations greatly reduced the number of airworthy aircraft in the J/88 inventory. In the 1. Staffel there were only four serviceable aircraft, while the 2. Staffel's strength was down to seven machines. Needless to say, the situation had a great impact on the unit's operational capabilities. Things began to look up when a new batch of Bf 109 C and Ds was delivered in the second half of the month, which allowed the 3. Staffel to convert to the Messerschmitt. On June 25, 1938 Oblt. Schellmann became the last Bf 109 pilot to score a kill that month when he successfully engaged a Rata fighter.

The early days of July, 1938 saw intense air activity over Valencia. on July 12, 1938 Lt. Keidel and Fw. Ihlefeld fought a victorious battle against I-15s and shot down two Republican fighters over Valencia harbor. Another encounter with the Red fighters took place when a large formation of I-15s attacked He 111s escorted by the Bf 109s. In the ensuing fight the Germans dispatched nine enemy aircraft. It was during that engagement that the future Condor Legion leading ace, Oblt. Werner Mölders from 3.J/88 scored his first aerial victory. Mölders was at the controls of a Bf 109 D (6•79) and this is how he remembered the fight: *What I saw took my breath away: over Valencia, still some distance away, I spotted a multitude of little black specks in the sky – enemy aircraft! So the long awaited moment has finally arrived. I climbed another 500 m constantly giving the attack signal. The dots in the sky were getting bigger and bigger – now I could recognize the type: some forty, maybe forty five Curtiss fighters. There were only six of us, all rookies, but so far the enemy pilots had not detected our presence. Let's go get them!*

I closed in undetected, but out of excitement I opened fire much too soon. The guy quickly turned around and headed straight for me. Within seconds I was staring into four machine guns spewing volleys of bullets.

Damn it, I was really scared. It looked like shooting down an enemy aircraft is not so easy after all! I caught a glimpse of a burning Curtiss falling to the ground and a deployed parachute canopy – my guys must have scored their first kill. I was wondering who the lucky man was. I throw the aircraft into a wild turn and mix it up with the enemy once again. For a split second I can see two Curtiss fighters running straight into me. Sweat is flooding my eyes as the two Reds zoom right past my Messerschmitt. Suddenly there is a Bf 109 in a vertical dive. I'm just hoping the pilot will recover before hitting the ground. Thank God, he pulls out just in time. I really don't want to lose anybody in the first fight. Now I kick myself for jumping those fighters: 45:6 is not exactly great odds. Well, all I can do now is fight. Suddenly I feel completely calm and composed. Keeping a careful lookout I spot two enemy fighters heading upstairs. I drop the nose to pick up some speed and then pull up sharply.

Lt. Hartmann Grasser from 3./JGr. 152 poses for the camera with the Iron Cross 2nd Class, which he received for a successful attack against an observation balloon on September 16, 1939. The aircraft behind him is a Messerschmitt Bf 109 D-1.

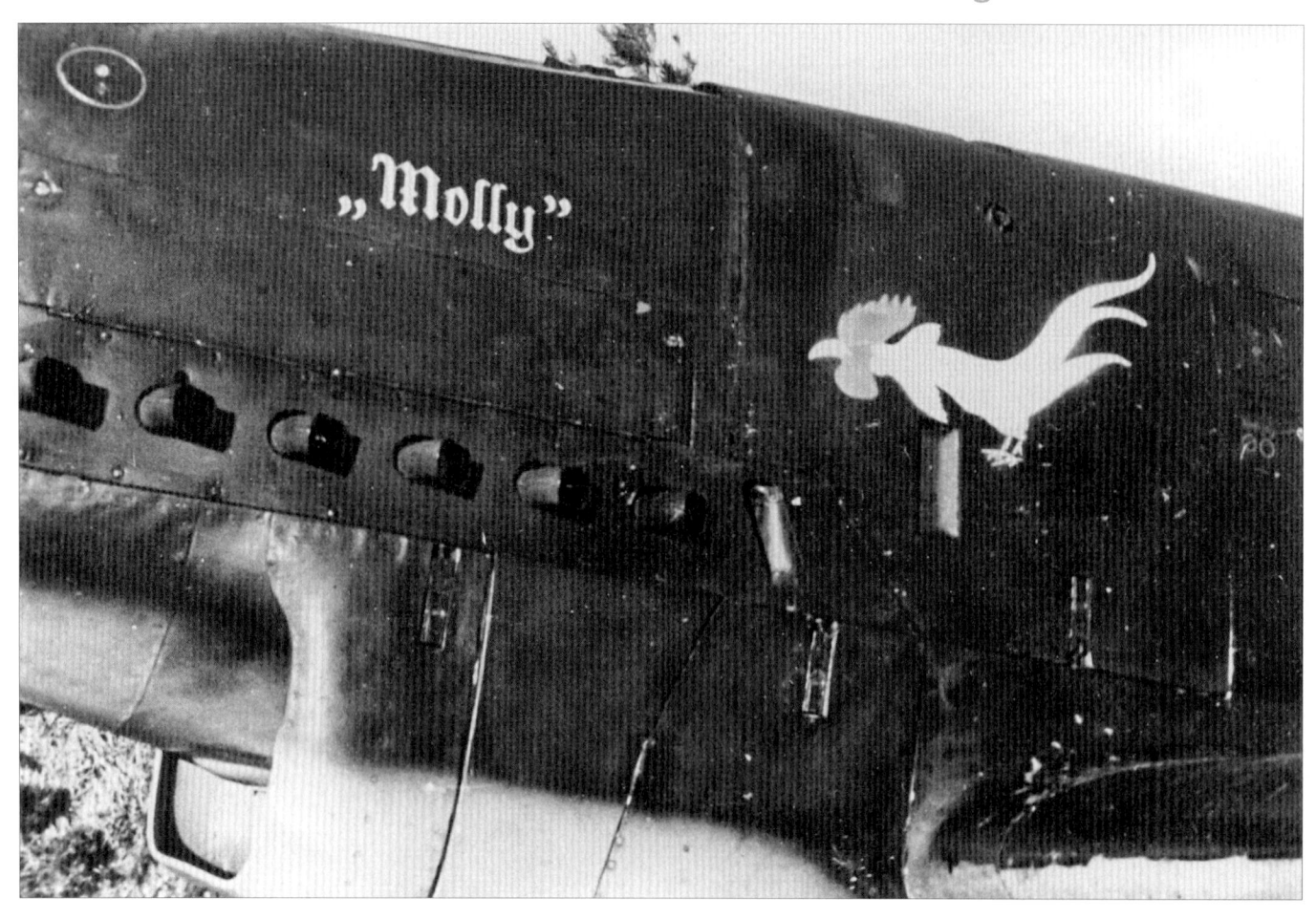

"Molly" – the Messerschmitt Bf 109 D-1, W.Nr. 2723, "yellow 3" from 3./JGr. 126 photographed in September 1939.

The second guy saw me coming and bogged out, but I get the other one in my sight. At fifty meters my guns begin to rattle. The enemy goes vertical and tumbles down in a mad dive. I follow suit and squeeze of another burst from all four guns. The Curtiss lights up and sends off a plume of black smoke. My first kill! I am on cloud nine! But where are my Messerschmitts?

All remaining Curtiss made a run for the deck. I form up with four of my fighters and together we set course for home. Over the field I rock my fighter's wings to signal a good kill. Another Messerschmitt in the formation does the same – that's Leutnant Lippert who shot down the first Curtiss. Down below I can see the ground crews jumping up and down with joy. My crew chief Meier could now paint the first white bar on my Bf 109's fin. Leutnant Oesau also bagged a Red fighter, so I could proudly report to the CO and claim three kills during our first combat sortie.[31]

Two days later, on July 17, 1938 the Bf 109 pilots downed six I-15 fighters, including Oblt. Werner Mölders' second kill: *The next day was pretty quiet, but on July 17, on a return leg from Valencia, I stumbled upon two flights of Curtiss fighters. Without hesitation we jumped the enemy and within minutes Uffz. Bauer had his first combat kill. The enemy pilot wasted no time and bailed out of his aircraft seconds after Bauer's initial burst. Shortly thereafter I put my sights on another Curtiss. The biplane immediately caught fire, the star-board wing separated from the fuselage and what remained of the aircraft tumbled to the ground. The pilot must have been killed instantly. Leutnant Oesau also scored a good kill during the fight.*[32]

On the second anniversary of the outbreak of the civil war (July 18, 1938) heavy air-to-air fighting took place over Segorbe. In several engagements with the Republicans the German pilots shot down three Rata fighters. On the following day a formation of Heinkel He 111s escorted by Bf 109s from 3.J/88 launched a strike against a road intersection between Segorbe and Liria. Over the target area the Messerschmitt pilots engaged a formation of Rata fighters and downed four of them. More victories were added to German tallies on July 20, when Oblt. Schellmann claimed two I-16s, while Uffz. Brucks returned to base with a single I-16 kill.

Heavy fighting continued on July 23, 1938. Here is Oblt. Mölders again: *It's a beautiful day today and we'll be flying escort for a bomber formation. Over the target area I noticed a flight of Messerschmitts mixing it up with some forty Curtiss and Rata fighters just north of Viver. I quickly take my guys right into that mess, but I soon realize that the Curtiss pilots have definitely done their homework: they maneuvered beautifully in the vertical and spread out in all directions at 1 000 meters. Mixed between them were Ratas that constantly kept popping up from the formation. In the mean-*

Messerschmitt Bf 109 D-1 from 3./JGr. 126 parked at Bönninghardt airfield.

time my first flight also showed up. I was trying to give Jänisch, my wingman, a clear shot of one of the Curtiss, but he was a bit late and too far behind. To make things worse our first flight got between us and the enemy fighters effectively ruining our chances for a clean shot.

Now all Messerschmitts were above the defensive circle formed by the enemy fighters. One by one the Bf 109s dropped down right in the middle of the Republican formation firing from a long distance and scoring no hits. Our machine guns worked from above, but when we targeted one enemy fighter we were immediately jumped by two or three others. The stalemate continued. At times one of our guys would fly right into the middle of the enemy circle and had to hightail immediately chased by hundreds of bullets fired from Republican guns.

I finally managed to maneuver into a good firing position behind one of the Curtiss fighters. In a wide turn I was closing the distance to the Curtiss: 200 meters, 100 meters, 50 meters – he still doesn't know I' behind him. Now the enemy fighter completely fills my gun sight. What a great opportunity! I can clearly see the enemy pilot looking forward and to the left as if he was trying to spot something in the distance. I know I just can't miss. I squeeze the trigger and... there's silence. What on earth is going on? The enemy in front of me performs a gentle, shallow turn. I try to re-cock the guns – still nothing. I am now working frantically to unjam the guns while at the same trying to keep the enemy in my gun sight. The red guns ready light is out – must be a short in the gun charging circuits. I pass the enemy fighter, unable to do anything else. For a mo-ment we fly side by side and I can see the pilot's petrified face for a brief moment, just before he drops the wing and peels off. My dear boy, you don't even know how lucky you are! What do I do now? Go back home? Impossible. The fight's still going on. Being the squadron's CO I can't just turn around and head back to base. But at the same time I'm in a very uncomfortable position – surrounded by enemy aircraft and unable to fight back. All I have left is the agility of my aircraft.[33]

After the fight the Germans claimed four enemy aircraft, but only two of those were eventually confirmed (Fw. Menge and Lt. Lippert). The Bf 109 pilots fought again on August 1, 1938 during an air battle over the Ebro and achieved three confirmed kills. On the following day Oblt. Kroeck shot down a Republican Rata fighter.

After the Republican offensive ground to a halt, the operational momentum was once again on Franco's side. On August 12, 1938 the crews from 1.J/88 shot down three SB-2 bombers and a single I-16. Two of the SB-2s were credited to Oblt. Schellmann – his ninth and tenth aerial victories in Spain. Two days later the Germans claimed seven I-16 kills, followed by an I-16 and two I-15s shot down a day later. More fighting took place on August 19, 1938 when Bf 109 pilots dispatched four I-16s. The Republicans intensified their air campaign on August 23, 1938. Oblt. Werner Mölders from 3.J/88 remembers the events of that day: *August 23 was a day when just about everything went wrong. Still, it was an exceptionally lucky day for me.*

In the morning 1. and 2. Staffel were going on a 'free hunt' over the frontlines in hopes of getting the Martin bombers. The Reds did show up exactly when we expected them, but we were still sitting on the ground, since somebody higher up pushed back the take-off time by one hour. Had we launched as originally planned we would have stood a good chance of jumping the Martins. Now the odds were stacked against us, since the Martins would not show up twice over the same area. The 1. and 2. Staffeln were sitting at our airfield and I managed to convince the powers that be to put together a 'free hunt' sortie between 1315 and 1430.

Everything went to plan and we were hanging in the air like hawks waiting for their pray when, lo and behold, the Martins showed up! I spotted them some distance away, but I knew they would be difficult to see for the other guys in the flight. We were just making a wide turn away from the frontlines, which is why my signals to attack went unnoticed by some of the pilots. At that point our formation completely lost its integrity.

Closing in on the Martins we had to penetrate a thick wall of AA fire. The guys in my flight took longer than I to zigzag through the AA fire, which meant that at some point I was alone in the chase of the Martins. Flying behind me Scholz saw a flight of Ratas descending upon my aircraft like a hail storm.

When I spotted the Ratas I was already within range of the big bombers. I was trying to figure out if I was closer to the bombers than Ratas were to me. I decided I had the upper hand and pressed on towards the Martins. I was well within enemy territory when I saw the Martins split up into two sections flying in a tight formation. I quickly closed up on them and opened up on the middle aircraft in the right section from about 200 meters. My cockpit canopy was soon enveloped in white tracer trails coming from the Martin's gunner. He quickly fell silent after I had responded with a short burst from my guns. After I fired another burst my windshield got instantly covered with oil. I managed to catch a glimpse of the bomber's port engine catching fire before I flew right on top of the Martin and maneuvered to target the section lead.

At that very instant I spotted a Rata coming in straight at me, slightly from the right. As I turned into the Red fighter, two more Ratas jumped me from the other side. I threw the aircraft into a series of evasive maneuvers, but then I saw yet another pair of Ratas screaming towards me. I twisted and turned like a beast in a trap, desperately trying to shake off the enemy fighters. However, they held on to me like a swarm of angry bees. Finally I dropped to the deck and lost them in one of the deep valleys.

I quickly set course back towards the frontline and pressed on at full speed, just 10 meters off the deck. All the while I was praying for the engine not to quit on me. When I was positive there was nobody chasing me, I throttled back to give the motor some rest. I climbed a little and quickly covered the last 50 km of enemy territory.[34]

During the encounter the German Bf 109 pilots scored four confirmed kills. The Repub-

The engine cowling of a Bf 109 D-1 "Christel" from 3./JGr. 126 featuring the unit's badge.

lican aircraft fell victim to Oblt. Mölders, Oblt. Müller, Lt. Bertram and Lt. Ensslen.

In early September 1938 the Bf 109s from J/88 operated mainly out of La Cenia airfield in support of bombers from K/88. During one of the operations, on September 5, 1938 the German bombers were attacked by a formation of some 50 Republican fighters. During the fight Lt. Ensslen downed a single I-15.

The only kill recorded on September 9, 1938 belonged to Oblt. Molders. During the same battle one of the Bf 109s (flown by Lt. Lutz) was hit by a well-placed burst fired by an I-16. Lutz managed to make it across the frontlines and landed safely on friendly territory. Uffz. Kiening's Messerschmitt also suffered in the encounter with the Republicans forcing the pilot down behind friendly lines. The aircraft was extensively damaged in a forced landing attempt.

On September 10, 1938 Hptm. Walter Grabmann took over as the CO of J/88, while the unit's previous commander, Hptm. Handrick returned to Germany. Another flyer who finished his combat tour on that day was the CO of 1.J/88, Hptm. Schellmann, who was replaced by Hptm. Siebelt Reents.

On September 13 Oblt. Mölders shot down an I-16 during a routine combat patrol over the frontline. There were also several skirmishes on September 23: the J/88 crews achieved eight confirmed kills (three claimed by Hptm. Grabmann, two credited to Lt. Goy, and single kills reported by Oblt. Mölders, Uffz. März and Uffz. Braunshirn). On the following day Uffz. Schob returned to base with a single confirmed victory. On September 27 the German fighters fought against a large formations of I-16s and downed four of them. This time, however, there were also losses on the German side: having shot down two I-16s Lt. Horst Tietzen was hit by a Rata fighter and wounded in the arm. Tietzen's Messerschmitt was completely destroyed during a forced landing attempt. The German pilot spent two months in the hospital recovering from his wounds.

On October 4, 1938 the Germans shot down three Republican fighters, but in the process lost one of the leading Condor Legion aces: Lt. Otto Bertram (nine confirmed kills) was jumped by an I-15 and had to bail out from his burning fighter (Messerschmitt Bf 109 D-1, 6•67). Bertram was captured and became a POW. On October 15, 1938 the J/88 pilots scored ten air-to-air kills, including three victories achieved by Oblt. Mölders).

When the Nationalist offensive along the Ebro got underway on October 30, the Republican air did everything they could to stop Franco's progress. In a series of aerial battles that took place between October 30 and November 16 the J/88 pilots scored no fewer than 24 air-to-air kills. The fighting over the Ebro ended on November 16 in a crushing defeat of the Republican forces.

Messerschmitt Bf 109 D-1 featuring late exhaust stack arrangement. "Martel" belonged to 3./JG 126.

This Messerschmitt Bf 109 D-1 "yellow 5" from 3./JGr. 126 features large Belkenkreuz markings on the lower wing surfaces, which were introduced in the fall of 1939. The propeller spinner is painted yellow.

After the hectic battles over the Ebro the J/88 pilots enjoyed a quiet month of rest. It was not until December 20, 1938 that new kills were added to the unit's tally, when Lt. Rossiwell from 3. Staffel claimed a single I-16, followed a day later by another I-16 downed by Lt. Tietzemen. The last four days of 1938 saw a flurry of air battles in the Spanish skies. During the fighting the J/88 pilots claimed no fewer than 17 enemy aircraft.

In early January 1939 the Republicans made one more desperate attempt to gain the upper hand in Catalonia by launching an offensive effort in the province of Estermadura. During the first few days of fighting they even managed to break through a thirty kilometer-long stretch of frontline and move 20 km into Nationalist-held territory. Franco immediately threw his air assets into the fray to provide support for the ground troops defending their positions against the Reds. Among the units taking part in air battles was also J/88, whose pilots scored eleven air-to-air kills. In addition, the German pilots destroyed 12 enemy aircraft in air-to-ground attacks.

In late January 1939 the Messerschmitt pilots returned to the skies over Catalonia and downed seven more Republican aircraft. By February 13, 1939 Catalonia was under Nationalist control and J/88 traded their Messerschmitt 109 A/B/C/Ds for the newer E-1 and E-3 versions.

Bf 109 C/D in the Polish campaign – September 1939[35]

Two Luftwaffe *Luftflotte* were deployed in Poland during the 1939 campaign: Luftflotte 1 Ost under General Albert Kesselring operated in the northern sector, while Luftflotte 4 Südost, commanded by General Alexander Löhr covered the southern sector. Two units operating in Poland were equipped with the Messerschmitt Bf 109 C/D: I./JG 21 commanded by Hptm. Martin Mettig and operating in the north as part of Luftgaukommando I (Ostpreußen), and I./ZG 2 under Hptm. Johannes Genzen. The latter was based in the south and operated under the command of Fliegerführer z.b.V.

Shortly before the outbreak of war I./JG 21 deployed to Gutenfeld airfield in East Prussia. On August 26, 1939 the unit fielded 39 Messerschmitt Bf 109 D-1 fighters split between three flights: 1. Staffel – CO Oblt. Günther Scholz, 2. Staffel – CO Oblt. Leo Eggers and 3. Staffel commanded by Oblt. Georg Schneider.

On August 26, 1939 I./ZG 2 operated out of Groß-Stein airfield and was equipped with 45 Bf 109 C/Ds.[36] Commanding the Staffeln were: 1. Staffel – Oblt. Waldermar von Roon, 2. Staffel – Oblt. Erich Groth, and 3. Staffel – Oblt. Josef Kellner-Steinmetz.

Lt. Hans-Ekkehard Bob, at the time technical officer with 3./JG 21, remembers his first combat sortie of the war: *In the early afternoon all three Staffeln launched from our base at Arys-Rostken and set course for Warsaw. Our task was to provide top cover for Heinkel He 111 from KG 27. When we reached the rendezvous point the Heinkel gunners opened up on us, but luckily missed by miles. It later turned out the gunners mistook us for Polish fighters, unaware that the Poles had no low-wing, retractable gear fighters in their inventory. Since we had no radio communication with the bombers our CO, Maj. Martin Mettig tried to use a flare gun to fire a prescribed signal to the bomber crews – it was supposed to be a white flare. The flare gun was mounted in a fixed position, just underneath the right side of the windshield, with the barrel sticking out of the cockpit. The barrel was evidently blocked by some foreign object, because as soon as the CO pulled the trigger the cartridge tore the breech apart and the flare shot into the cockpit severely burning his right hand. The white ball of fire kept bouncing off the cockpit walls for a while before it finally burnt out. However, in the next moment it shot up flames again and released three small red balls into the cockpit. Suffocating with smoke, the CO immediately jettisoned the canopy to get rid of the three burning red balls. With severe burns to his hands, he aborted the mission and returned to base, followed by his wingman, Oblt. Schelcher and the other two aircraft from the HQ flight.*

The rest of us pressed on towards Warsaw, but just in case remained well clear of the bombers, whose crews still thought we were the enemy and continued to take pot shots at us. Over the outskirts of Warsaw we spotted Polish PZL 24 fighters, which were setting up to attack our bombers.[37]

A ferocious fight began, which quickly developed into a series of 1v1 engagements. Our formation was now in total disarray, but we managed to engage all enemy fighters, which meant they couldn't get to the Heinkels. However, the prolonged fight ate into our fuel reserves and by the time we reached Warsaw we had barely enough gas left to make it back to base. Since we were scattered all over the sky it was each man for himself to find the way back to Arys-Rostken. For many of the rookie pilots getting their bearings right turned out to be an impossible task. I had no such problems and, having positively established my position, quickly found my way home. Just before 1800 hours and with little more than fumes in my fuel tank, I was the first pilot from the 3. Staffel to land back at Arys-Rostken. My squadron CO, Oblt. Schneider, was forced to make a refueling stop at another Luftwaffe airfield and didn't arrive at the base until later that night.

At the end of the day only two of the eight aircraft returned to base that night. The remaining pilots ran out of fuel and were forced to land somewhere along the way. As far as I can remember two of them became POWs and one was interned in Lithuania. As soon as fighting in Poland came to an end they all returned to combat flying.[38]

In the aftermath of fighting over Warsaw the crews of I./JG 21 claimed five Polish

A Krigsmarine NCO visiting the base takes a peek into the cockpit of the Messerschmitt Bf 109 D-1, "yellow 15" "Della" from 3./JGr. 126.

A photograph of Lachen-Speyerdorf airfield taken in October 1939. On the left is the Messerschmitt Bf 109 D-1, W.Nr. 2621 assigned to the CO of JGr. 102 (earlier I./ZG 2), Hptm. Johannes Gentzen.

PZL fighters. Four of those claims were subsequently confirmed: Lt. Fritz Gutezeit from 3./JG 21 - good kill at 1655 over Warsaw; Lt. Gustav Rödel from 2./JG 21 - air-to-air kill at 1708 over Warsaw; Oblt. Georg Schneider from 3./JG 21 - a confirmed kill at 1710 over Marki and Uffz. Heinz Dettmer from 3./JG 21 – a victory scored at 1719 north of Warsaw. The kill claimed by Oblt. Albrecht Dresz from 2./JG 21 was not confirmed or credited to the pilot.

At 1719 on September 2, 1939 the HQ flight from I./ZG 2 launched from their base to attack Polish positions near the railroad bridge at Dąbrówka, west of Radomsko. The mission to stop Polish army engineers from blowing up the bridge was a total success. On their return to base the Luftwaffe pilots encountered a single PZL P.23B, nr 44.185, from 1. Eskadra Bombowa (1st Bomber Squadron). The CO of I./ZG 2, Hptm. Johannes Gentzen, immediately attacked the Polish aircraft and shot it down in just one pass. The Polish crew (obs. ppor. Rudolf Wilczak, pil. sierż. Wojciech Uryzaj, strz. sam. kpr. Władysław Scibich) perished with their aircraft. The fight was later described by a German war correspondent Karl Georg von Stackelberg: *Up in the blue autumn sky a fighter appears rocking its wings. This is to signal a success to everybody waiting down below. Soon dozens of people run towards the taxiing aircraft to welcome back their commander.*

It is the unit's first combat kill. The commander, who is presently climbing out of the cockpit with a big smile on his face, has just destroyed the first Polish bomber. Hi adjutant offers a quick recap of the fight: from the tactical perspective everything went smoothly. As soon as the enemy aircraft was detected, the Luftwaffe fighters attacked it with a vengeance. The Hauptman's aircraft, spewing fire from all its guns, descended upon the bomber like a hawk. In no time at all the enemy aircraft was tumbling to the ground engulfed in flames. The first kill! Carefully and with precision, a ground crew member paints a white victory bar on the aircraft's fin. [39]

On September 3, 1939, between 847 and 1000, eleven Bf 109s from 1. Staffel flew an escort sortie in support of eleven Ju 87s from I./St.G 77 attacking targets near Łask. Simultaneously nine aircraft from 3. Staffel and several machines from 2./JG 76 provided top cover for a formation of 17 Henschel Hs 123s from II.(Sch)/LG 2. On their returned leg the crews from 3./ZG 2 stumbled upon a flight of PZL P.23 Karas bombers from the Polish Brygada Bombowa (Bomber Brigade). Lt. Reinhold Meßner launched a successful attack against a P.23 from 55. Eskadra Bombowa (55th Bomber Squadron) and downed the Polish bomber after a single gun pass. The P.23 crew (obs. por. Tadeusz Frąckowiak, pil. plut. Czesław Borzecki, strz. sam. kpr. Czesław Buziuk) were listed as KIA. Just minutes later the CO of 3./ZG 2 achieved his first air-to-air kill when he downed a Karas fro 1. Eskadra Bombowa (1st Bomber Squadron). The bomber's gunner, pchor. rez. Mieczysław Mazur, was killed in action, while the other two crew members (obs. kpt. Stefan Alberti and pil. plut. Wacław Buczyłko) managed to bail out of the burning aircraft.

On September 3, 1939 the HQ flight from I./ZG 2 flew a combat patrol in support of the *XVI Panzerkorps*, when the pilots spotted a single P.23 bomber north east of Radomsko. The Karas from 55. Eskadra Bombowa (55th Bomber Squadron) was on a reconnaissance sortie flying a route from Częstochowa to Radomsko. After a short chase the P.23 was downed by Hptm. Johannes Gentzen becoming the CO's second air-to-air kill.

The Bf 109 pilots from 1./ZG 2 scored a major success on September 4, 1939. On that day seven of the unit's Messerschmitt fighters launched an attack against a Polish forward airfield at Widzew. The Germans first fired upon several fighters in the landing pattern and then proceeded to strafe the aircraft parked on the ground. The Luftwaffe pilots eventually claimed the destruction of nine Polish fighters in the air-to-ground attacks. Lt. Hans Nocher shot down a PZL P.11 flown by por. Tadeusz Jeziorowski, who was on a short final to land. Another Polish fighter engaged just over the airfield was a PZL P.7 from 162. Eskadra Myśliwska (162nd Fighter Squadron). The fire from Uffz. Georg Schuch's guns was very accurate and quickly destroyed the Polish fighter's engine. Ppor. Zdzisław Zadroziński, wounded in the legs, did manage to land the crippled fighter and jump out of the cockpit before the machine was lit up by the Messerschmitts. Contrary to German pilots' claims, only five Polish aircraft were destroyed on the ground (four P.11s and a single P.7). Another P.7 could also be added to that number as the fighter was forced down in an air-to-air fight and later destroyed on the ground in a strafing pass.

Having finished their work over Widzew airfield, the German fighters set course for their base at Groß-Stein. Several minutes later they spotted a formation of five PZL P.37 Łoś aircraft from 12. Eskadra Bombowa (12th Bomber Squadron) returning home after a raid against the German *XVI Panzerkorps* columns. Using a 300 meter altitude advantage the Messerschmitt pilots split into two sections and attacked the Polish formation. The first Łoś to go down was PZL P.37B nr 72.43. Having received multiple hits from Uffz. Hans Katzmann's guns the bomber rolled and crashed near the village of Śladkowice killing the entire crew: obs. por. Kazimierz Żukowski, pil. sierż. Józef Siwik and strz. sam. kpr. Władysław Kramarczyk.

Shortly thereafter the unit's CO, Oblt. Waldemar von Roon, got on the tail of the PZL P.37A bis, nr 72.16. The first burst ruptured the bombers port wing fuel tank. The aircraft crashed almost immediately, but both gunners, kpr. Aleksander Danielak and kpr. Konstanty Gołębiowski managed to bail out. Miraculously, the pilot and navigator (pchor. Feliks Mazak and obs. ppor. Kazimierz Dzik) survived the crash and were pulled from the burning wreckage by Polish forest rangers.

The third Łoś (PZL P.37B, nr 72.91) went down near the village of Patoki. Three of the crew members were killed in the crash (obs. ppor. Mieczysław Bykowski, strz. sam. kpr. Marian Gargol and strz. sam. kpr. Lucjan Zimmermann), while the pilot, kpr. Kazimierz Kaczmarek, managed to bailout safely. The kill was credited to Uffz. Karl Schuch.

The fourth bomber (PZL P.37B, nr 72.111) was shot down by Uffz. Hans Katzmann. After several bursts of machine gun fire killed the bomber's gunner (kpr. Władysław Wojdat) and set the aircraft on fire. The navigator, por. Jan Kazimierz Lekszycki tried to bail out at low altitude, too low for his parachute to deploy. He was killed on impact with the ground. The bomber's pilot, pchor. Michał Ostrowski managed to put the bomber down near the village of Wygiezów. Both Ostrowski and the gunner kpr. Stanisław Wrzeszcz suffered major injuries, but survived the crash.

Between 1345 and 1530 on September 4, 1939 eight Bf 109s from 2./ZG 2 provided top cover for a formation of 27 Do 17s from III./KG 76. The German bombers were flying a raid

Messerschmitt Bf 109 D-1 from I./ZG 26 pictured at Jever airfield in December 1939.

against Kielce-Masłów airfield, home to Polish Szkoła Lotniczego Przysposobienia Wojskowego (Aviation Training School). The German fighters performed several strafing passes over the field and claimed the destruction of two PZL P.37 bombers and a single PZL P.24 fighter. In fact eight aircraft were destroyed on the ground that day, but all of them were RWD and PWS trainers.

On Tuesday, September 5, 1939 the crews of 2./JG 21 flew a "free hunt" sortie over the city of Grudziądz. Later on the same day three flights sections from 3./JG 21 attacked Polish columns on the roads between Lipno, Płock, Sierpiec and Rypin. This is how Lt. Hans-Ekkehard Bob remembers the day's events: *There were countless horse-drawn carts on the roads, all that remained of Polish divisions that had been crushed in the first days of the war in the Pomeranian corridor. They were all making their way towards Warsaw. Our strafing attacks were hampered by rows of trees on each side of the roads. Our appearance over enemy columns caused immediate panic: people would scatter in all directions, seeking shelter in ditches alongside the road; the galloping horses sent the carriages crashing into one another causing mayhem and havoc. I think that panic and fear of aerial attack inflicted more damage to the Poles than did the fire from our machine guns. I don't remember ever being shot at during those attacks.*

What I do remember are long columns of Polish cavalry units, who apparently were famous for launching attacks against our armored vehicles using nothing but swords. They must have believed in the pre-war Polish propaganda that tried to picture the Wehrmacht as a paper army armed with wooden tanks. I will never forget attacking a Polish cavalry unit: I can still see the horses galloping in panic, throwing off their riders or just rolling on the ground in the grip of pre-mortal convulsions. It was then that I realized for the first time how horrific a war could be.[40]

On September 6, 1939 the crews from 2./JG 21 flew an afternoon patrol over Ciechanów. At around 1440 the German pilots attacked a lone PZL P.23B bomber from 55. Eskadra Bombowa (55th Bomber Squadron). The aircraft was shot down by the unit's CO, Oblt. Leo Eggers. The Polish crew (obs. ppor. Stanisław Pytlakowski, pil. kpr. Stanisław Zarzecki, str. sam. szer. Antoni Iwaniuk) did not survive the attack.

The crews from 3./JG 21 had a good day on Thursday, September 7: the squadron's CO, Oblt. Georg Schneider downed a PZL P.23 Karaś from 4. Eskadra Bombowa (4th Bomber Squadron). The bomber's pilot and navigator (obs. ppor. Jan Ząbik and pil. ppor. Kazimierz Bilecki) were wounded in the fight, but bailed out successfully. The gunner, kpr. Roman Stronczak, was listed as KIA.[41]

On the same day, between 1214 and 1434, eight Messerschmitt Bf 109s from 1./ZG 2 escorted a formation of 21 Heinkel He 111s from I./KG 4 during an attack against Dęblin and river crossings on the Vistula. Over the target area the Luftwaffe bombers were attacked by PZL P.11s from 121. and 122. Eskadra Myśliwska (121st and 122nd Fighter Squadron). After the fight the German crews were credited with three good kills (two victories scored by Lt. Hartwig Domeier from the HQ of I./ZG 2 and a single kill claimed by Fw. Fritz Griehl from 1. Staffel).

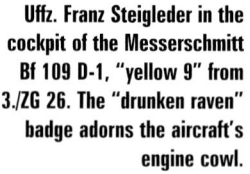

Uffz. Franz Steigleder in the cockpit of the Messerschmitt Bf 109 D-1, "yellow 9" from 3./ZG 26. The "drunken raven" badge adorns the aircraft's engine cowl.

Bf 109 C/D in the Polish campaign – September 1939

On Monday, September 11, Fw. Fritz Griehl from 1./ZG 2 scored another victory when he shot down a lone PZL P.37B over Jarosław. The bomber belonged to 31. Eskadra Bombowa (11th Bomber Squadron). On the following day three Bf 109 Ds from 1./ZG 2 jumped a pair of PZL P.23Bs just west of Karakowice. Uffz. Hans Katzmann and Gefr. Siegfried Becker were each credited with a single kill. One of the bombers crashed near the village of Czaplaki, killing the entire crew (obs. ppor. Leon Nowicki, pil. st. sierż. Konstanty Korzeniowski and strz. sam. plut. pchor. rez. Mariusz Pszenny). The bodies were recovered by the locals and buried at the Lubaczow cemetery.[42] The other PZL P.23 suffered heavy damage, but kpr. Andrzej Kuźniacki managed to nurse the bomber to Batiatycze airfield, where he made a successful landing. The navigator, ppor. Stefan Szczepański, suffered gunshot wounds to his right hand.[43]

Early in the morning on September 14, 1939 eight Messerschmitt fighters from ZG 2 attacked Ławrów airfield near Łuck. The Germans claimed two kills during the battle: Lt. Franz Menzel from 3./ZG 2 added a Lublin R-XIII to his tally while Lt. Heinz Wilberg from 2./ZG 2 downed a trainer aircraft. In addition as many as eleven Polish aircraft were destroyed on the ground. The machines most likely belonged to Eskadra Sztabowa (HQ Flight), which on September 10 still had an inventory of 25 airworthy aircraft of different types, including RWD 14 Czapla, Lublin R XIII, RWD 8, PWS 26 and RWD 13. When the unit was evacuated to Romania on September 17, 1939 it had only seven serviceable aircraft.[44]

In the afternoon the Luftwaffe pilots from I./ZG 2 launched a raid against another Polish airfield. Their target this time was Hutniki, just south west of Brody. When the Germans arrived over the field a number of Karaś aircraft from Eskadra Ćwiczebna (Training Squadron) were just launching for a short hop to Horodenko. There were also seven PZL P.23A aircraft in the area, enroute from Wielick to Stanisławów. Two of the P.23s belonging to Dęblin's Rezerwowa Eskadra Rozpoznawcza (Reserve Reconnaissance Squadron) were downed in the engagement. There are no confirmed reports on the losses suffered by the Training Squadron. The Germans claimed 14 kills in the fight, although only eight of those were later confirmed: the CO of I./ZG 2, Hptm. Johannes Gentzen was credited with four air-to-air victories, Uffz. Karl Schuch from 1./ZG 2 achieved two kills, while Lt. Hartwig Domeier from Stab I./ZG 2 and Fw. Wolfgang Brachs from *1. Staffel* each scored a single kill. The Luftwaffe lost one Bf 109 D-1 in the engagement (W.Nr. 507, "white 4" from 1./ZG 2, flown by Fw. Wolfgang Koch).

The aircraft in the background is a Messerschmitt Bf 109 D-1 belonging to one of the flight schools. Germany, 1941.

The panels covering top of the engine cowl and MG 17 bays have been removed on this aircraft. In the background is a Messerschmitt Bf 109 D-1.

The fighter was shot down by one of the Karas gunners and crashed. The pilot survived and returned to his unit on October 5, 1939.[45]

On Friday, September 15, 1939 five Bf 109s fro 1. and 3./ZG 2 took off from their base at Dębica and again set course for Hutniki airfield. In a strafing attack that followed the Germans destroyed a single P.37 Łoś bomber and lit up three PZL P.23 Karas aircraft. The Germans also claimed a probable destruction of eleven more aircraft concealed in the woods surrounding the airfield. On the ground a Polish navigator obs. pchor. Zdzisław Kaniewski from 5. Eskadra Bombowa (5th Bomber Squadron) showed remarkable bravery when he jumped into one of bombers and proceeded to fire at the German fighters from the top gunner's position. After he had expended all ammunition, Kaniewski quickly ran to another parked bomber and continued to fire away at the attacking Luftwaffe aircraft. One of the Messerschmitts (Bf 109 D-1, W.Nr. 2972, flown by Lt. Hans Rosenkranz) suffered substantial damage from Kaniewski's fire, which forced the pilot to put the fighter down at Dębica airfield. The *3. Staffel* pilot walked away from the crash landing without injuries. Ofw. Kurt Müller claimed the destruction of a Lublin R-XIII that he bounced near the airfield. In fact the aircraft claimed by Müller was most probably an RWD-14 Czapla from 23. Eskadra Obserwacyjna (23rd Observer Squadron). The aircraft's crew obs. por. Radomir Walczak and pil. ppor. Tadeusz Kaszycki did manage to nurse the damaged machine back to base, where they landed safely.

When considering the combat record of the two Luftwaffe fighter Bf 109 units operating over Poland in 1939, one has to bear in mind that the Jumo-powered C and D models, although largely obsolete at that time, were still vastly superior to anything that Polish Air Force could muster. During the September campaign the pilots from I./JG 21 scored six air-to-air kills and suffered surprisingly high losses, albeit mostly in various mishaps and accidents. Of the nineteen fighters lost by the unit, only five were destroyed in action. Two of the crews were listed as KIA (victims of a mid-air collision on September 21), one pilot was wounded, five became POWs and one was interned. The captured and interned personnel returned to their unit after the fighting had come to an end.

On the other hand, the crews of I./ZG 2 achieved much better results in combat over Poland. The unit's pilots were credited with 29 air-to-air kills and the destruction of 49 enemy aircraft on the ground. The leading ace of the campaign was the CO of I./ZG 2 Hptm. Johannes Gentzen, who scored seven air-to-air kills. One of the unit's pilots was killed in action, while two were initially listed as missing (both later returned to their squadron). I./ZG 2 lost twelve aircraft, while additional nineteen fighters suffered various degrees of damage.

The Messerschmitt Bf 109 D during the Phony War

When France and Great Britain joined the war on September 3, 1939 the Luftwaffe had the following Bf 109 C/D units deployed on the Western Front:

During the first weeks of the war one of the most active Bf 109 D units was I./ZG 52 operat-

Unit	Operating base	Commanding Officer	Inventory total/airworthy
Stab ZG 26	Varel	Obst. von Döring	3/1
I./ZG 26	Varel	Hptm. Kaschka	43/39
JGr. 126	Neumünster	Hptm. Schalk	46/41
11.(NJ)/LG 2	Köln-Ostheim	Oblt. Bascilla	9/9
II./ZG 26	Werl	Maj. Vollbracht	48/45
I./ZG 52	Biblis	Hptm. Lessmann	48/45
JGr. 176	Gablingen	Hptm. Schmidt-Coste	50/42
I./JG 71	Fürstenfeldbruck	Maj. Kramer	34/34
I./JG 70	Herzogenaurach	Maj. Kithil	50/21
		Total:	331/277

ing out of Biblis under the command of Hptm. Wilhelm Lessmann. On September 9 Lessmann scored the unit's first kill when he downed a French Bloch MB.200 bomber west of Landau. Another MB.200 was shot down in the same engagement by Oblt. Friedrich-Karl Rhinow from 4./ZG 76. A week later, on September 16, 1939 Lt. Hartmann Grasser from 3. *Staffel* successfully attacked a French observation balloon. The first major air battle took place on September 20, 1939 west of Saarbrücken. In the afternoon three Battle bombers from RAF 88 Squadron were bounced by Bf 109 Ds belonging to I./ZG 52. Hptm. Lessmann and Oblt. Dietrich von Bothmer both claimed single kills in the engagement.

On Sunday, September 24, 1939 six Morane MS.406 fighters from GC I./3 provided top cover for a Mureaux aircraft on a reconnaissance sortie. The French were attacked west of Saarbrücken by eight Bf 109 Ds from JGr. 152 (up until that day that was the official designation of I./ZG 52). Within seconds one of the French aircraft went down near Etting killing its pilot, Sgt. Jean Garnier. Another Morane was hit just moments later, but the pilot managed to safely crash-land his stricken fighter. The destruction of both aircraft was credited to Lt. Kurt Rosenkrantz, who himself was shot down just moment later by Cne. Roger Gerard. Gerard had a lot of time to enjoy his success, because within minutes after scoring a kill he was on the way down to earth under a fully deployed parachute, courtesy of Oblt. Werner Schnoor's accurate fire. While Adj. Antonin Combett scored good hits on Gefr. Adolf Hesselbach's Messerschmitt, he too had to bail out just seconds later having been hit by Lt. Lothar Hagen. The fifth Mo-

Messerschmitt Bf 109 D-1 in service with the fighter school at Werneuchen.

The Messerschmitt Bf 109 D during the Phony War

rane kill was credited to Ofw. Johannes Oertel. Both Bf 109s that suffered damage in the fight landed behind the enemy lines. The pilots were captured, but returned to their unit after the French surrender in June 1940. Two other Messerschmitt fighters made it safely back to German bases, although both sustained various degrees of damage. Lt. Hartmann Grasser brought his Bf 109 into Bingen, while Lt. Horst Elstermann landed at Weitersbach.

After the end of the Polish campaign, I./ZG 2 was deployed to the Western Front. Prior to that the unit had been brought up to full strength and received the designation of JGr. 102 on September 21, 1939. The squadron's new home would be Lachen-Speyerdorf with the area of responsibility covering much of Saarland. On September 25, 1939 III./ZG 26 was renamed JGr. 126.

At 1230 on September 26, 1939 Oblt. Lothar Ehrlich from 2./JGr. 176 shot down a Bloch MB.131 from GR II./55 performing a reconnaissance mission over Freiburg. Another French reconnaissance machine, a Potez Po.637 from GR I./52, was downed ten minutes later over Sigmaringen by Lt. Werner Güth from 3./JGr. 176.

On September 27, 1939 Gefr. Josef Scherm from JGr. 152 was killed by a burst from a rear gunner of a Battle bomber from RAF 88 Squadron (K9271, pilot F/O Vipan). Scherm's Bf 109 D-1 crashed 8 km west of Hornbach.

On September 29, 1939, just west of Helgoland, the crews of 3./ZG 26 intercepted a formation of Hampden bombers from 144 Squadron. Five British aircraft were shot down in the fight: Oblt. Günther Specht claimed two kills, while Hptm. Friedrich-Karl Dickoré, Uffz. Helmut Pisch and Uffz. Pollack were all credited with single victories. The Germans lost two fighters (Bf 109 D-1, W.Nr. 481 and Bf 109 C-1, W.Nr. 1749) and one of their aircrews (Uffz. Helmut Haugk) suffered wounds in the engagement.

On November 6, 1939 a formation of 27 Bf 109 Ds from JGr. 102 launched from their base at Lachen-Speyerdorf led by the leading Luftwaffe ace of the Polish campaign, Hptm. Johannes Gentzen. Shortly thereafter the Germans bounced a formation of nine Curtiss H-75As from GC II./5 providing top cover for a Potez Po.64 from GR II./22 on a reconnaissance mission to photograph German defenses along the Saar river. The French pilots under the command of Lt. Houzé quickly spotted twenty Luftwaffe fighters approaching them at the same level and seven more German machines flying some 700 meters above. Within minutes a fierce air battle ensued.

Sgt. Salés got on the tail of one of the Bf 109s and chased it almost all the way to the ground. He finally managed to get a bead on the German fighter just 200 meters off the deck. The Messerschmitt pilot bailed out at the last possible moment and safely landed near Hunnenberg. Before long another Messerschmitt went down hit by bursts of fire from Salés' guns. The fighter crashed on the banks of the Saar, near Eincheville. The next French pilot to achieve a good kill was Asp. Lefol, whose victim crashed and burned near Anzeling. Another Luftwaffe fighter was downed by Sgt.Chef Tremolet. After the dust settled four of the JGr. 102 machines were lost and one sustained severe

Messerschmitt Bf 109 D-1s operated by a flight school at Zerbst.

Paint schemes and markings

Messerschmitt Bf 109 D-1 marked 'Yellow 2' of 3./JG 21 photographed over Poland in September 1939. Noteworthy aspects include the early-style crosses and position of the swastika.

damage. Three other Messerschmitts limped back to their base riddled with bullet holes. Two German pilots were killed in the fight: Oblt. Josef Kellner-Steinmetz, the CO of *3. Staffel* and Oblt. Waldemar von Roon, the commander of *1. Staffel*. Lt. Günther Voigt, the squadron's Technical Officer and Fw. Fritz Giehl from *1. Staffel* were captured and became POWs. Uffz. Hans Hennings suffered injuries during a forced landing attempt at Mannheim-Sandhofen.

The results of the encounter with the French fighters clearly showed that the Jumo-powered Bf 109 Ds stood no chance against modern types operated by the Western Allies. Later that night Hptm. Gentzen traveled to Berlin to provide the brass with insight into what was to date the greatest defeat suffered by the Luftwaffe fighters in a single air-to-air engagement.

On November 8, 1939 Hptm. Johannes Gentzen downed a Morane MS.406 5 km north east of Edenkoben, while Oblt. Erich Groth dispatched a French observation balloon. Another balloon was downed two days later by Oblt. Wilhelm Hobein from 2./JGr. 176.

The last air-to-air battle fought by Messerschmitt Bf 109 D pilots was an encounter with a large formation of British Vickers Wellington bombers from 9, 38 and 149 Squadrons over Helgoland. The crews from 10.(N)/JG 26 "Schlageter" claimed five Wellingtons, including a double kill achieved by Oblt. Johannes Steinhoff. Three single victories were credited to Fw. Willy Szuggar, Uffz. Werner Gerhardt and Uffz. Robert Portz. The Messerschmitt Bf 109 D-1 flown by Pblt. Johann Fuhrmann sustained heavy battle damage forcing the pilot to ditch the fighter. The attempt was unsuccessful and Fuhrmann died in the crash.

On January 25, 1940 Fw. Walter Scherer from 2./JGr. 102 shot down a Bristol Blenheim over Duisburg (L1280 from 57 Squadron). The entire Blenheim's crew perished in the crash. It was most likely the last air-to-air kill by a Luftwaffe pilot at the controls of a Bf 109 D. The Jumo-powered Bf 109s were soon withdrawn from operational service and replaced with E models equipped with Daimler-Benz powerplants. The B, C and D versions soldiered on until the war's end in various training outfits scattered throughout the Reich.

Paint schemes and markings

The first Bf 109 prototype, the V1 (W.Nr. 758, D-IABI) featured overall DKH-Nitroemaillelack L40/52 Hellgrau paint scheme, which was a slightly lighter shade of RLM 63 Hellgrau. The civilian registration was painted in black letters (RLM 22 Schwarz) on each side of the fuselage and on the wing's upper and lower surfaces. The vertical fin featured a black swastika (RLM 22 Schwarz) in a white circle (RLM 21 Weiß) on a red tail band (RLM 23 Rot). Black (RLM 22 Schwarz) stenciling was added to the lower section of the rudder. The Messerschmitt Bf 109 V2 (W.Nr. 759, D-IILU) wore an identical paint scheme, although the L40/52 coat was highly polished.

The Bf 109 As serving with VJ/88 in Spain wore a one-tone silver coat of paint, or featured natural aluminum finish sprayed with a thin coat of semi-transparent protective paint of a slightly greenish hue. The national markings (Spanish Nationalist in this case) were added in the shape of black roundels with a white St. Andrew's cross to upper and lower wing's surfaces. Both fuselage sides featured a black roundel, while a white St. Andrew's cross was painted on the rudder. The aircraft had white wingtips on both upper and lower wing's surfaces. The aircraft's type number and individual code (separated by a dash – e.g. 6-4) were painted in black behind the fuselage roundel. At some point the fuselage marking convention changed and in-

Paint schemes and markings

Messerschmitt Bf 109 B-1, S2+M52 of JFS 1 aviation school.

cluded the type number, black roundel and then the individual aircraft number (e.g. 6•10).

The Bf 109 Bs that were deployed in Spain initially wore a standard splinter RLM 70/RLM 71 camouflage scheme covering the upper and side surfaces of the airframe. Lower surfaces sported a solid RLM 65 Hellblau paint job. Some of the aircraft later received additional mottles of RLM 63 Hellgrau on the wing's upper surfaces, although in most cases the upper and side surfaces of the Condor Legion Bf 109 Bs were painted RLM 63 Hellgrau, or perhaps (at least in some cases) RLM 62 Hellgrün. Very similar camouflage schemes were applied to Bf 109 C-1s and D-1s. The national markings and white quick identification features were applied in the same manner as on the Bf 109 As. The markings worn by the Bf 109s of the Condor Legion were supplemented by unit badges, personal pilot insignia and white or black victory bars painted on the vertical fin.

The Messerschmitt Bf 109 B/C/D were delivered to the Luftwaffe in factory-applied standard splinter camouflage of RLM 70 Schwarzgrün and RLM 71 Dunkelgrün covering the upper and side surfaces of the airframe. A solid coat of RLM 65 Hellblau was applied to the lower surfaces.

National markings were painted on the wing's upper and lower surfaces, as well as on both fuselage sides: the black Balkenkreuz featured a white outline and additional thin, black line. On October 24, 1939 a new version of the Balkenkreuz was introduced featuring wider arms and outlines. The swastika was initially painted in a white circle against a red tail band, but the design was changed on January 1, 1939. The new paint scheme saw a black swastika outlined in black and white painted on the vertical fin (both the white circle and the red tail band were discarded). After October 24, 1939 the swastika was moved from the rudder-fin line and was placed entirely on the vertical stabilizer surface.

The camouflage scheme was supplemented by a wide variety of tactical markings. Every *Gruppe* within a *Geschwader* had individual markings added behind the Balkenkreuz: *I.Gruppe* – no markings added, *II. Gruppe* – a horizontal bar (*Balke*), *III.Gruppe* – a horizontal squiggle (*Schlangenlinie*) and *IV. Gruppe* – a circle (*Kreis*). Before the Balkenkreuz the tactical numbers were painted using colors and numericals representing individual *Staffeln*: *1. Staffel* in each *Gruppe* used white numbers 1., 4., 7., 10., *2. Staffel* aircraft wore red numbers 2., 5., 8. and 11., while *3 Staffel*'s aircraft featured yellow numbers 3., 6., 9. and 12. The wing's and squadron's HQ aircraft used a combination of geometric symbols based on the chevron (*Winkel*) and vertical or horizontal bars. The aircraft also wore unit's badges, most typically painted either under the windshield or on the sides of the engine cowling.

The Messerschmitt Bf 109 C/Ds withdrawn from frontline units and handed over to training outfits eventually received a modified version of the standard camouflage. Starting in the spring of 1940 some aircraft would receive a splinter camouflage consisting of RLM 02 Grau and RLM 71 Dunkelgrün in place of the standard RLM 70 Schwarzgrün and RLM 71 Dunkelgrün. In such instances the RLM 65 Hellblau coat would extend over the fuselage side surfaces. Later, a new camouflage scheme was introduced, which consisted of RLM 74 Dunkelgrau and RLM 75 Grauviolett on the upper surfaces and RLM 76 Lichtblau covering the wings lower surfaces and the sides of the fuselage. In addition to the overall RLM 76 Lichtblau finish, the sides of the fuselage featured irregular mottles of RLM 02 Grau, RLM 74 Dunkelgrau or RLM 75 Grauviolett. The aircraft in service with flight training units wore a four-letter registration markings (*Stammkenzeichen*) or a two- or three-digit tactical numbers on both sides of the fuselage. Some flight schools also applied their own badges to various airframe surfaces.

Messerschmitt Bf 109 B-1 of J.88 Legion Condor takes off from Teruel airfield for another combat mission.

Bibliography

Ebert Hans J., Kaiser Johann B., Peters Klaus, *Willy Messerschmitt – Pionier der Luftfahrt und des Leichtbaues*, Bonn 1992.
Emmerling Marius, *Luftwaffe nad Polską 1939, cz. I Jagdflieger*, Gdynia 2002.
Forell Fritz von, *Mölders und seine Männer*, Graz 1941.
Green William, *The Augsburg Eagle, A Documentary History Messerschmitt Bf 109*, London 1980.
Hitchcock Thomas H., *Taifun*, Boylston 1979.
Jägerblatt, *Offizieles Organ der Gemeinschaft der Jagdflieger e. V.*, Nr. 6/1966.
Kosin Rüdiger, *Die Entwicklung der deutschen Jagdflugzeuge*, Die deutsche Luftfahrt, Band 4, Koblenz 1983.
Laureau Patrick, *Condor, The Luftwaffe in Spain 1936-1939*, Ottringham 2000.
Messerschmitt-Nachrichten nr 3/1963.
Michulec Robert, *Messerschmitt Me 109, cz. 1*, Gdynia 1997.
Nowarra Heinz J., *Die 109, Gesamtentwicklung eines legendären Flugzeugs*, Stuttgart 1979.
Prien Jochen, Stemmer Gerhard, Rodeike Peter, Bock Winfried, *Die Jagdfliegerverbände der Deutschen Luftwaffe 1934 bis 1945, Teil 1, Vorkriegszeit und Einsatz über Polen – 1934 bis 1939*, Eutin b.r.w.
Prien Jochen, Stemmer Gerhard, Rodeike Peter, Bock Winfried, *Die Jagdfliegerverbände der Deutschen Luftwaffe 1934 bis 1945, Teil 2, Der "Sitzkrieg" 1.9.1939 bis 9.5.1940*, Eutin b.r.w.
Radinger Willy, Schick Walter, *Messerschmitt Me 109, das meistgebaute Jagdflugzeug der Welt, Entwicklung, Erprobung und Technik, alle Varianten, von Bf (Me) 109 A bis Me 109 E*, Oberhaching 1997.
Ries Karl, Ring Hans, *Legion Condor 1936-1939, Eine Illustrierte Dokumentation*, Mainz 1979.
Ritger Lynn, *The Messerschmitt Bf 109, A Comprehensive Guide for the Modeller, Part 1: Prototype to 'E' Variants*, London 2005.
Shores C., Ehrengardt C.-J., Foreman J., Weiss H., Olsen B., *Fledgling Eagles*, London 1991.
Skotnicki Mariusz, Nowakowski Tomasz, Zalewski Krzysztof, *Legion Condor*, Warszawa 1994.
Stackelberg Karl Georg von, *Jagdgruppe G., Jäger an Polens Himmel*, Graz 1940.
Trautloft Hannes, *Als Jagdflieger in Spanien*, Berlin b.r.w.
www.valka.cz/clanek_12310.html.

Endnotes

[1] The account of an air-to-air battle fought on February 7, 1938 by Oblt. Wilhelm Balthasar of 2J/88 in: Ries Karl, Ring Hans, Legion Condor 1936-1939, Eine Illustrierte Dokumentation, Mainz 1979, pp.122-123.
[2] "Mitarbeiter berichten von den Anfängen des Messerschmitt-Flugzeugbaues" in: Messerschmitt-Nachrichten nr 3/1963.
[3] The letter "S" stood for Segelflugzeug, or a sailplane, while the letter "M" designated Motorflugzeug, a powered aircraft.
[4] The official name of the event was FAI – Challenge internationale des avions de tourisme.
[5] The winner of the 1929 and the 1930 editions of the vent was a German pilot Fritz Morzik.
[6] The M 31 prototype was in fact built as W.Nr. 607 and flight tested in early August 1932 by Erwin Aichele.
[7] Hitchcock Thomas H., Typhoon, Boylston 1979, p. 2
[8] Ebert Hans J., Kaiser Johann B., Peters Klaus, Willy Messerschmitt – Pionier der Luftfahrt und des Leichtbaues, Bonn 1992, p. 100.
[9] The Flugzeug-Beschaffungsprogramm 1935-1937 of November 1, 1935 (RLM, LC II/13271/35) also mentions 50 examples of the Junkers Ju 87, which actually never went into production at the BFW plant.
[10] A letter from Hermann Göring to Theo Croneiß, dated October 20, 1933. In: Ebert Hans J...., pp. 110-111.

Endnotes

[11] Many authors, including Robert Michulec (Messerschmitt Me 109, vol. 1, Gdynia 1997, p.. 9), maintain that BFW was in fact not invited to participate in the project, which would have been understandable given the animosity between Erhard Milch and Willy Messerschmitt. However, there is no support of that version in the historic data. In fact it was Focke-Wulf that received the fighter specs seven months later, the evidence of which can be found in Radinger Willy, Schick Walter: Messerschmitt Me 109, das meistgebaute Jagdflugzeug der Welt, Entwicklung, Erprobung und Technik, alle Varianten: von Bf (Me) 109 A bis Me 109 E, Oberhaching 1997, p. 15 and in: Ritger Lynn, The Messerschmitt Bf 109, A Comprehensive Guide for the Modeller, Part 1: Prototype to „E' Variants, London 2005, p. 8.

[12] Kosin Rüdiger, Die Entwicklung der deutschen Jagdflugzeuge, Die deutsche Luftfahrt, Band 4, Koblenz 1983, p. 108.

[13] The aircraft was initially designated Bf 109a.

[14] Op. cit., Radinger…, p. 27.

[15] Flight test center

[16] Op. cit., Radinger…, pp. 28-29.

[17] Many sources, including Green William, The Augsburg Eagle, A Documentary History Messerschmitt Bf 109, London 1980, p. 14, or Michulec Robert, Messerschmitt Me 109 vol. 1, Gdynia 1997, p. 18, quote the aircraft's registration as I-IUDE, which appears to be incorrect in light of the most recent research.

[18] D.-Ing. Wurster Hermann, Me 109 oder He 112 (Diskussionsbeitrag), Jägerblatt, Offizieles Organ der Gemeinschaft der Jagdflieger e. V., Nr. 6/1966, pp. 5-8.

[19] Some sources claim (e.g. Op. cit., Radinger…, p. 45) that the V10 was in fact a modified production Bf 109 A, designated Messerschmitt Bf 109 V10, W.Nr. 884, D-IXZA. The first flight of the machine took place on December 30, 1936 with Dr.-Ing. Hermann Wurster at the controls. On January 2, 1937 the prototype made a 90 minute test flight. A week later, on January 9, 1937 the machine was flown by one of the RLM officials. On January 19, 1937 the prototype was handed over to Rechlin flight test center. W.Nr. 1010 was to be designated V10a.

[20] In category B (multi-crew aircraft) the winner was the Dornier Do 17 M V1 crewed by Polte, Milch, Hänsgen and Franz

[21] Hannes Trautloft (March 3, 1912 – January 11, 1995) was one of the Luftwaffe's most accomplished fighter aces and field commanders. He scored 58 air-to-air kills during 560 combat missions. Among the units under his command was the famous JG 54 "Grün Herz".

[22] The aircraft that Trautloft is describing is the Bf 109 V3, which initially marked 6•2. After the loss of the Bf 109 V4, the V3's tactical code was changed to 6•1.

[23] A black top hat was the emblem of J/88.

[24] Rata – a nickname of the Russian Polikarpov I-16 fighter.

[25] Trautloft Hannes, Als Jagdflieger in Spanien, Berlin b.r.w.,p. 164-235.

[26] Op. cit., Ries…, p. 62

[27] Ibidem, pp. 79-83.

[28] Ibidem, pp. 91-92.

[29] Rojos – a common nickname of the SB-2 bombers operating in Spain.

[30] Op. Cit, Ries…,. pp. 121-122.

[31] Forell Fritz von, Mölders und seine Männer, Graz 1941, pp. 40-41.

[32] Ibidem, pp. 43-44

[33] Ibidem, pp. 43-44

[34] Ibidem, pp. 45-46

[35] For a detailed description of Bf 109 C/D units operating in Poland in September 1939 see: Marek J. Murawski, Messerschmitt Bf 109 C/D w kampanii wrześniowej 1939 roku, seria Bitwy Lotnicze 13, Wydawnictwo Kagero, Lublin 2009.

[36] There must have been at least several C-3 models in the mix equipped with wing-mounted MG FF 20 mm cannon.

[37] The Luftwaffe pilots fighting in Poland invariably identified all P series fighters with Puławski's wing as P 24s.

[38] From the author's interview with Bob Hans-Ekkehard, August 25, 2007.

[39] Stackelberg Karl Georg von: Jagdgruppe G., Jäger an Polens Himmel, Graz 1940, pp. 37-38

[40] From the author's interview with Bob Hans-Ekkehard, August 25, 2007.

[41] Emmerling Marius, Luftwaffe nad Polską 1939, cz. I Jagdflieger, Gdynia 2002, p. 100.

[42] Cumft Olgierd, Kujawa Hubert Kazimierz, Księga lotników polskich poległych, zmarłych i zaginionych 1939-1945, Warszawa 1989, p. 144.

[43] Ryszard, Armia „Karpaty" w Wojnie Obronnej 1939 roku, Rzeszów 1989, p. 211.

[44] See: www.valka.cz/clanek_12310

[45] Emmerling claims (p. 161) that Koch's aircraft made a forced landing north west of Garwolin. It cannot be true, since the I./ZG 2 area of operations was some 200 km south west of Garwolin. The Gesamtverluste der Luftwaffe, a report prepared by Generalquartiermeister 4 Abteilung, does mention a loss of an unidentified Bf 109 near Garwolin-Borowo. The aircraft in question was most likely a Bf 109 E from I./JG 76 that was shot down on September 12, 1939.

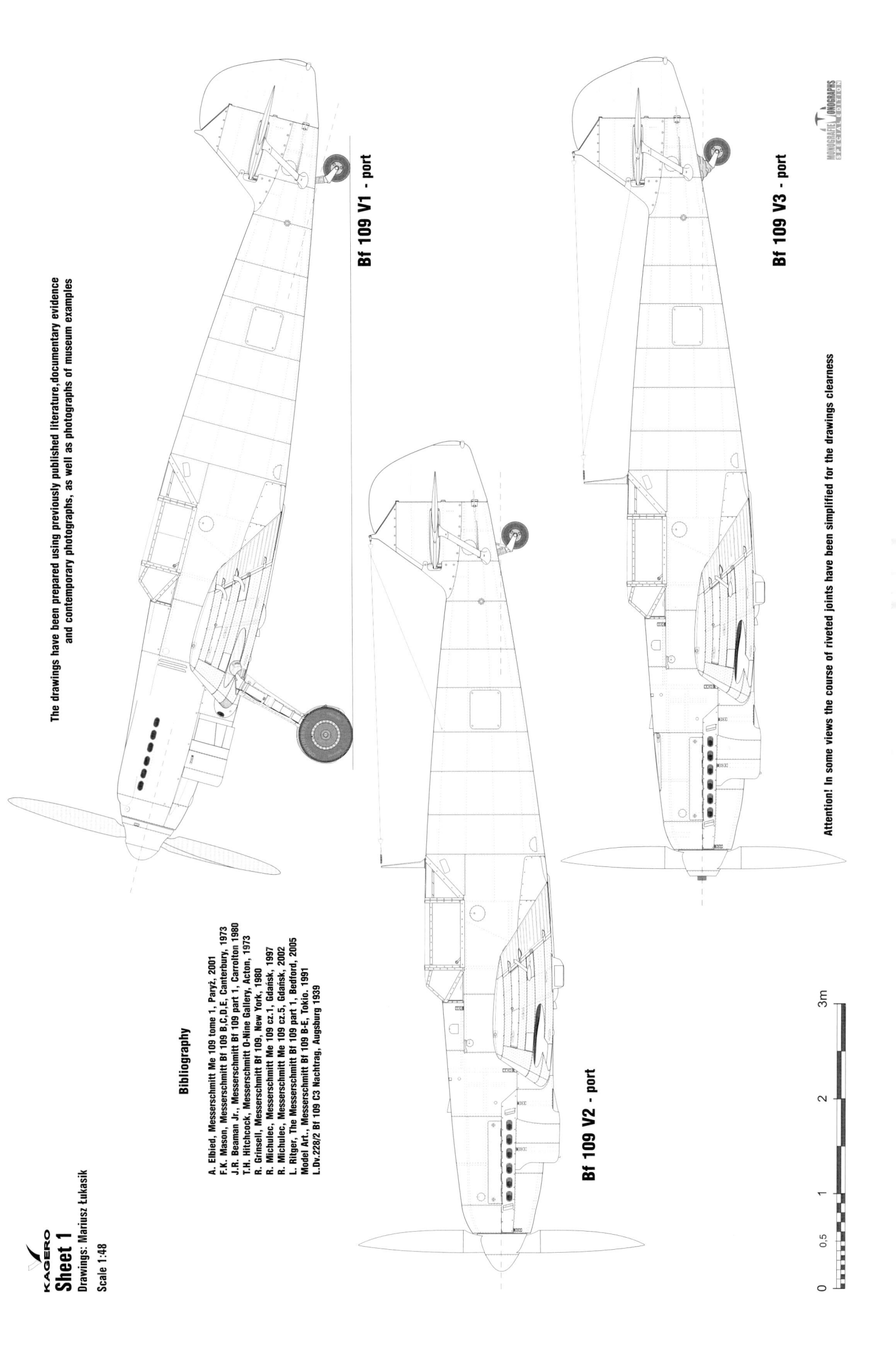

KAGERO
Sheet 1
Drawings: Mariusz Łukasik
Scale 1:48

The drawings have been prepared using previously published literature, documentary evidence and contemporary photographs, as well as photographs of museum examples

Bf 109 V1 - port

Bf 109 V2 - port

Bf 109 V3 - port

Bibliography

A. Elbied, Messerschmitt Me 109 tome 1, Paryż, 2001
F.K. Mason, Messerschmitt Bf 109 B,C,D,E, Canterbury, 1973
J.R. Beaman Jr., Messerschmitt Bf 109 part 1, Carrolton 1980
T.H. Hitchcock, Messerschmitt 0-Nine Gallery, Acton, 1973
R. Grinsell, Messerschmitt Bf 109, New York, 1980
R. Michulec, Messerschmitt Me 109 cz.1, Gdańsk, 1997
R. Michulec, Messerschmitt Me 109 cz.5, Gdańsk, 2002
L. Ritger, The Messerschmitt Bf 109 part 1, Bedford, 2005
Model Art., Messerschmitt Bf 109 B-E, Tokio. 1991
L.Dv.228/2 Bf 109 C3 Nachtrag, Augsburg 1939

Attention! In some views the course of riveted joints have been simplified for the drawings clearness

MONOGRAFIE MONOGRAPHS SPECJALNE EDITION

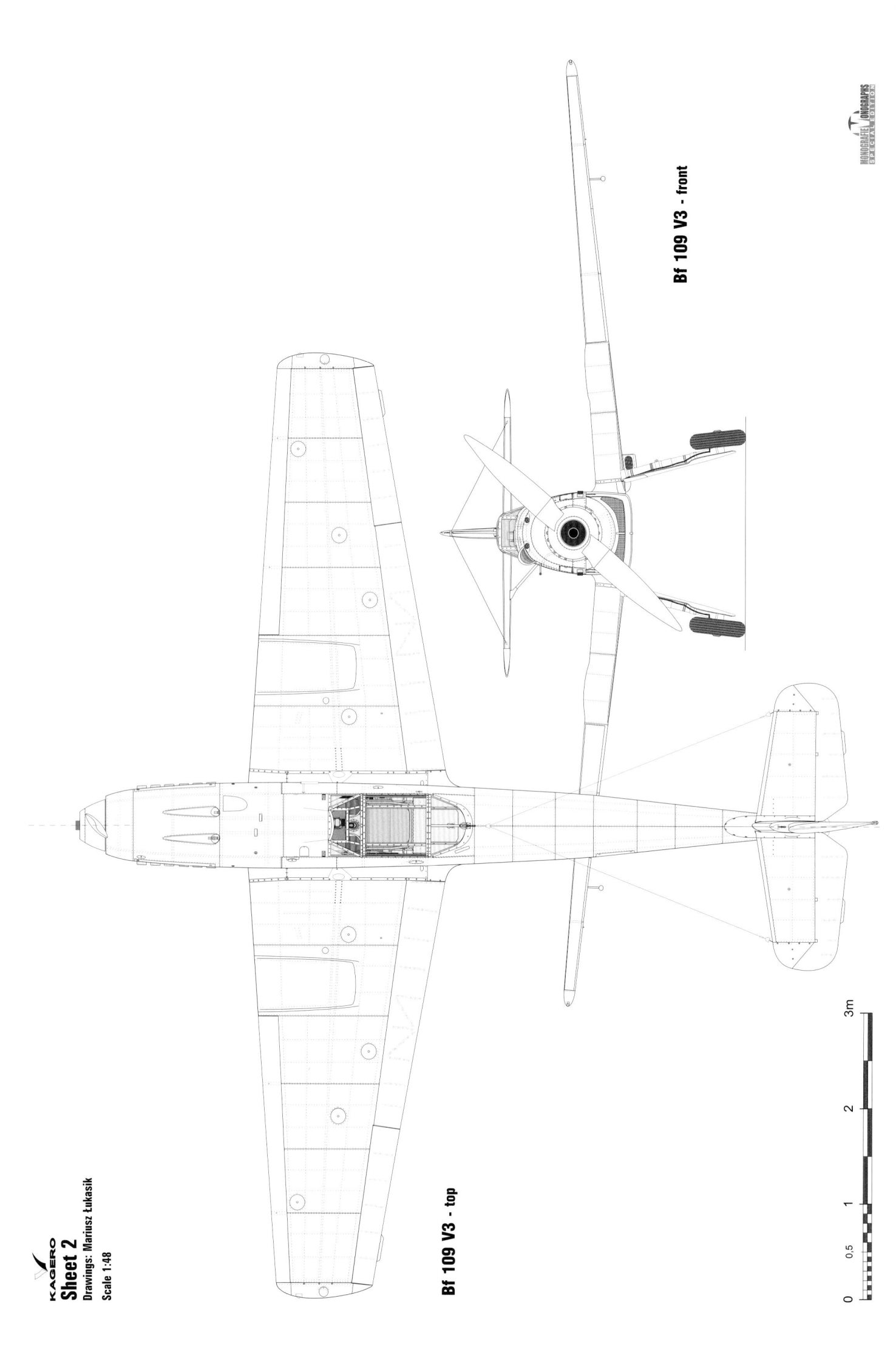

KAGERO
Sheet 2
Drawings: Mariusz Łukasik
Scale 1:48

Bf 109 V3 - front

Bf 109 V3 - top

0   0,5   1   2   3m

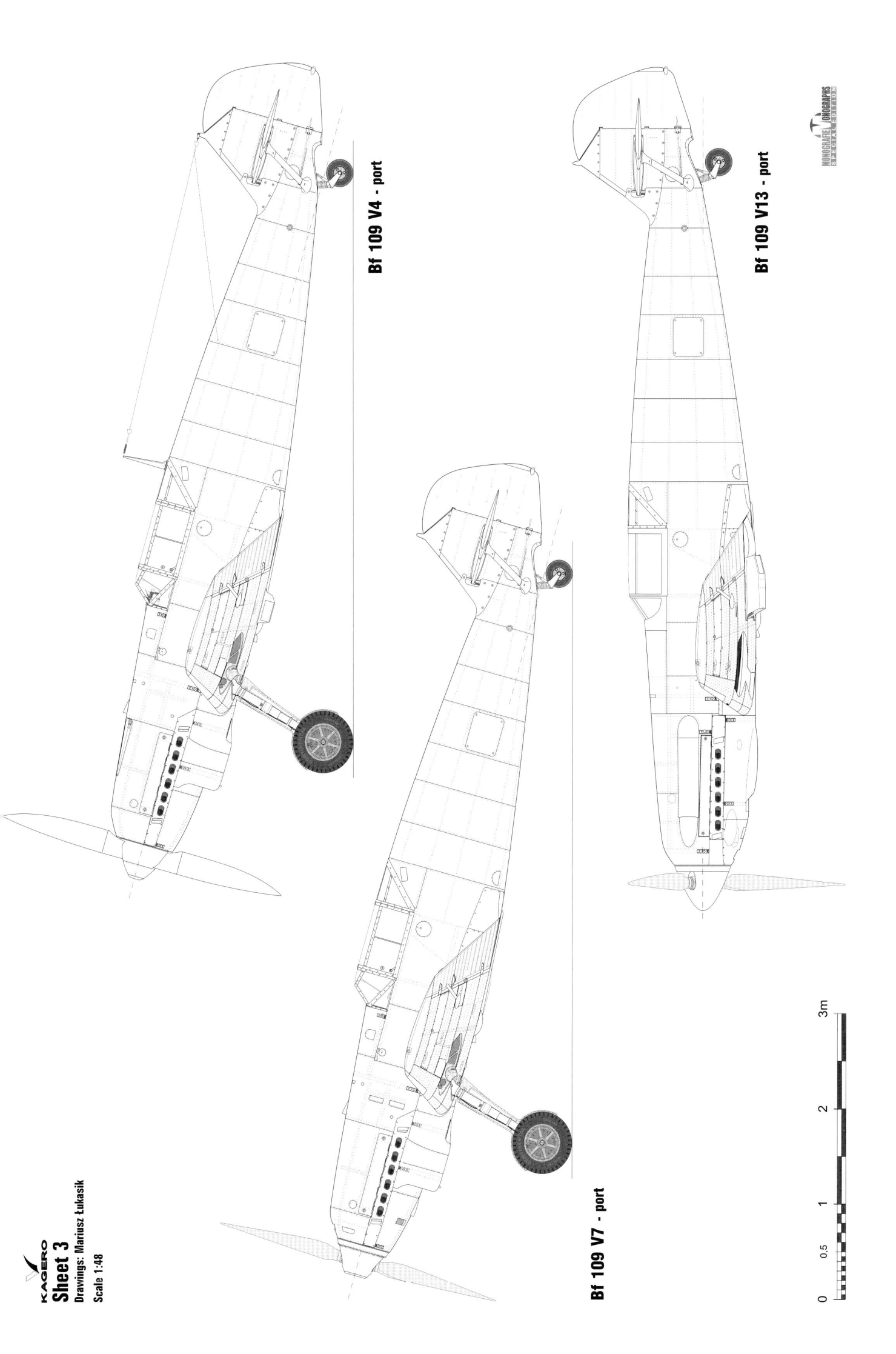

Sheet 3
Drawings: Mariusz Łukasik
Scale 1:48

Bf 109 V4 - port

Bf 109 V7 - port

Bf 109 V13 - port

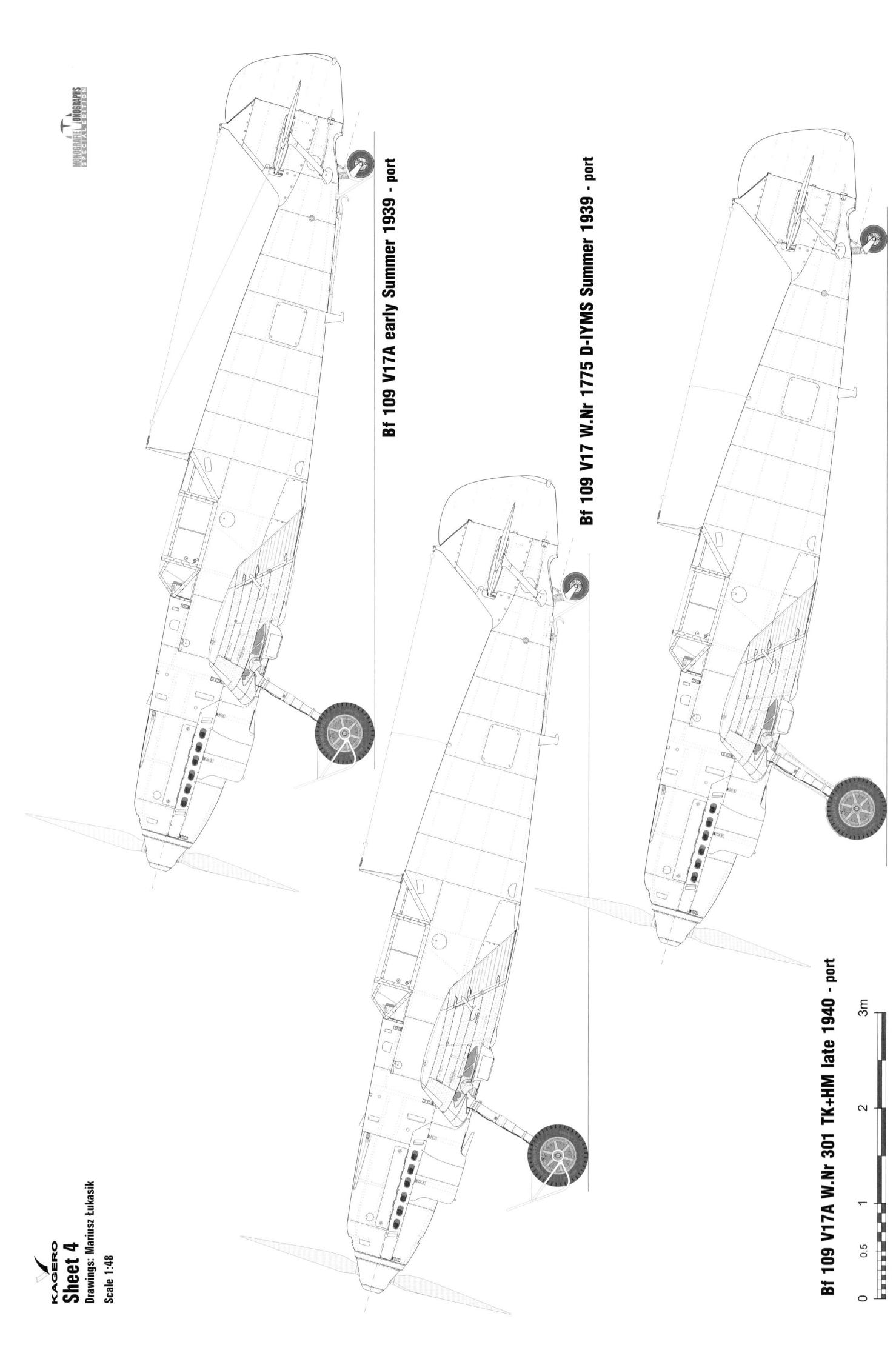

Sheet 4
Drawings: Mariusz Łukasik
Scale 1:48

Bf 109 V17A early Summer 1939 - port

Bf 109 V17 W.Nr 1775 D-IYMS Summer 1939 - port

Bf 109 V17A W.Nr 301 TK+HM late 1940 - port

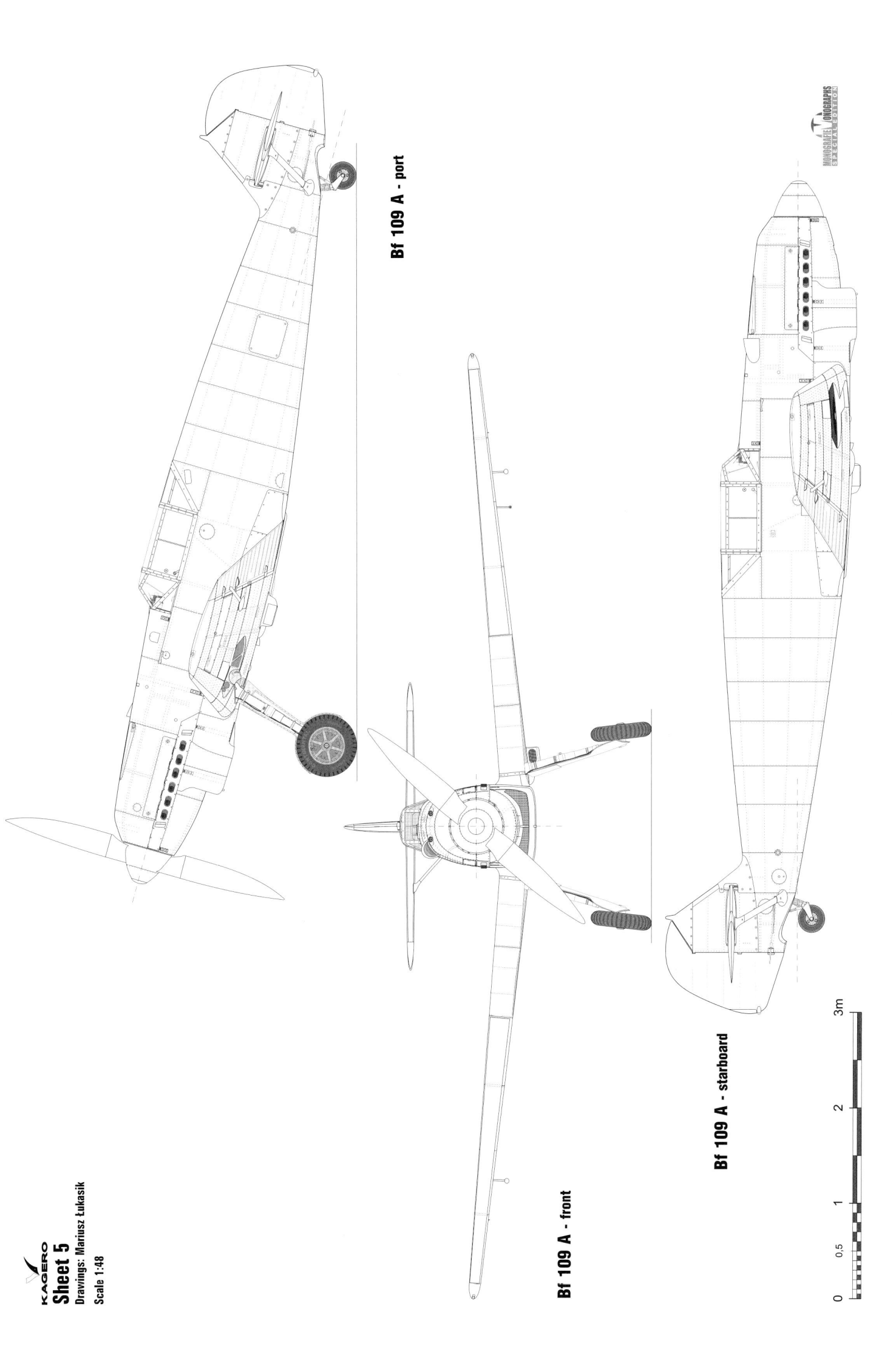

Sheet 5
Drawings: Mariusz Łukasik
Scale 1:48

Bf 109 A - port

Bf 109 A - front

Bf 109 A - starboard

Bf 109 A - rear

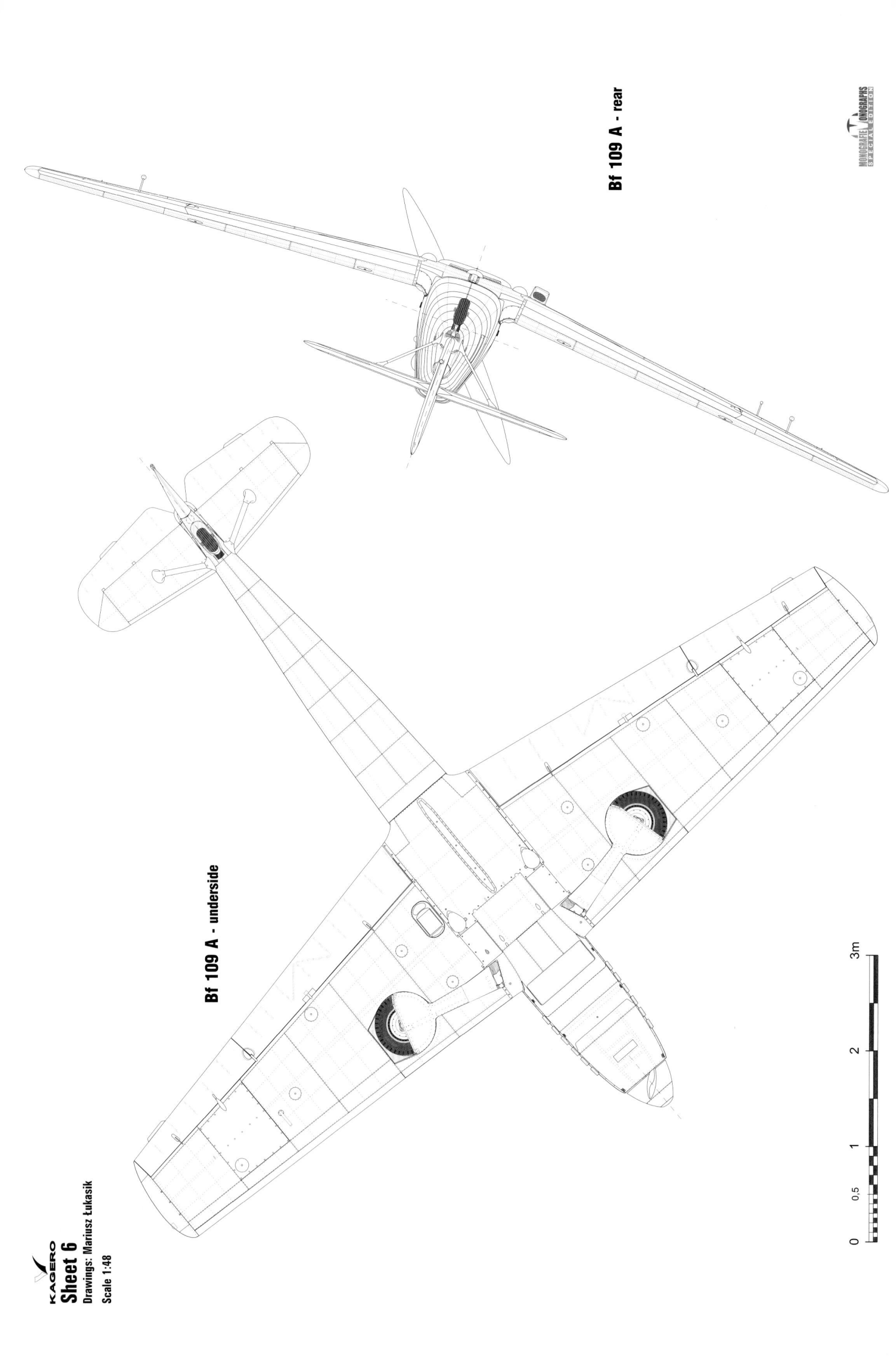

Bf 109 A - underside

KAGERO
Sheet 6
Drawings: Mariusz Łukasik
Scale 1:48

Sheet 7

Drawings: Mariusz Łukasik
Scale 1:48

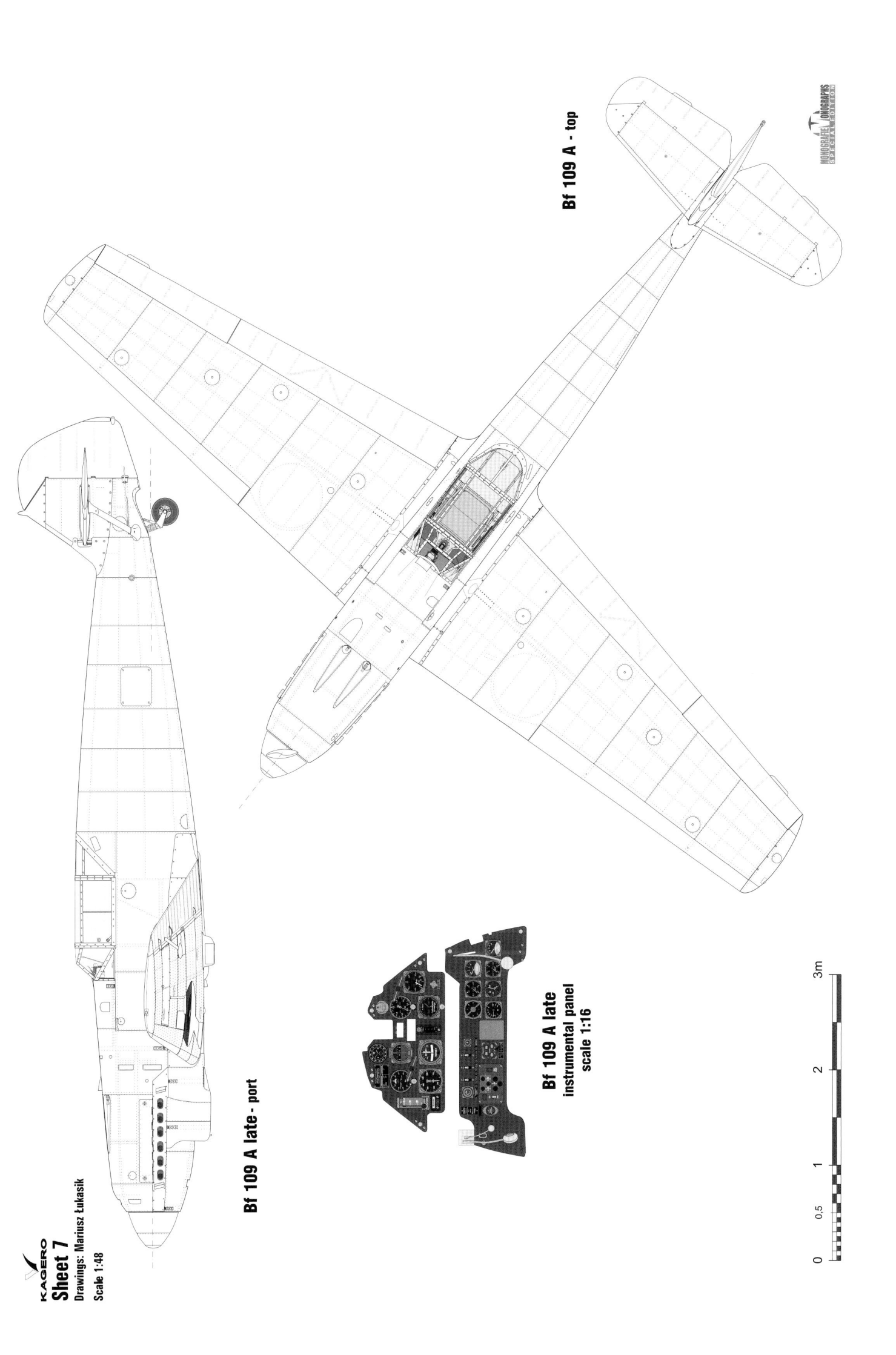

Bf 109 A - top

Bf 109 A late - port

Bf 109 A late instrumental panel
scale 1:16

Sheet 8

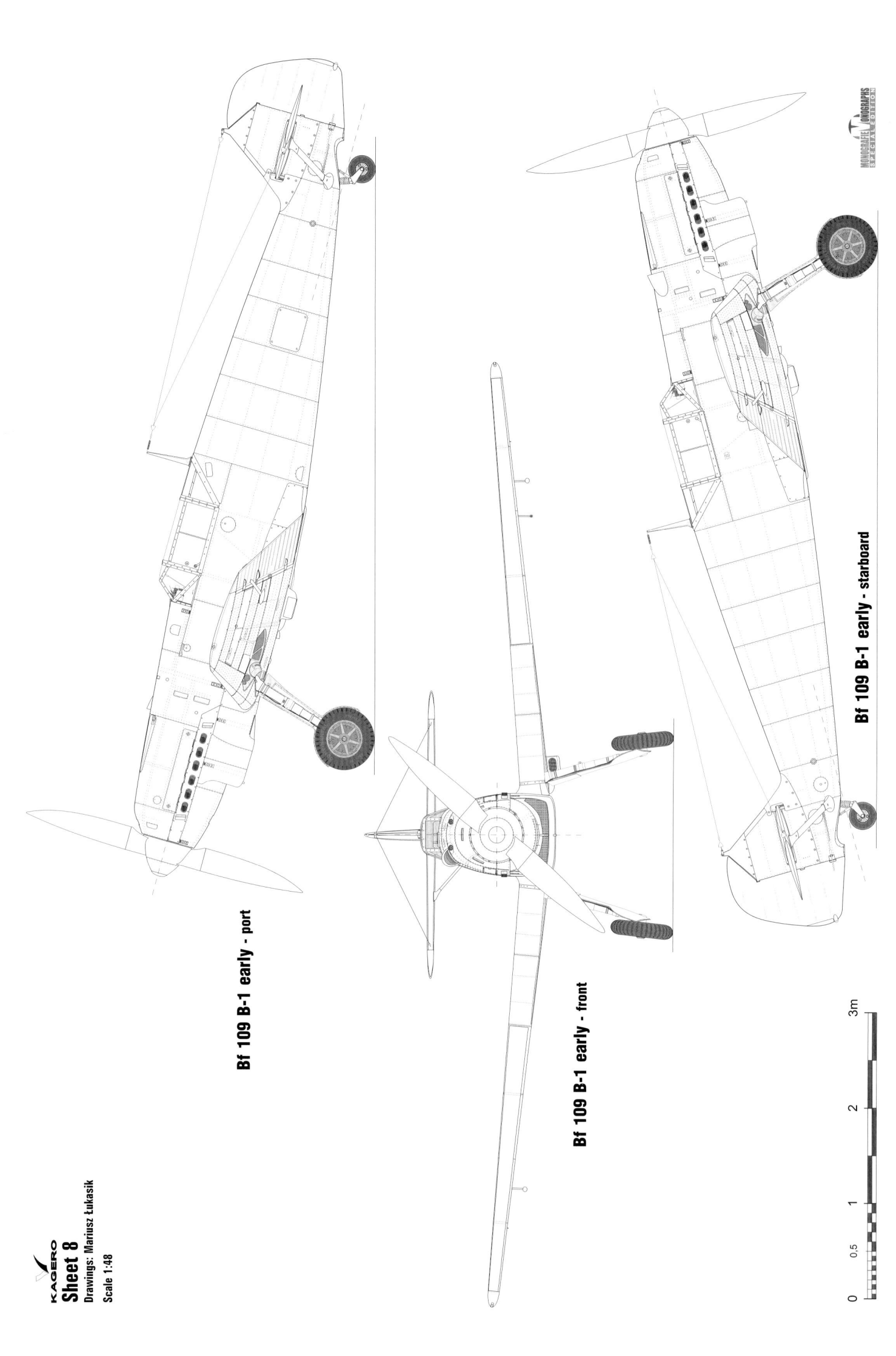

Drawings: Mariusz Łukasik

Scale 1:48

Bf 109 B-1 early - port

Bf 109 B-1 early - front

Bf 109 B-1 early - starboard

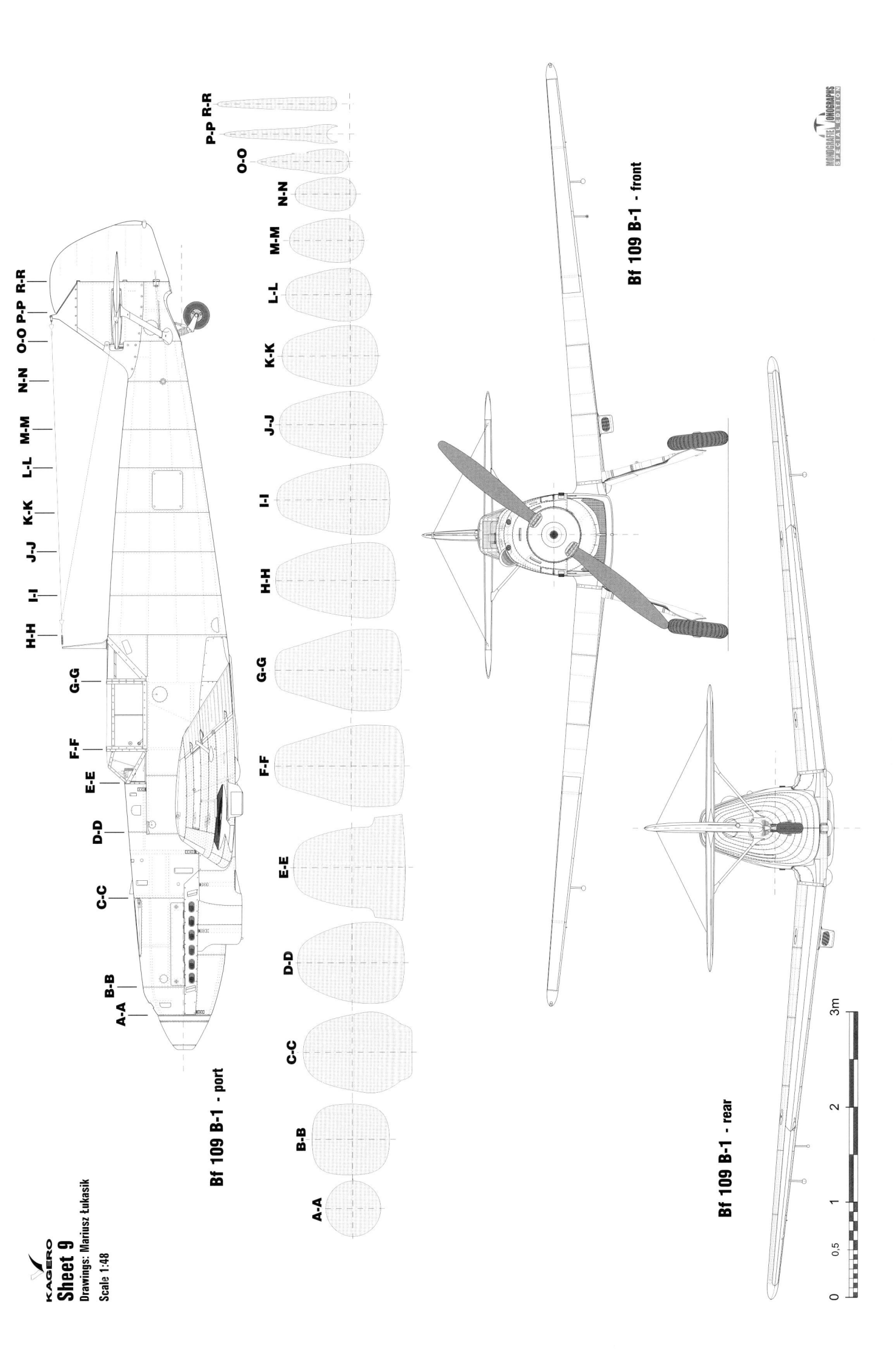

KAGERO
Sheet 9
Drawings: Mariusz Łukasik
Scale 1:48

Bf 109 B-1 - port

Bf 109 B-1 - front

Bf 109 B-1 - rear

Bf 109 B-1 - top

S1
S2
S3

S3
S2
S1

Scale 1:72
Scale 1:48
Scale 1:32

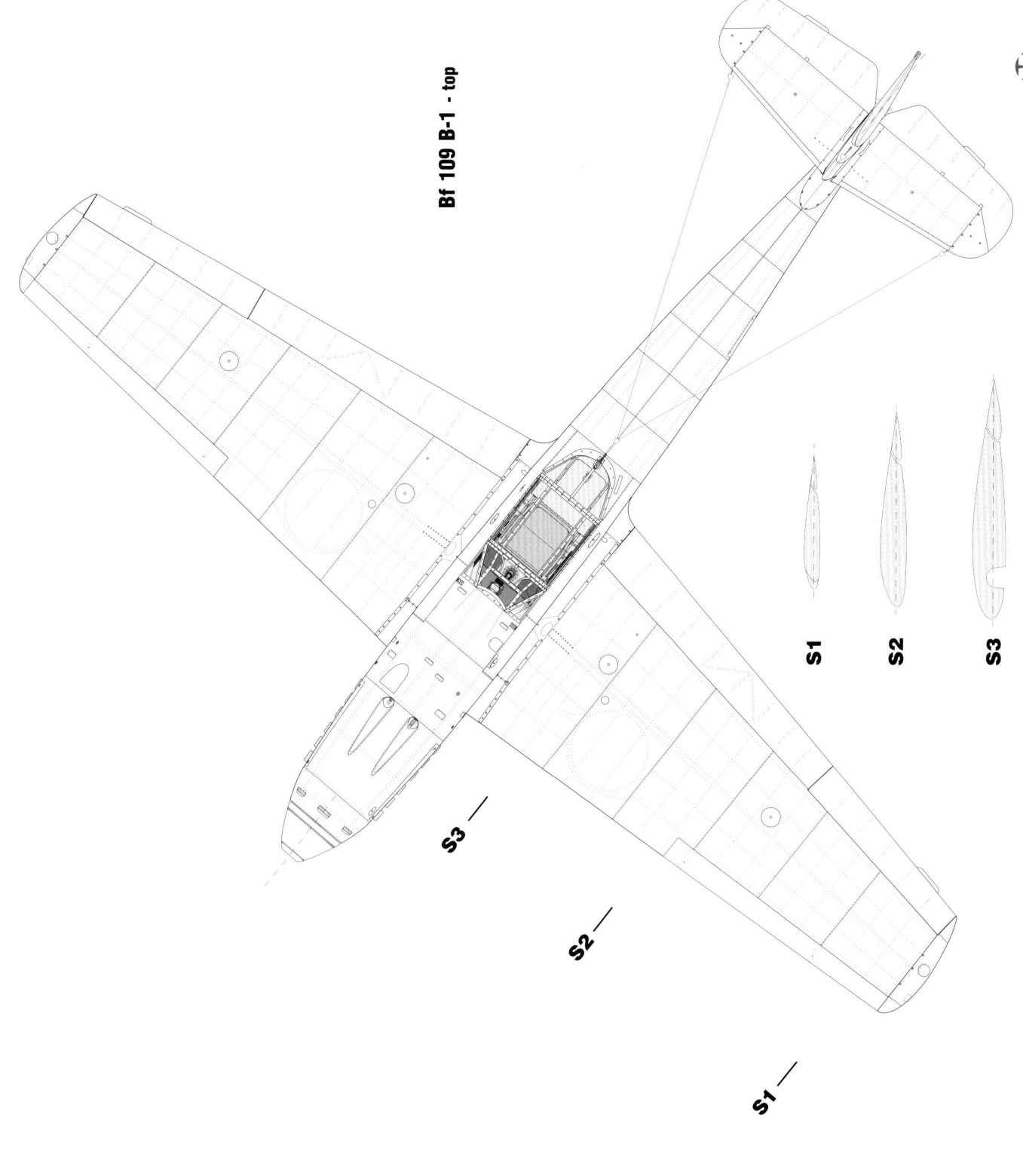

Bf 109 B-1 instrumental panel

KAGERO
Sheet 10
Drawings: Mariusz Łukasik
Scale 1:48

Sheet 11

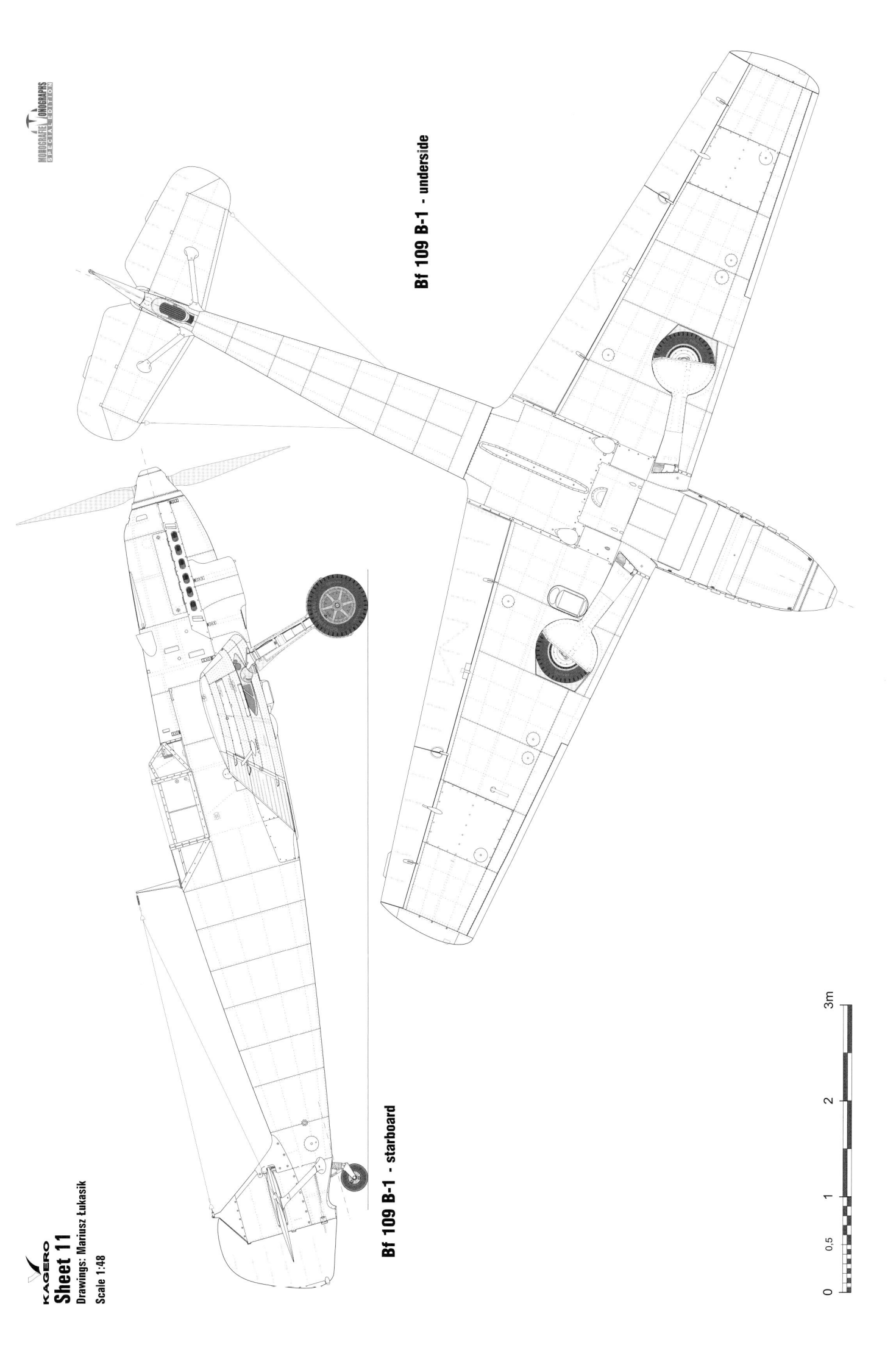

Drawings: Mariusz Łukasik
Scale 1:48

Bf 109 B-1 - underside

Bf 109 B-1 - starboard

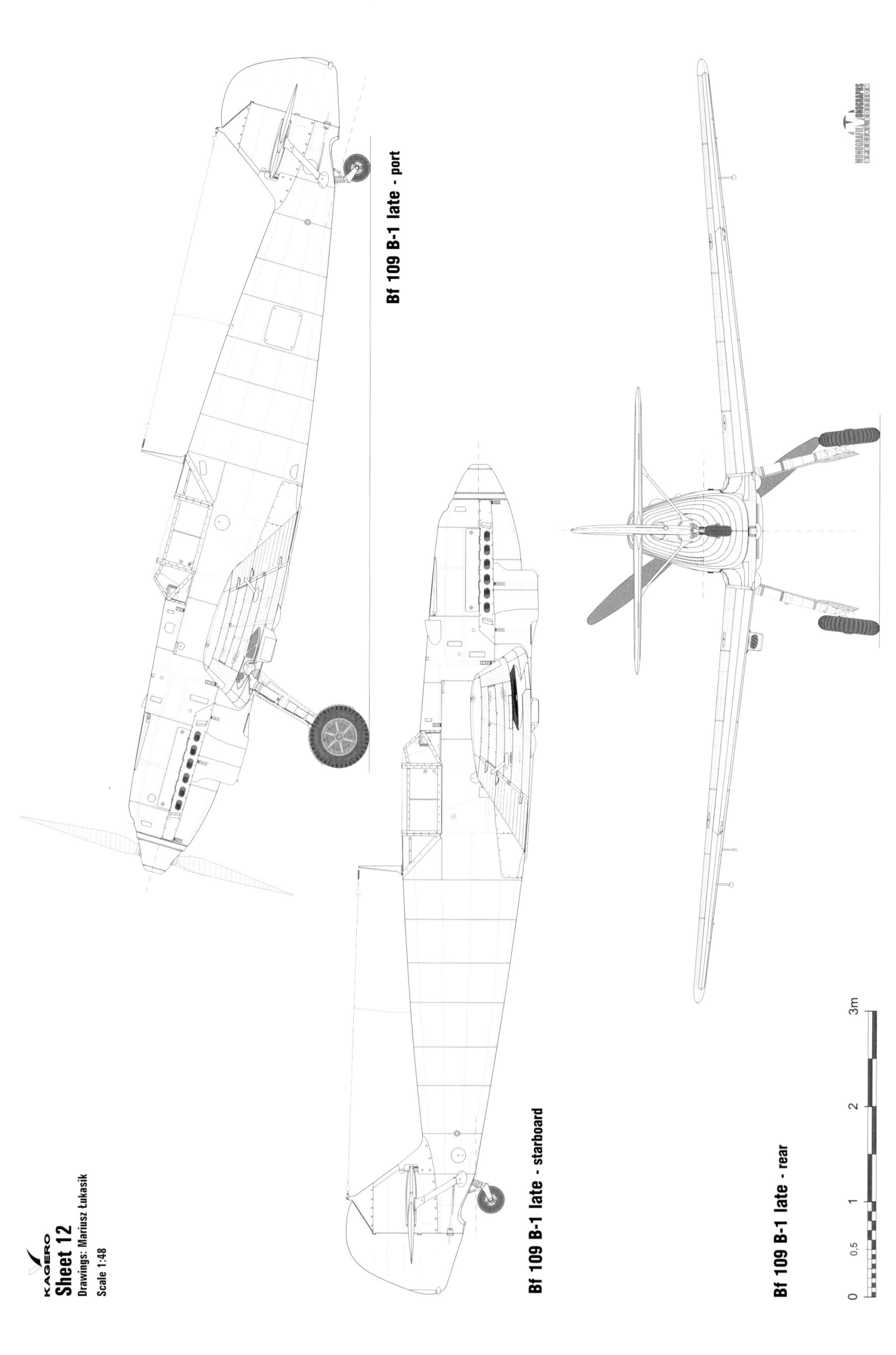

KAGERO
Sheet 12
Drawings: Mariusz Łukasik
Scale 1:48

Bf 109 B-1 late - port

Bf 109 B-1 late - starboard

Bf 109 B-1 late - rear

Bf 109 C-1 - port

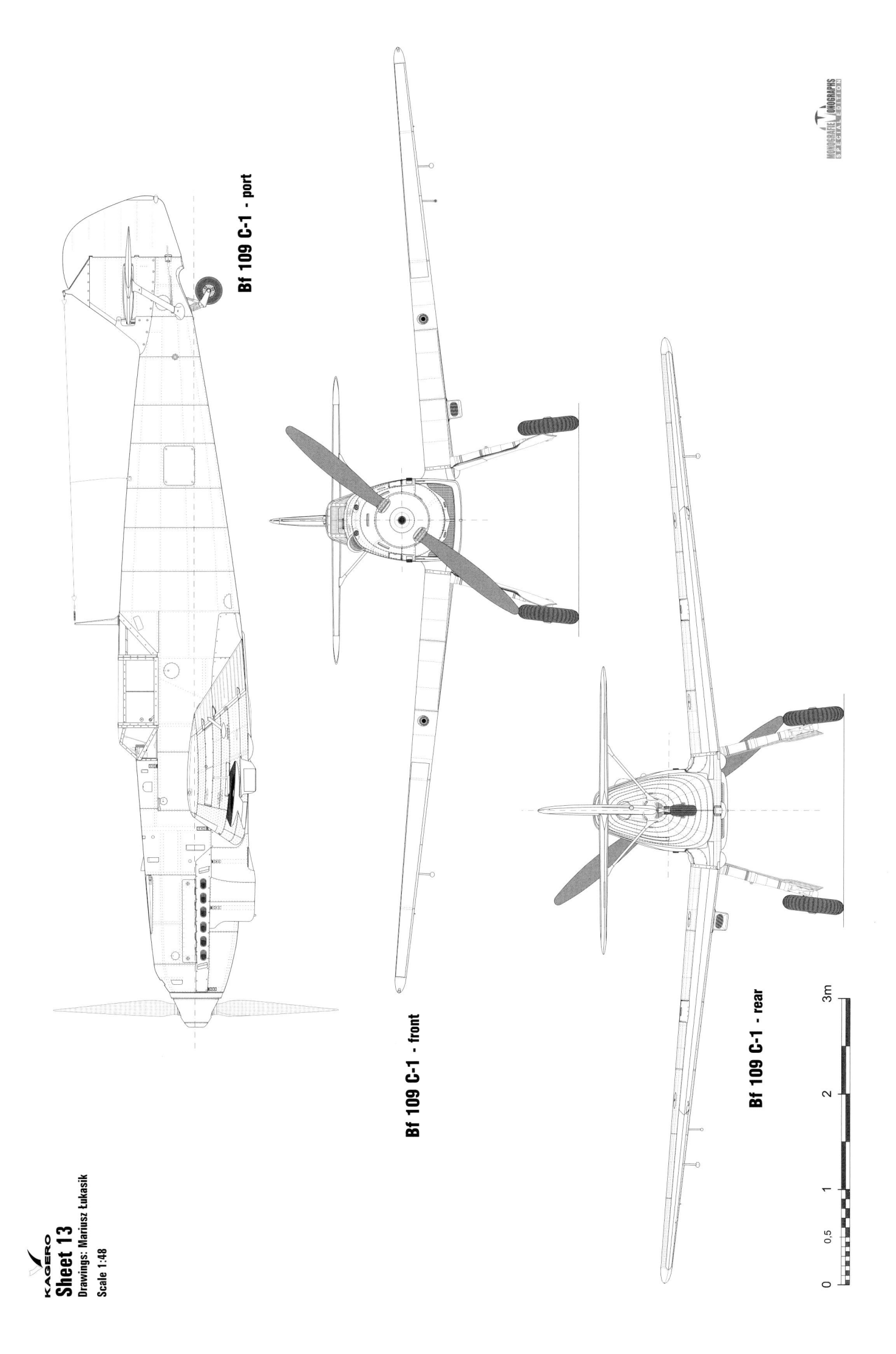

Bf 109 C-1 - front

Bf 109 C-1 - rear

KAGERO
Sheet 13
Drawings: Mariusz Łukasik
Scale 1:48

KAGERO
Sheet 14
Drawings: Mariusz Łukasik
Scale 1:48

Bf 109 C-1 - top

Bf 109 C-1 - starboard

Scale 1:72
Scale 1:48
Scale 1:32

MG 17 7,92mm

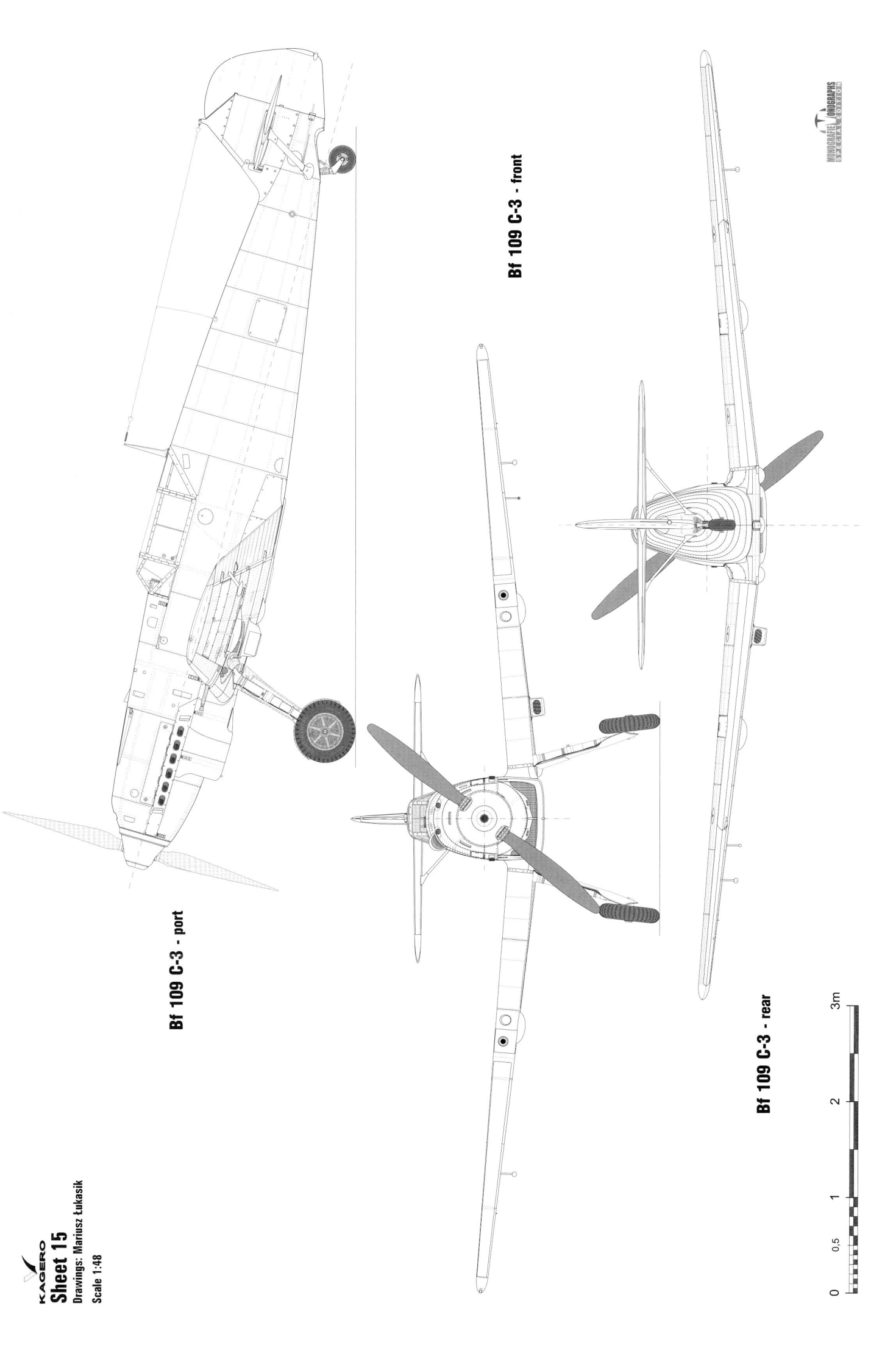

KAGERO
Sheet 15
Drawings: Mariusz Łukasik
Scale 1:48

Bf 109 C-3 - port

Bf 109 C-3 - front

Bf 109 C-3 - rear

Sheet 16
Drawings: Mariusz Łukasik
Scale 1:48

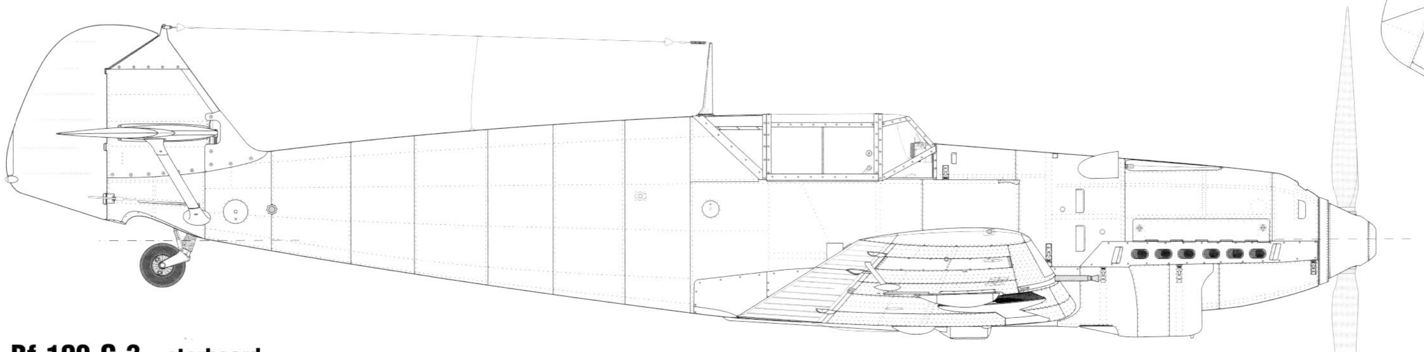

Bf 109 C-3 - underside

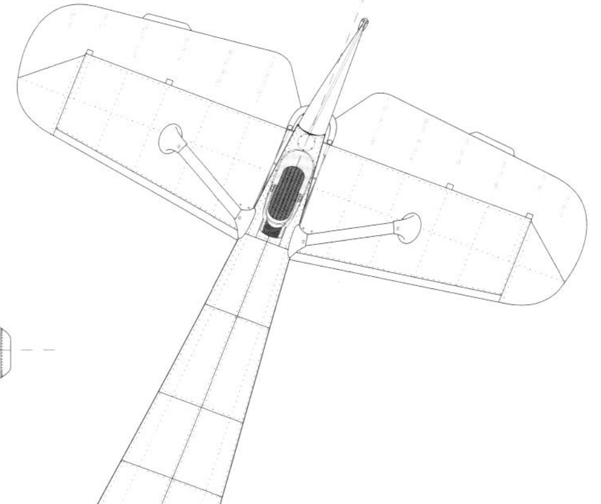

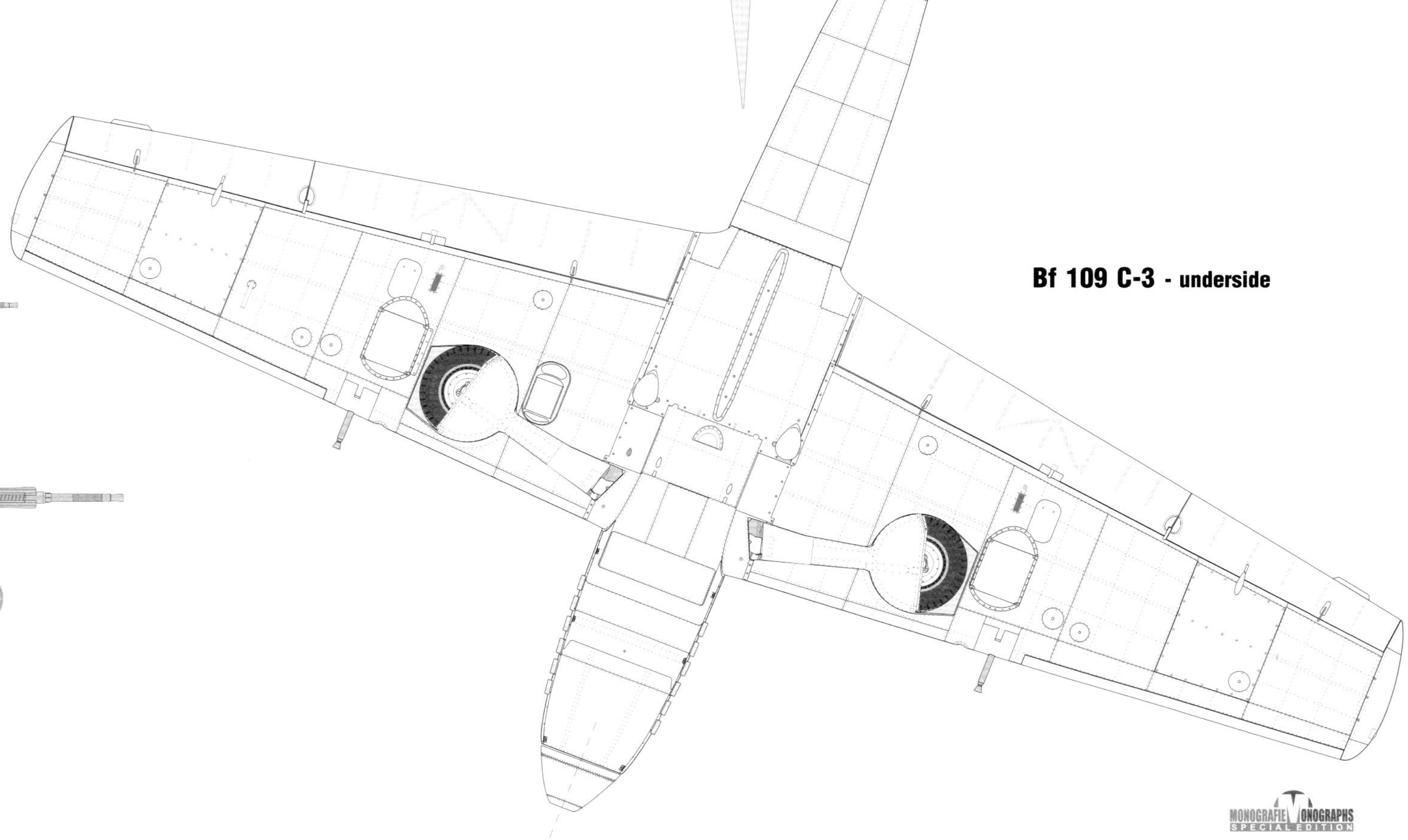

Bf 109 C-3 - starboard

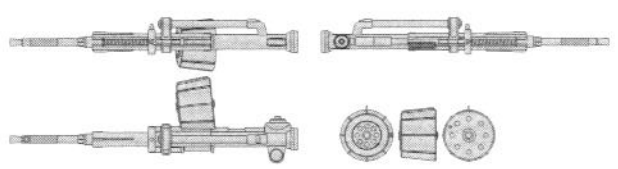

Scale 1:72

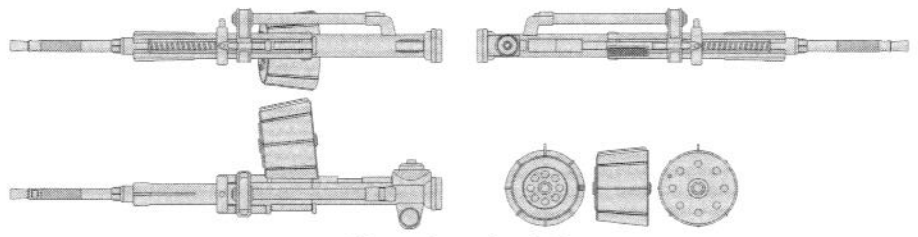

Scale 1:48

Scale 1:32

MG 17 7,92mm

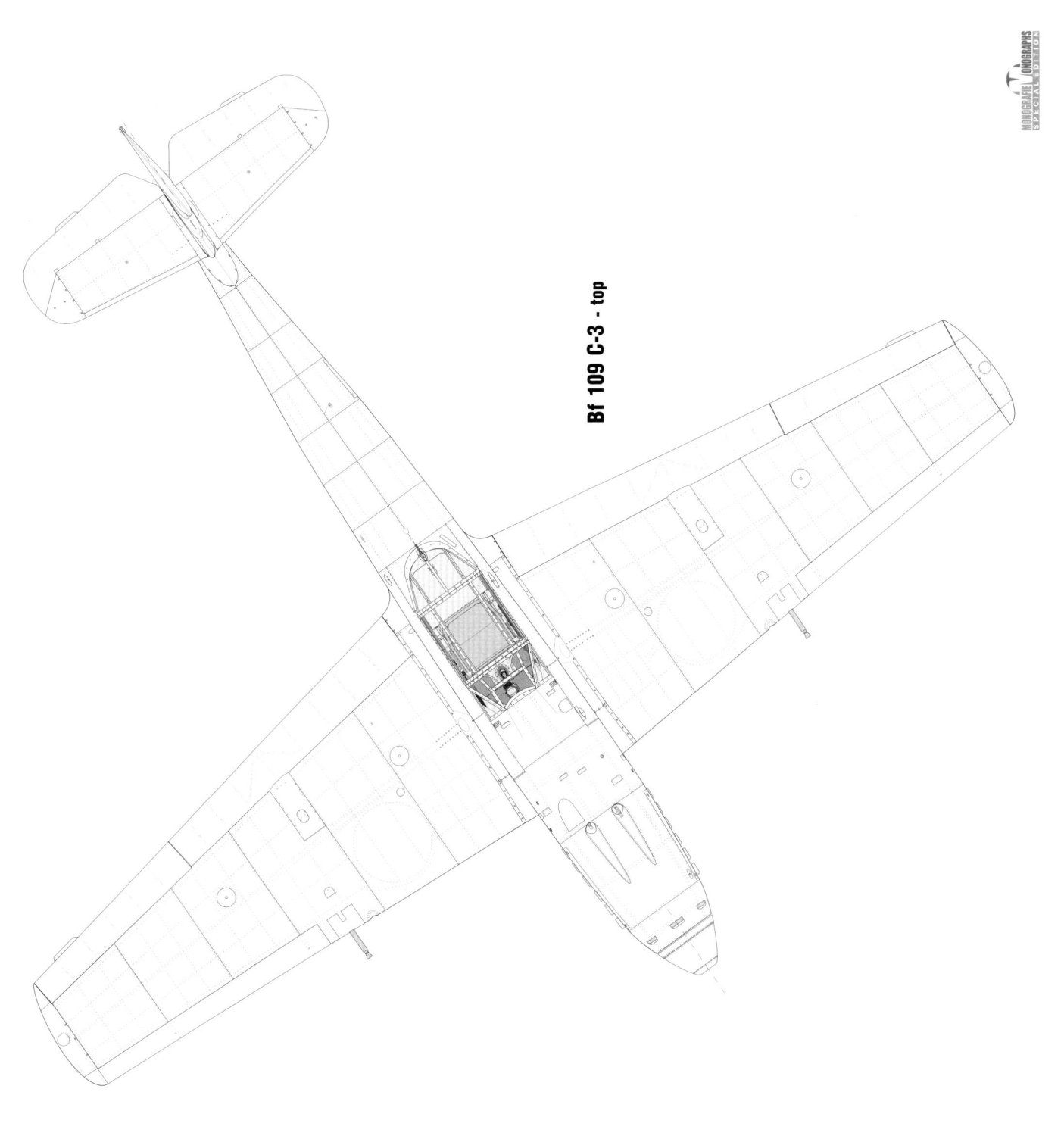

KAGERO
Sheet 17
Drawings: Mariusz Łukasik
Scale 1:48

Bf 109 C-3 - top

Revi C/12 D
scale 1:16

Bf 109 C-3
instrumental panel
scale 1:16

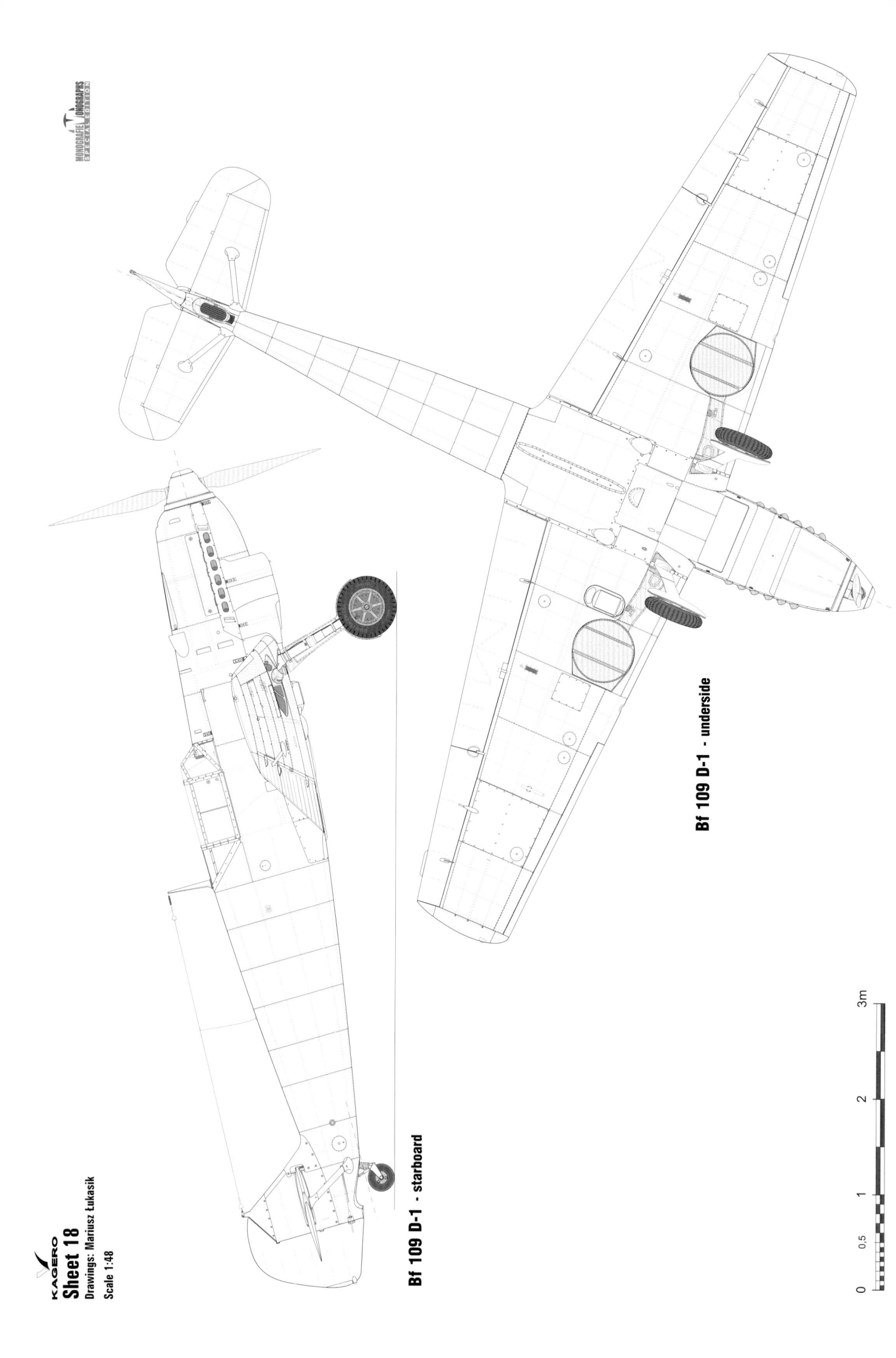

Sheet 18
Drawings: Mariusz Łukasik
Scale 1:48

Bf 109 D-1 - starboard

Bf 109 D-1 - underside

Sheet 19
Drawings: Mariusz Łukasik
Scale 1:48

Bf 109 D-1 - port

Bf 109 D-1 - top

Bf 109 D-1 - front

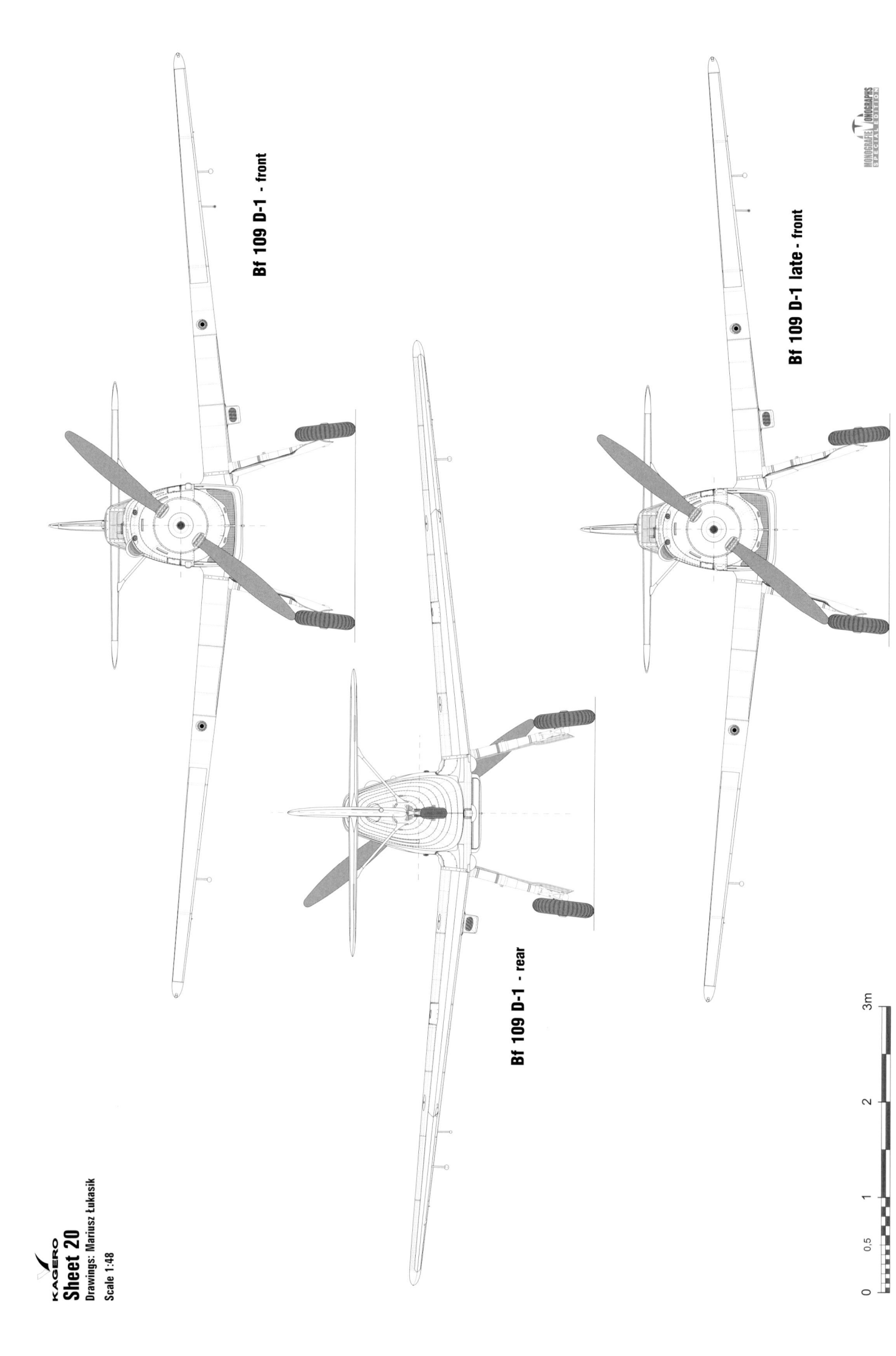

Bf 109 D-1 late - front

Bf 109 D-1 - rear

KAGERO
Sheet 20
Drawings: Mariusz Łukasik
Scale 1:48

Sheet 21

Drawings: Mariusz Łukasik Scale 1:48

Bf 109 D-1 late - top

Bf 109 D-1 late - port

Bf 109 D-1 instrumental panel
scale 1:16

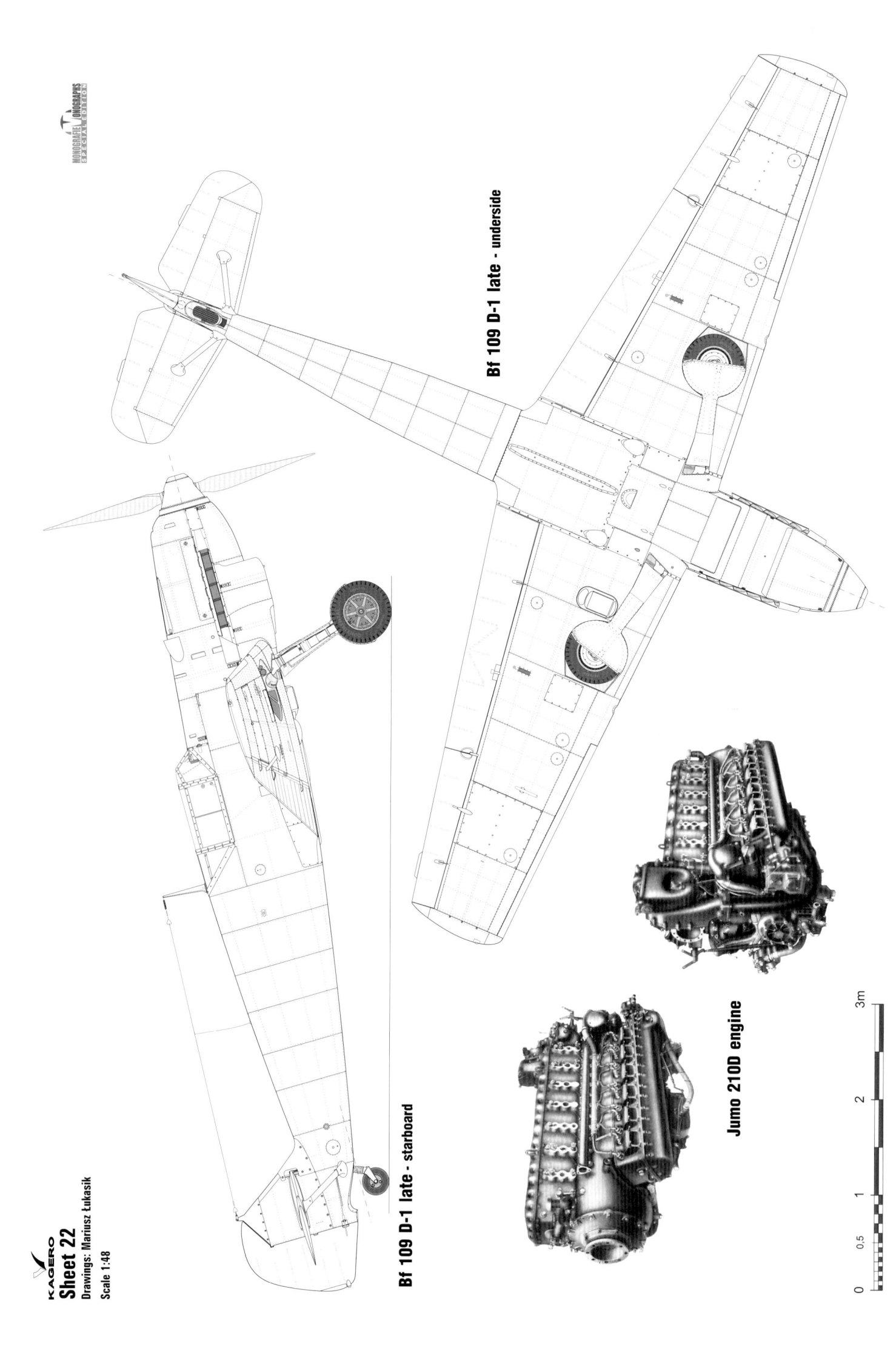

Sheet 22
Drawings: Mariusz Łukasik
Scale 1:48

Bf 109 D-1 late - underside

Bf 109 D-1 late - starboard

Jumo 210D engine

KAGERO
Sheet 23
Drawings: Mariusz Łukasik

Bf 109 A-D Fuselage

Undercarriage door
Scale 1:16

Main undercarriage 650x150 wheel
Scale 1:16

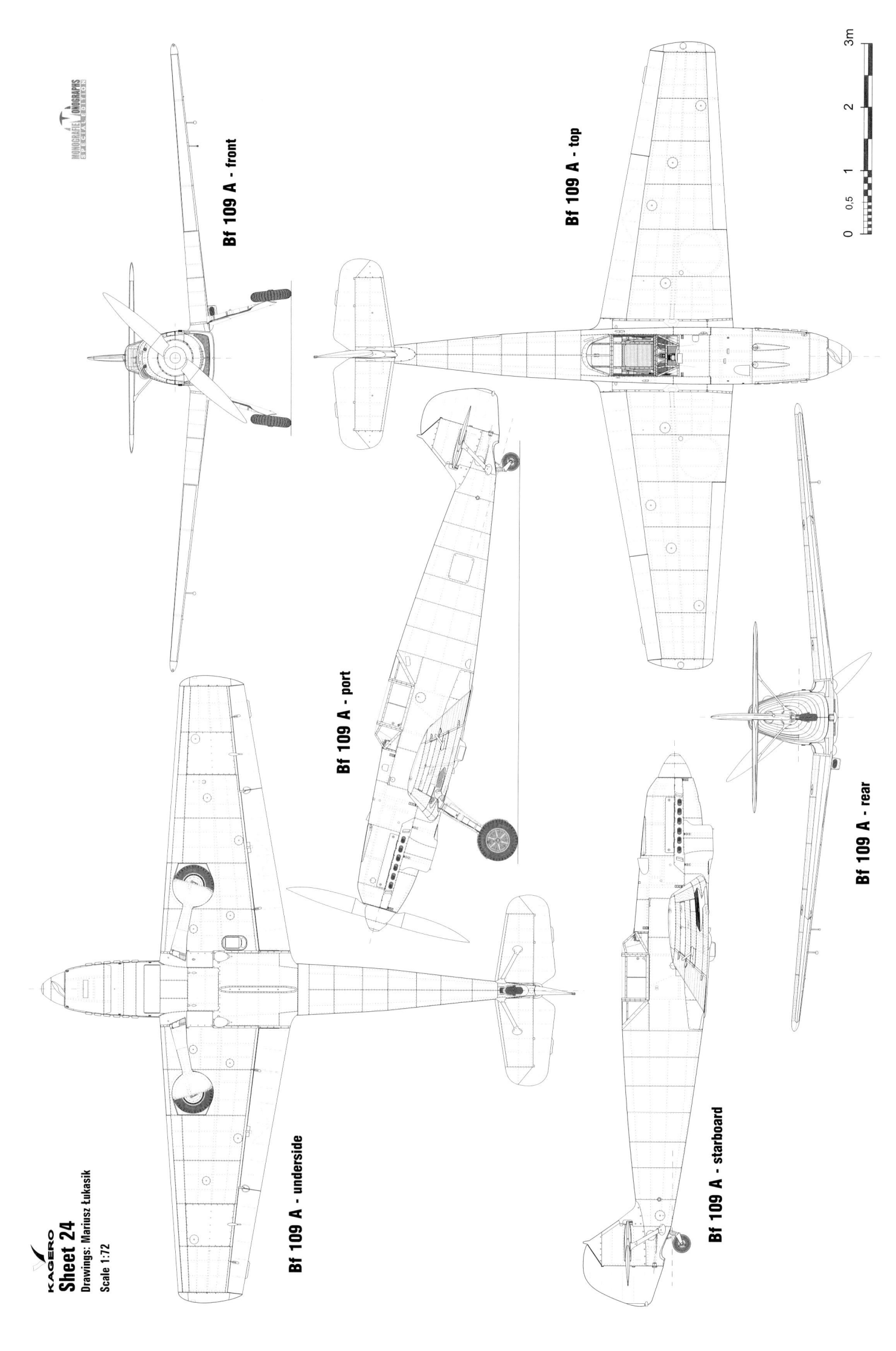

Kagero
Sheet 24
Drawings: Mariusz Łukasik
Scale 1:72

Bf 109 A - front
Bf 109 A - top
Bf 109 A - port
Bf 109 A - rear
Bf 109 A - underside
Bf 109 A - starboard

Bf 109 B-1

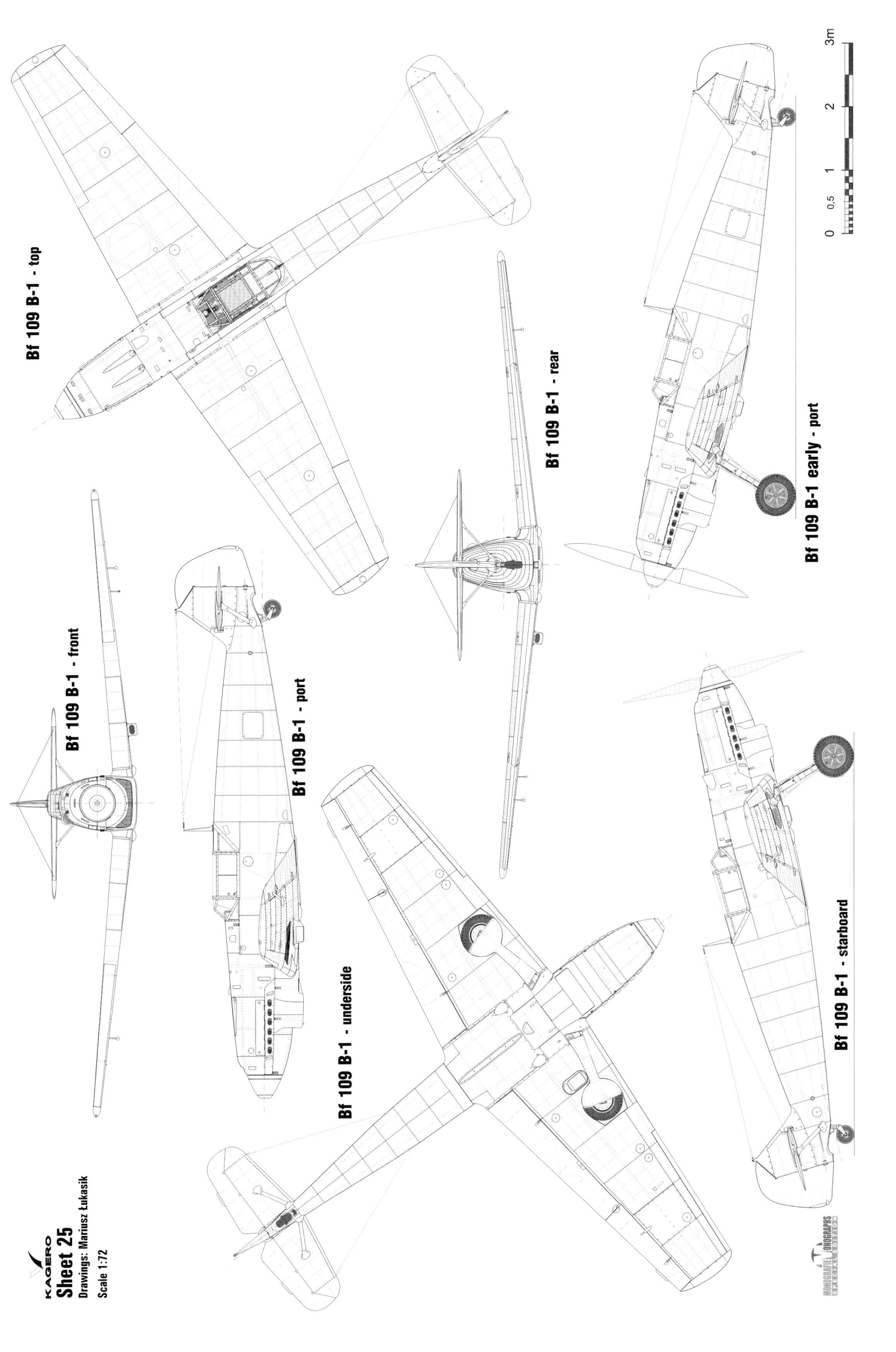

KAGERO Sheet 25
Drawings: Mariusz Łukasik
Scale 1:72

- Bf 109 B-1 - top
- Bf 109 B-1 - front
- Bf 109 B-1 - port
- Bf 109 B-1 - underside
- Bf 109 B-1 - rear
- Bf 109 B-1 early - port
- Bf 109 B-1 - starboard

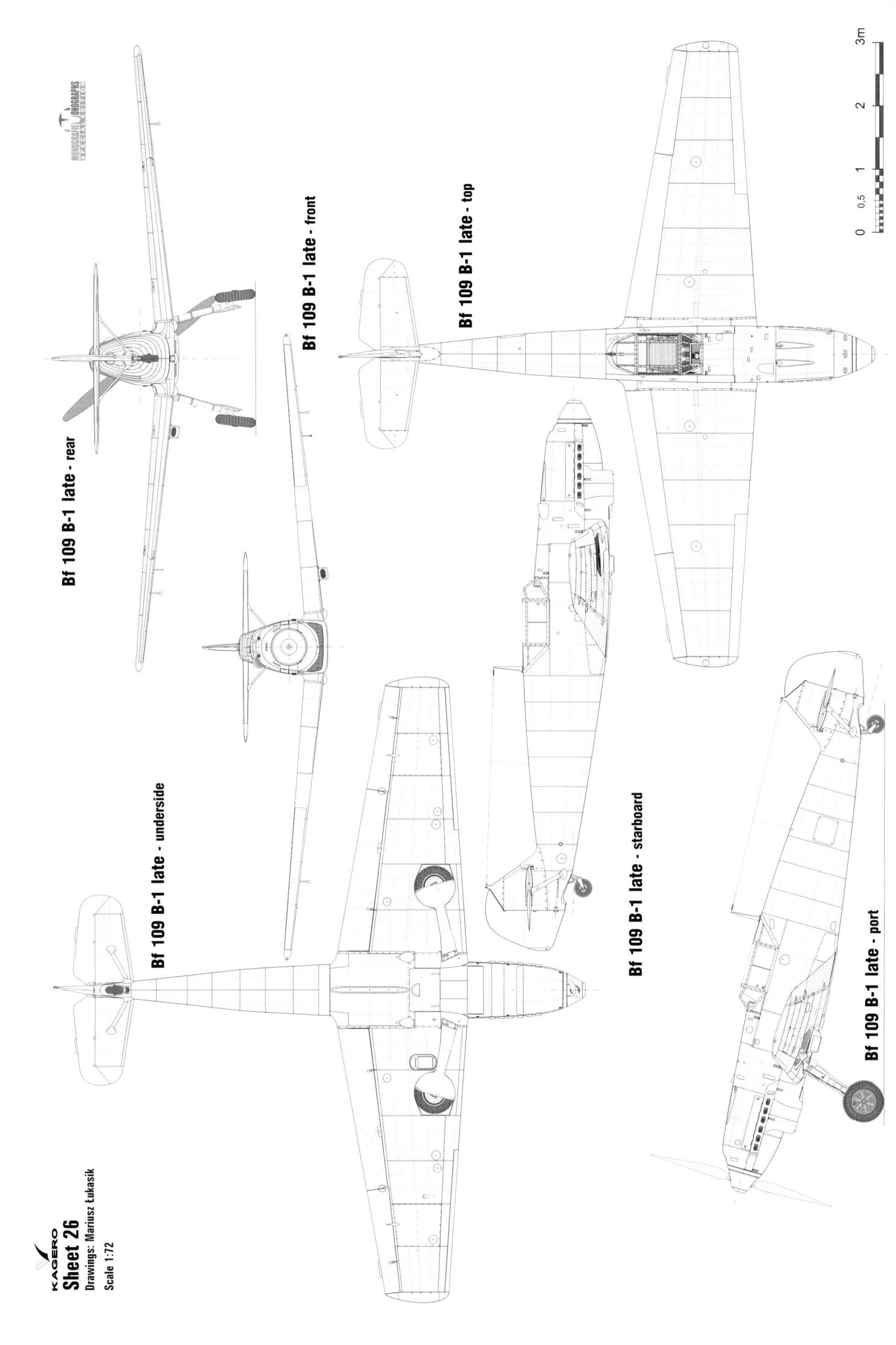

Bf 109 B-1 late - rear
Bf 109 B-1 late - front
Bf 109 B-1 late - top
Bf 109 B-1 late - underside
Bf 109 B-1 late - starboard
Bf 109 B-1 late - port

KAGERO
Sheet 26
Drawings: Mariusz Łukasik
Scale 1:72

Sheet 27

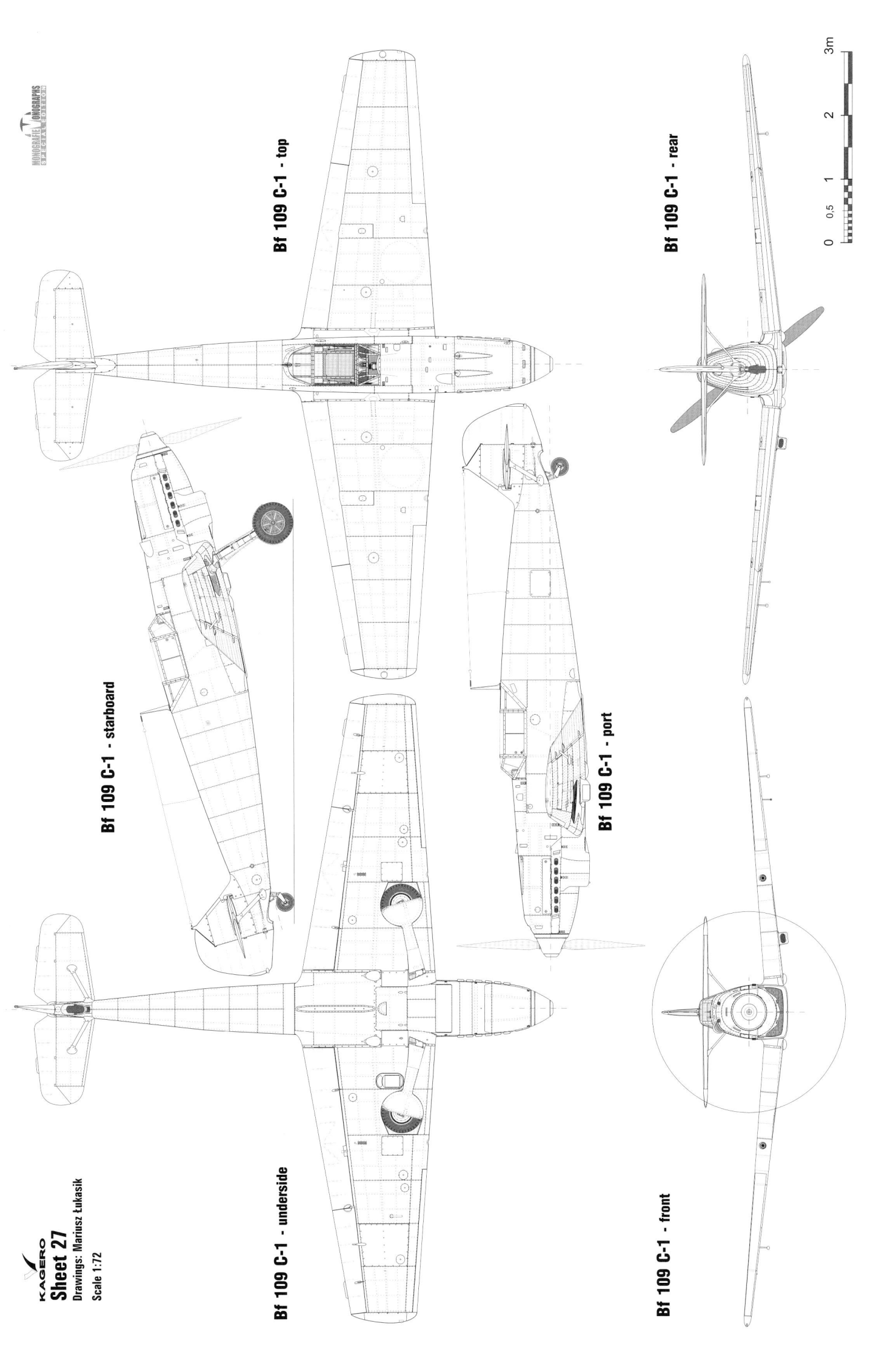

Drawings: Mariusz Łukasik
Scale 1:72

Bf 109 C-1 - top
Bf 109 C-1 - starboard
Bf 109 C-1 - port
Bf 109 C-1 - underside
Bf 109 C-1 - rear
Bf 109 C-1 - front

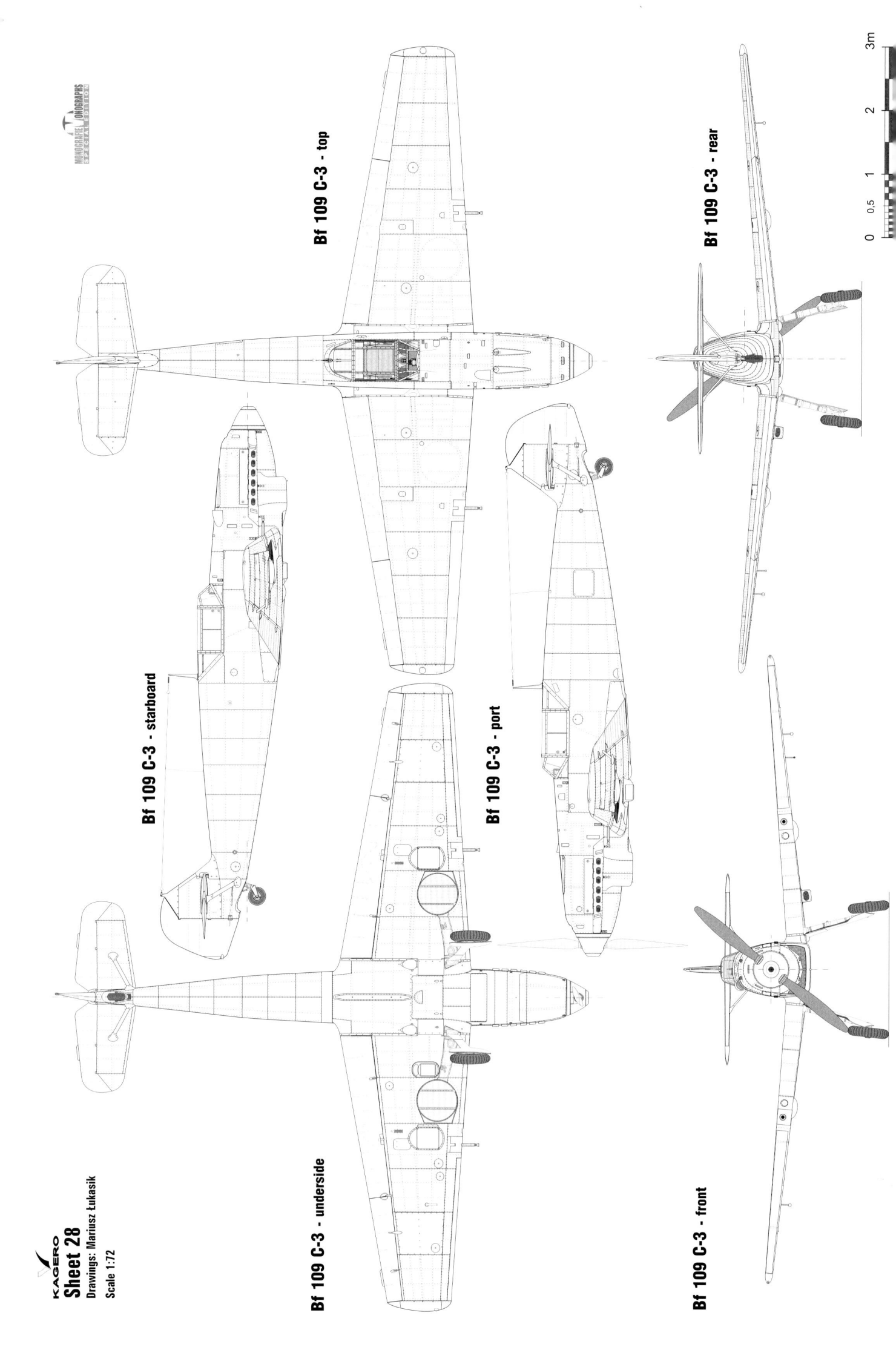

KAGERO
Sheet 28
Drawings: Mariusz Łukasik
Scale 1:72

Bf 109 C-3 - top
Bf 109 C-3 - starboard
Bf 109 C-3 - port
Bf 109 C-3 - underside
Bf 109 C-3 - rear
Bf 109 C-3 - front

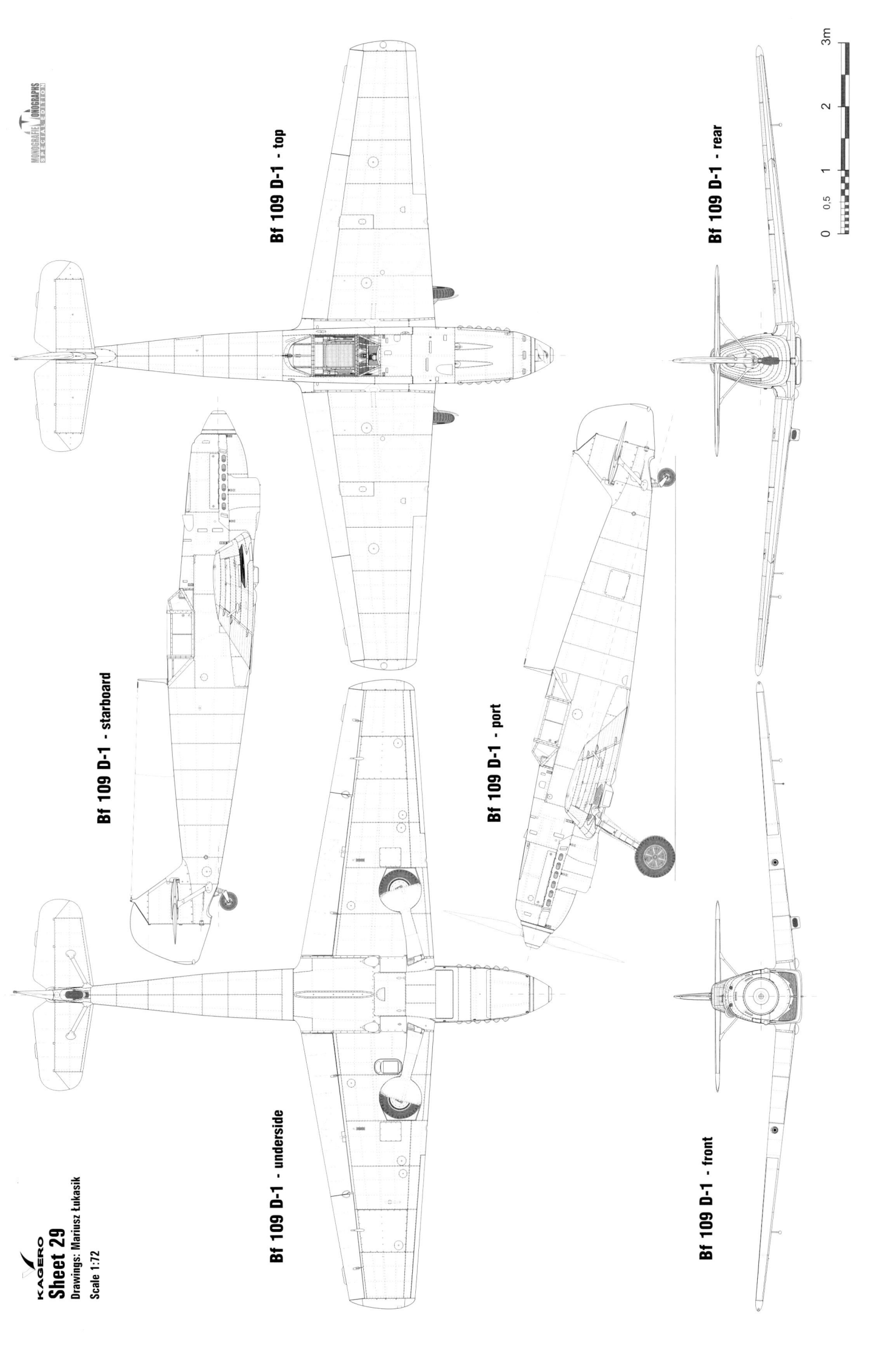

KAGERO
Sheet 29
Drawings: Mariusz Łukasik
Scale 1:72

Bf 109 D-1 - top
Bf 109 D-1 - starboard
Bf 109 D-1 - underside
Bf 109 D-1 - port
Bf 109 D-1 - rear
Bf 109 D-1 - front

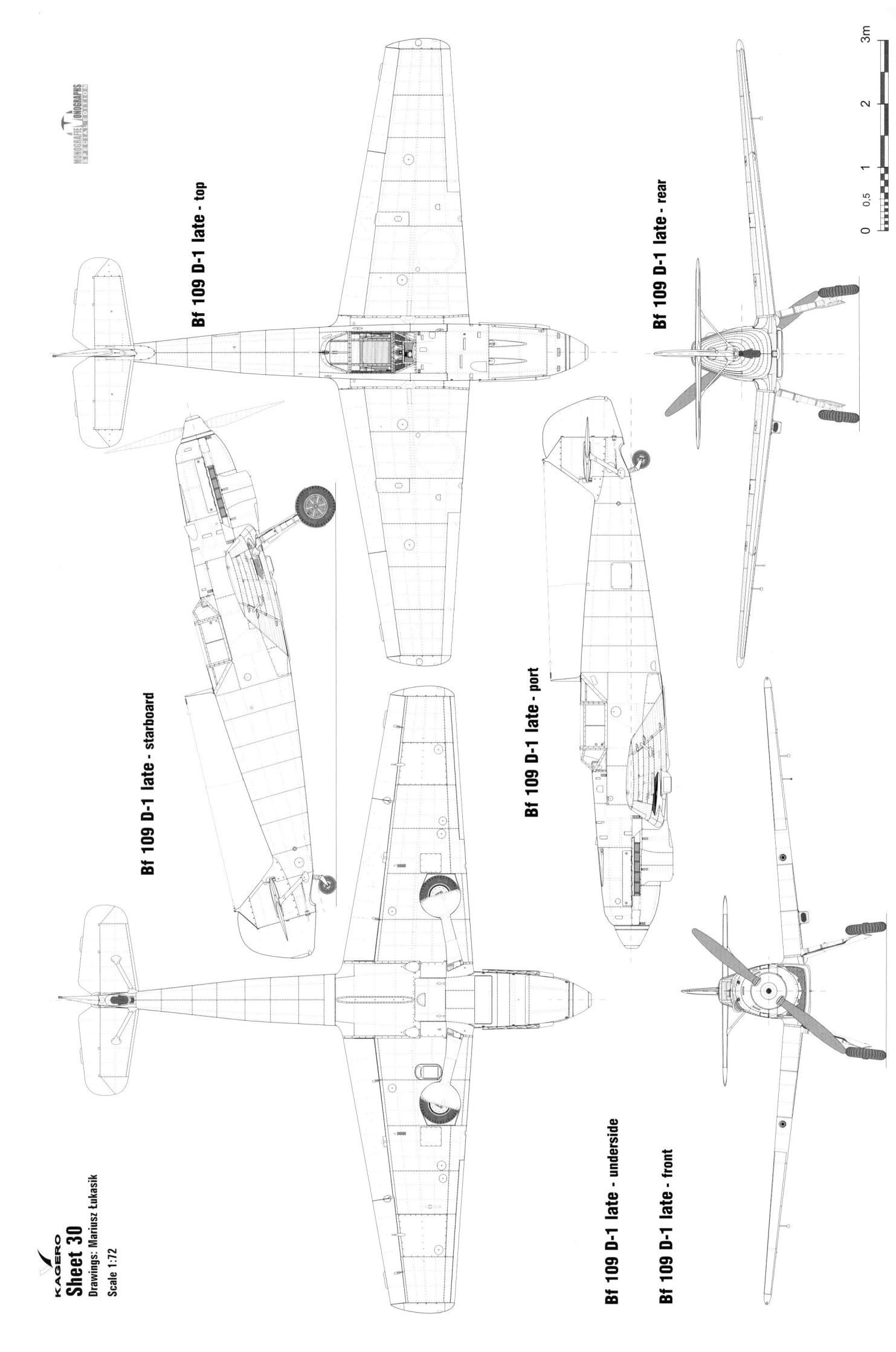

Sheet 30
Drawings: Mariusz Łukasik
Scale 1:72

Bf 109 D-1 late - top
Bf 109 D-1 late - rear
Bf 109 D-1 late - starboard
Bf 109 D-1 late - port
Bf 109 D-1 late - underside
Bf 109 D-1 late - front

Specification of external changes

N.B.
All modifications depicted herein were introduced at production plants. Many of them were subsequently retrofitted under field conditions in earlier models during overhauls or when such need arose.

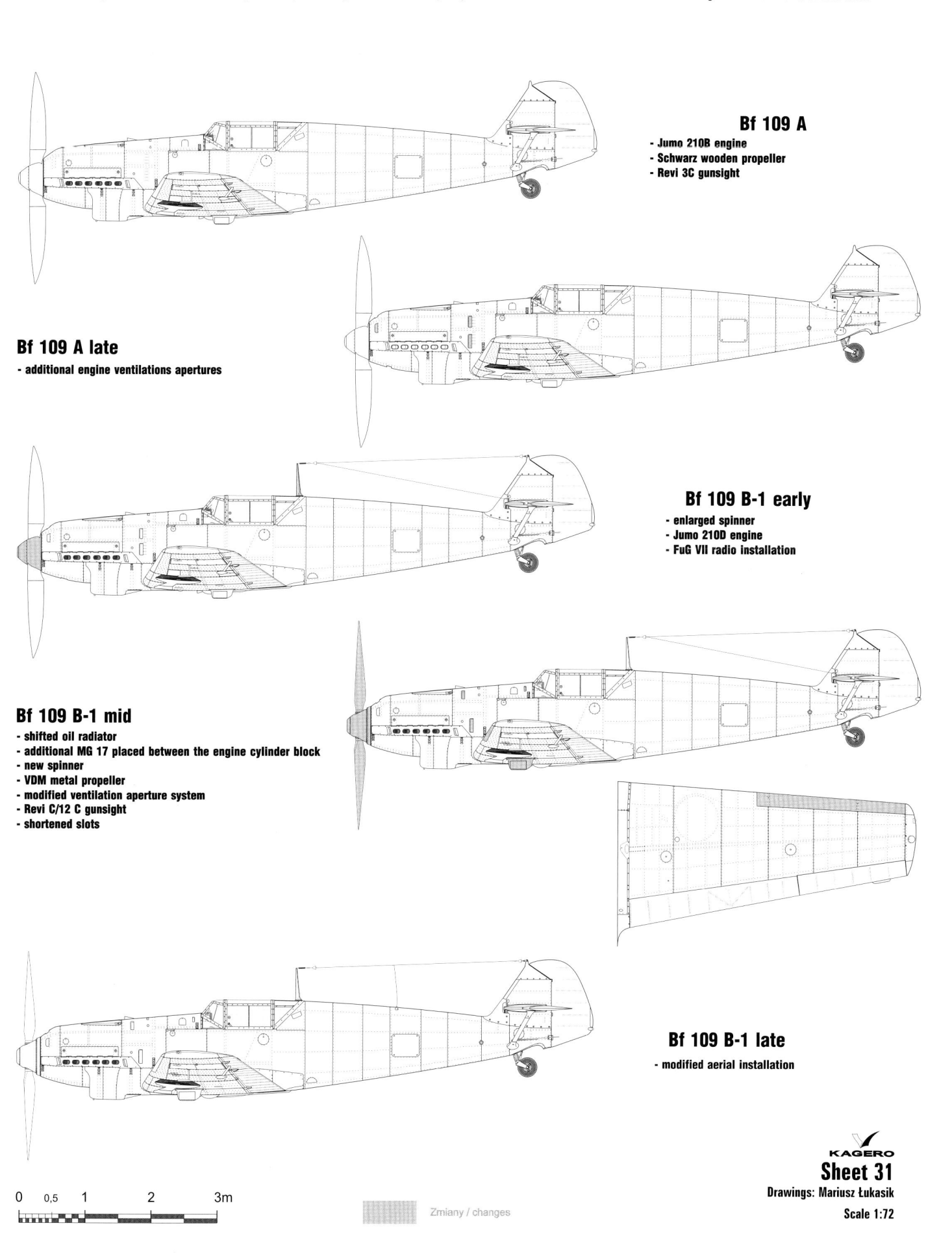

Bf 109 A
- Jumo 210B engine
- Schwarz wooden propeller
- Revi 3C gunsight

Bf 109 A late
- additional engine ventilations apertures

Bf 109 B-1 early
- enlarged spinner
- Jumo 210D engine
- FuG VII radio installation

Bf 109 B-1 mid
- shifted oil radiator
- additional MG 17 placed between the engine cylinder block
- new spinner
- VDM metal propeller
- modified ventilation aperture system
- Revi C/12 C gunsight
- shortened slots

Bf 109 B-1 late
- modified aerial installation

Zmiany / changes

Sheet 31
Drawings: Mariusz Łukasik
Scale 1:72

Specification of external changes

N.B.
All modifications depicted herein were introduced at production plants. Many of them were subsequently retrofitted under field conditions in earlier models during overhauls or when such need arose.

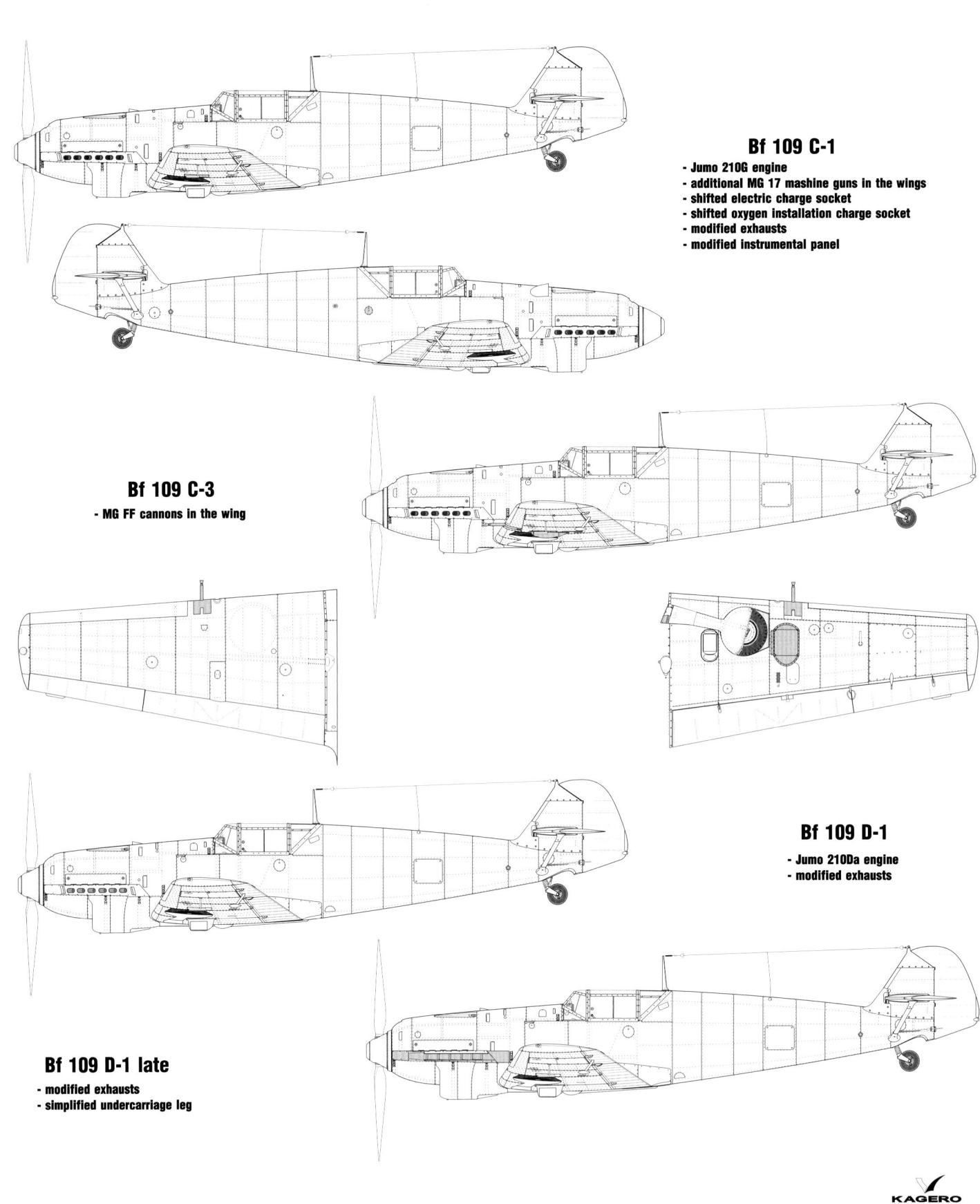

Bf 109 C-1
- Jumo 210G engine
- additional MG 17 mashine guns in the wings
- shifted electric charge socket
- shifted oxygen installation charge socket
- modified exhausts
- modified instrumental panel

Bf 109 C-3
- MG FF cannons in the wing

Bf 109 D-1
- Jumo 210Da engine
- modified exhausts

Bf 109 D-1 late
- modified exhausts
- simplified undercarriage leg

Sheet 32
Drawings: Mariusz Łukasik
Scale 1:72

Zmiany / changes

Visualization 3D Asen Atanasov

Messerschmitt Bf 109 A was powered by Junkers Jumo 210 engine (B and D variant).

Messerschmitt Bf 109 A, W.Nr. 808, D-IIBA after a landing accident.

Messerschmitt Bf 109 A fitted with Schwarz wooden fixed-pitch propeller.

Messerschmitt Bf 109 A viewed from below, small oil radiator can be seen under the left wing.

Messerschmitt Bf 109 Early Versions 109

Cross-section of a Messerschmitt Bf 109 A.

Cross-section views of a Messerschmitt Bf 109 A with fuselage armament visible (two MG 17 cal. 7.92 mm).

Messerschmitt Bf 109 B-1 early production series fitted with Schwarz wooden propeller and three antenna lines.

Messerschmitt Bf 109 B-1 early production series armed with two machine guns MG 17 cal. 7.92 mm.

Messerschmitt Bf 109 B-1 with VDM metal propeller and single radio antenna wire. Renderings shows the shortened slots on leading edges

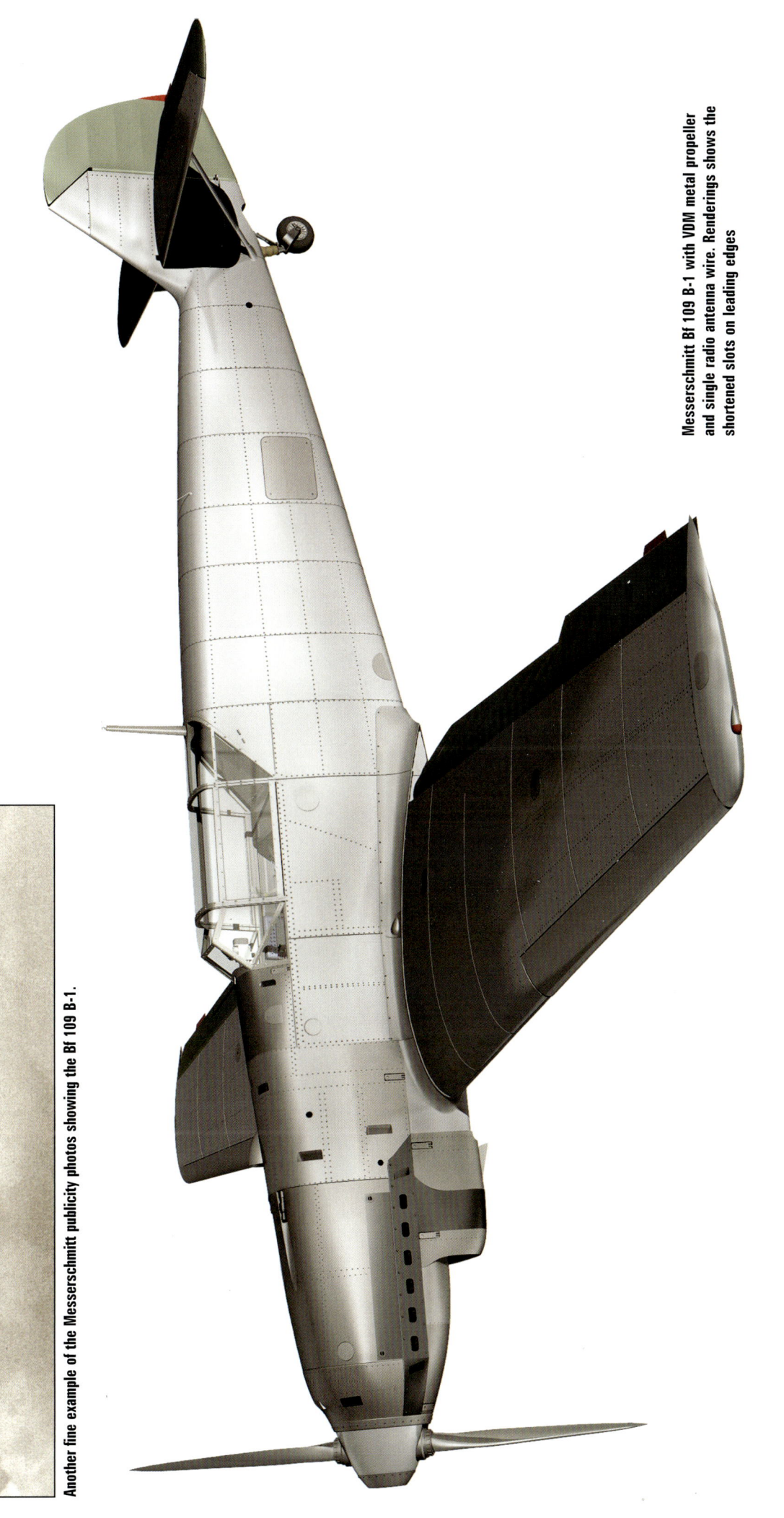

Messerschmitt Bf 109 B-1 with VDM metal propeller and single radio antenna wire. Renderings shows the shortened slots on leading edges

Another fine example of the Messerschmitt publicity photos showing the Bf 109 B-1.

Messerschmitt Bf 109 Early Versions

Cross-section of a Messerschmitt Bf 109 B-1 late production series.

Cross-section of a Messerschmitt Bf 109 B-1. Except of two MG 17 cal. 7.92 mm machine guns, most Bf 109's were also armed with third MG 17 machine gun, fitted between engine cylinders.

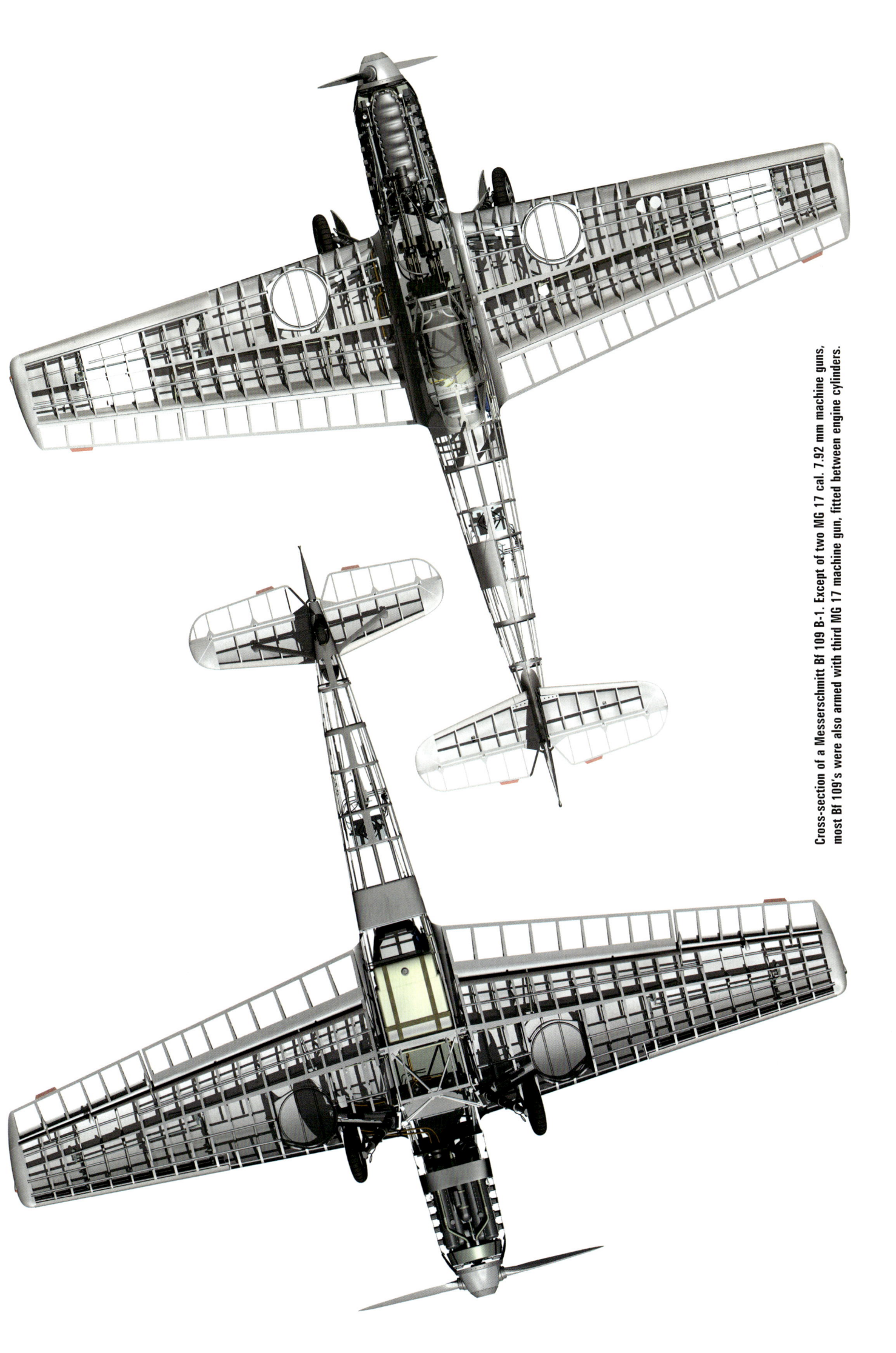

Messerschmitt Bf 109 C-1 powered by Junkers Jumo 210 G engine.

Messerschmitt Bf 109 C-1 was armed with four MG 17 cal. 7.92 mm machine guns – two mounted in the fuselage and two in the wings

Cross-section drawing of a Messerschmitt Bf 109 C-1.

Messerschmitt Bf 109 Early Versions

Cross-section of a Messerschmitt Bf 109 C-1, note four MG 17 cal. 7.92 mm mounted in the nose section and wings.

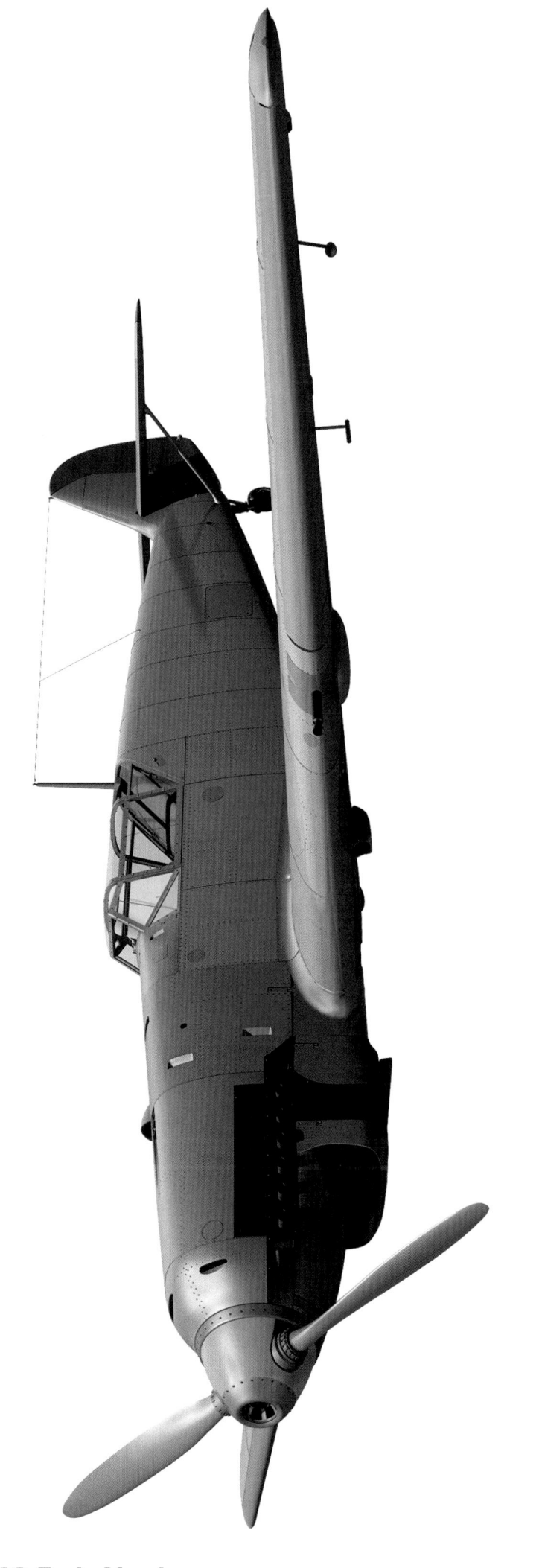

Messerschmitt Bf 109 C-3 armed with two fuselage MG 17 cal. 7.92 mm machine guns and two MG FF cal. 20 mm cannons mounted in the wings.

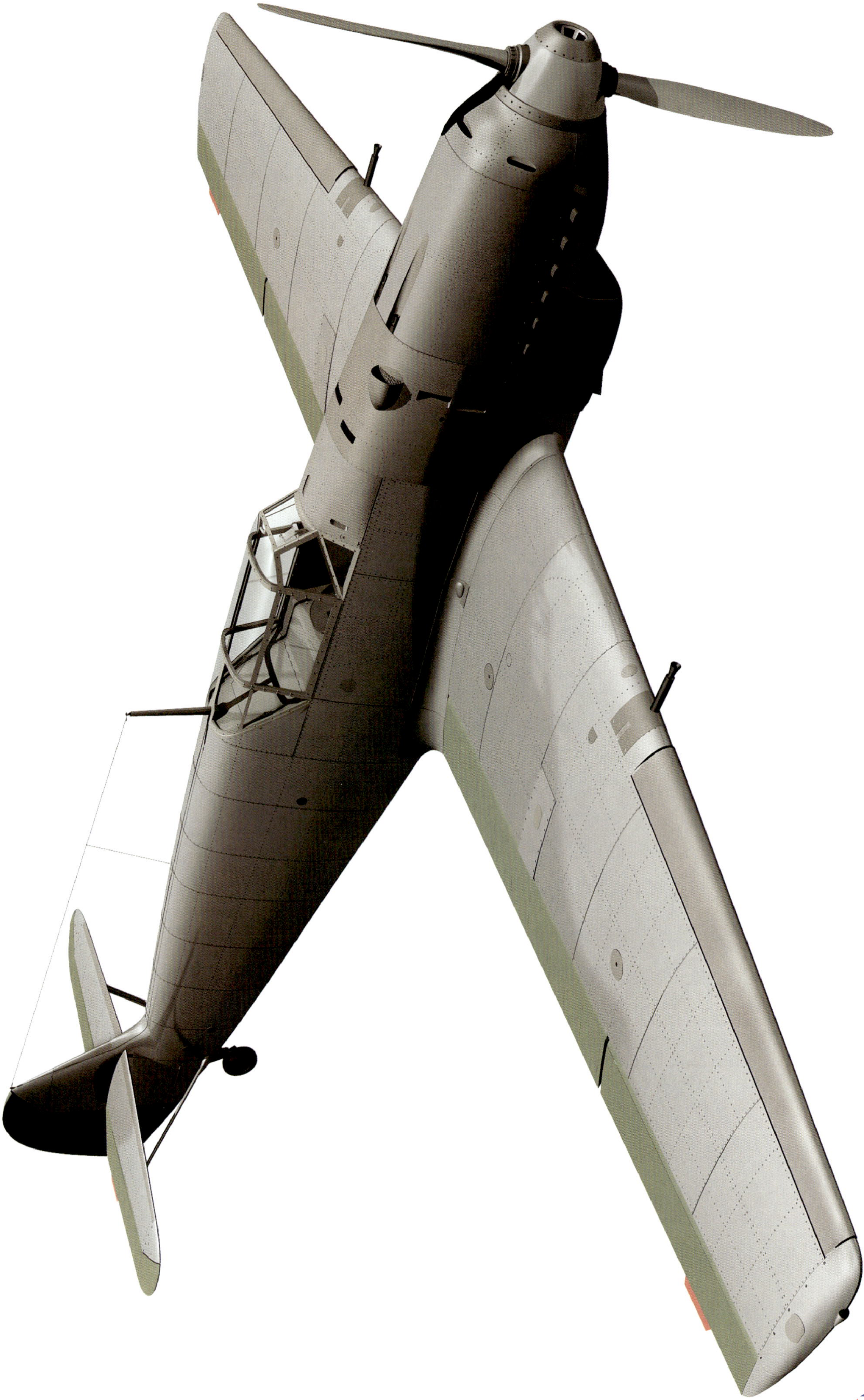

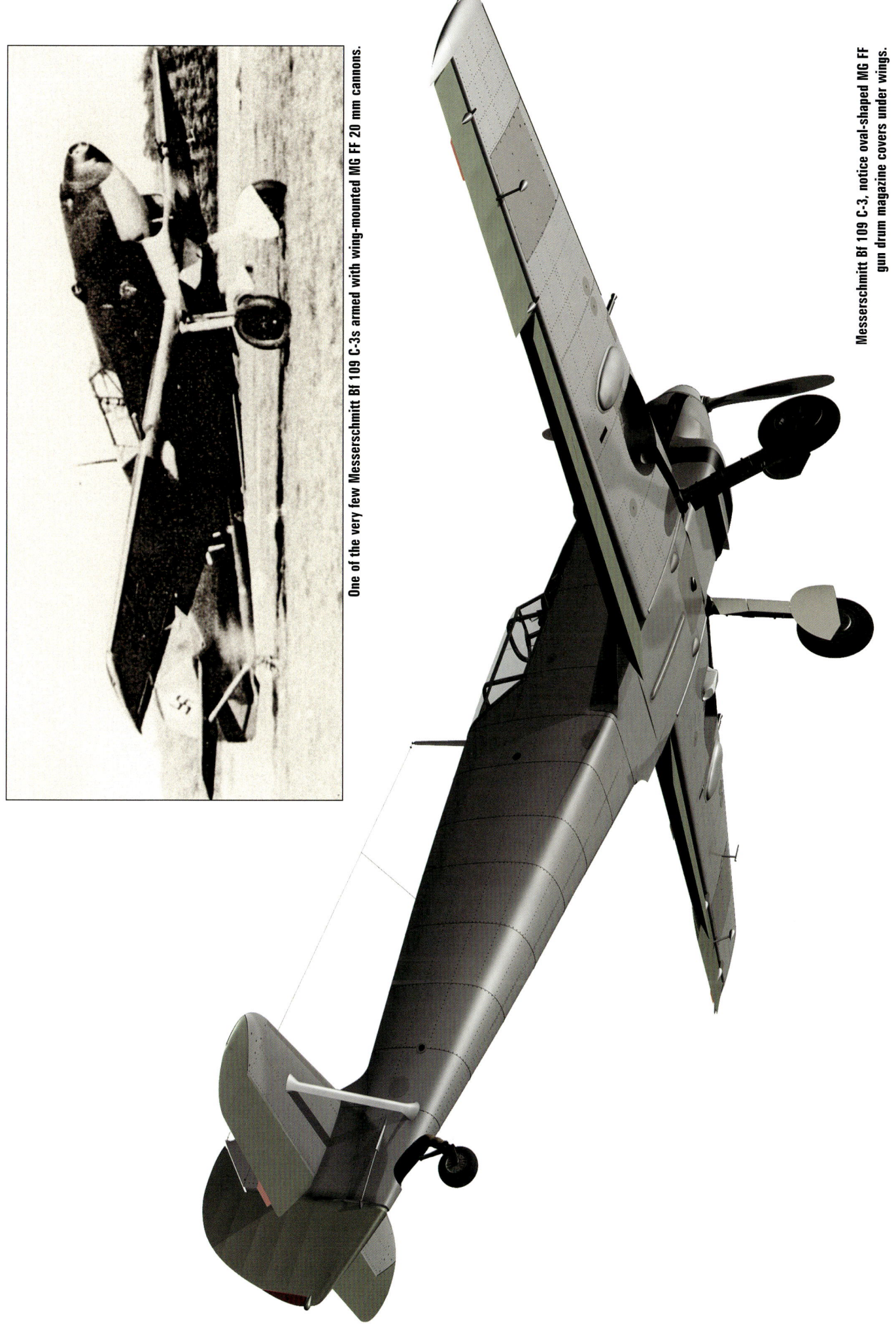

One of the very few Messerschmitt Bf 109 C-3s armed with wing-mounted MG FF 20 mm cannons.

Messerschmitt Bf 109 C-3, notice oval-shaped MG FF gun drum magazine covers under wings.

Messerschmitt Bf 109 Early Versions

Cross-section drawing of a Messerschmitt Bf 109 C-3.

Cross-section of a Messerschmitt Bf 109 C-3. Two MG 17 cal. 7.92 mm machine guns are mounted in the nose section, while in wings armament bays there are two MG FF cal. 20 mm cannons fitted.

Messerschmitt Bf 109 D-1 armed with four MG 17 cal. 7.92 mm machine guns.

Messerschmitt Bf 109 D-1s from 10./JG 132 en-route to Karslbad on October 5, 1938.

View from below of a Messerschmitt Bf 109 D-1.

Messerschmitt Bf 109 Early Versions 127

Messerschmitt Bf 109 D-1 equipped with new engine exhaust system – identical to those mounted on Bf 109 E-1.

Messerschmitt Bf 109 D-1 with exhaust from Bf 109 E-1, view from back.

Messerschmitt Bf 109 D-1 with modified exhausts

Messerschmitt Bf 109 Early Versions — 129

Cross-section of a Messerschmitt Bf 109 D-1.

Cross-section of a Messerschmitt Bf 109 D-1, plan view.

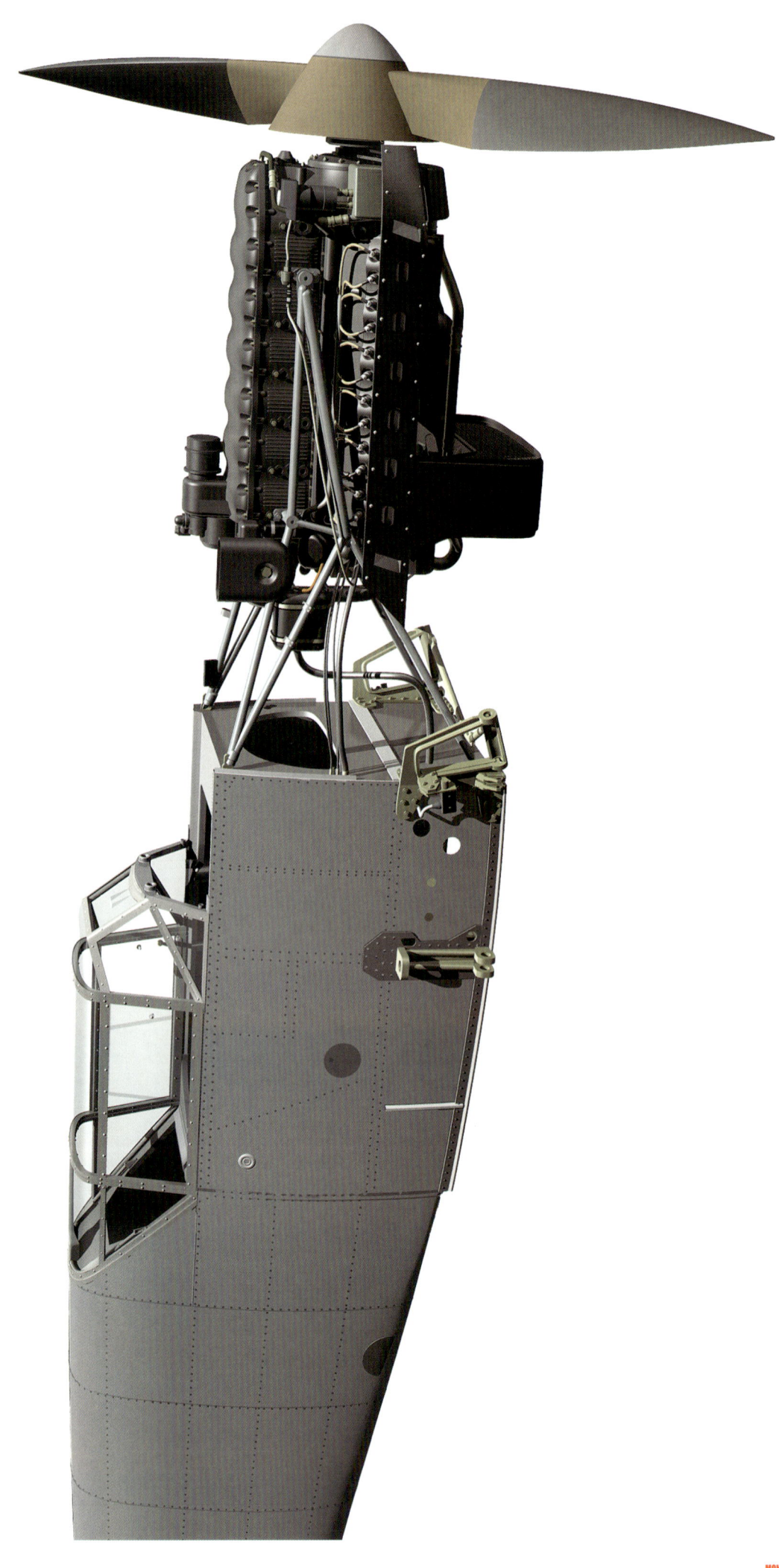

Junkers Jumo 210 B engine fitted with Schwarz wooden propeller.

Junkers Jumo 210 B engine fitted with Schwarz propeller powered a Messerschmitt Bf 109 A, in the fuselage, in front of cockpit, there are two MG 17 cal. 7.92 mm machine guns.

Messerschmitt Bf 109 Early Versions

Messerschmitt Bf 109 D-1 with Junkers Jumo 210 D engine and exhaust from Bf 109 E-1.

Junkers Jumo 210 D engine and fuselage machine guns MG 17 cal. 7.92 mounted on Messerschmitt Bf 109 D-1.

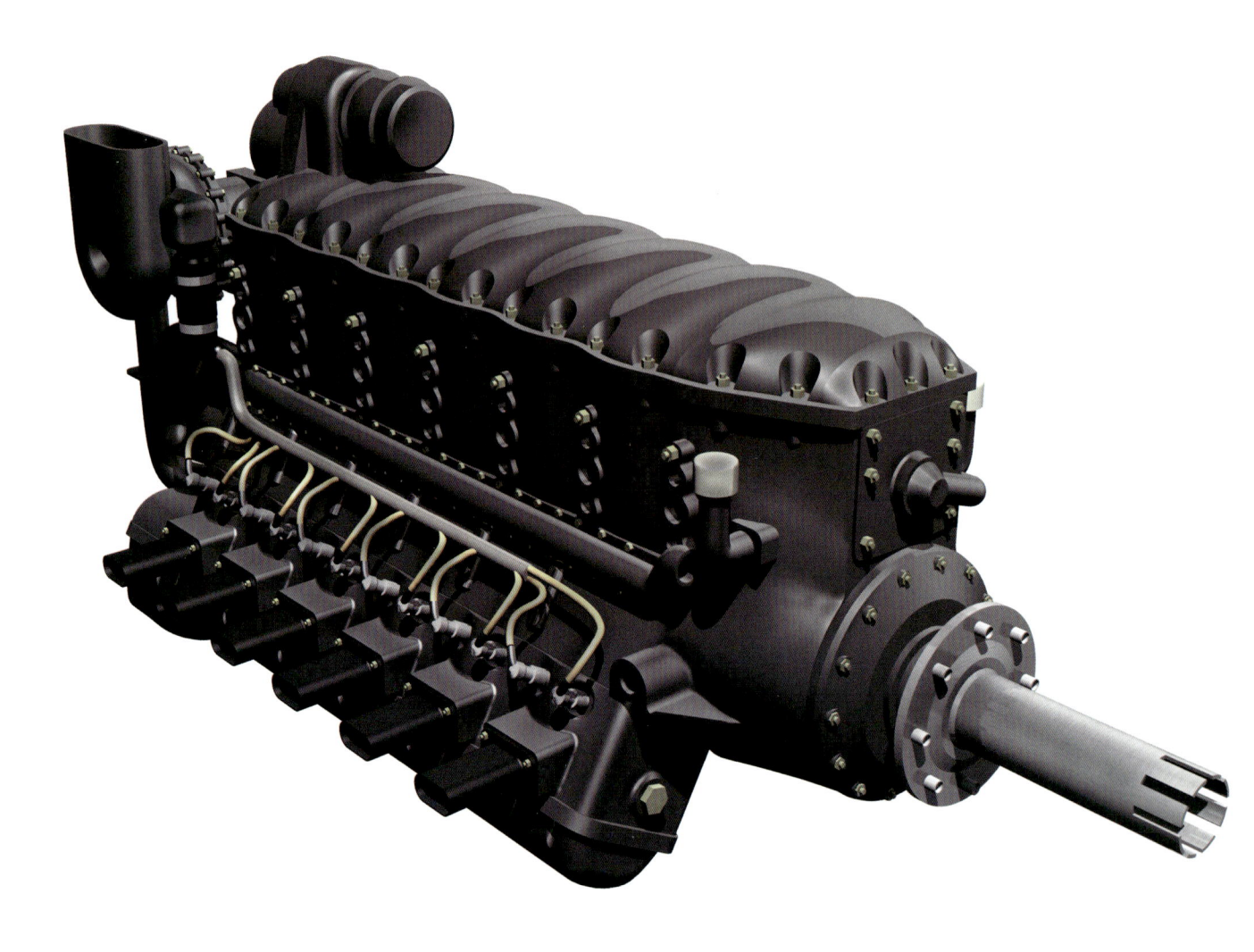

Junkers Jumo 210 D engine.

Junkers Jumo 210 D engine with coolant reservoir and coolant radiator.

Messerschmitt Bf 109 Early Versions 137

Fully equipped Junkers Jumo 210 D engine mounted on Messerschmitt Bf 109 D-1.

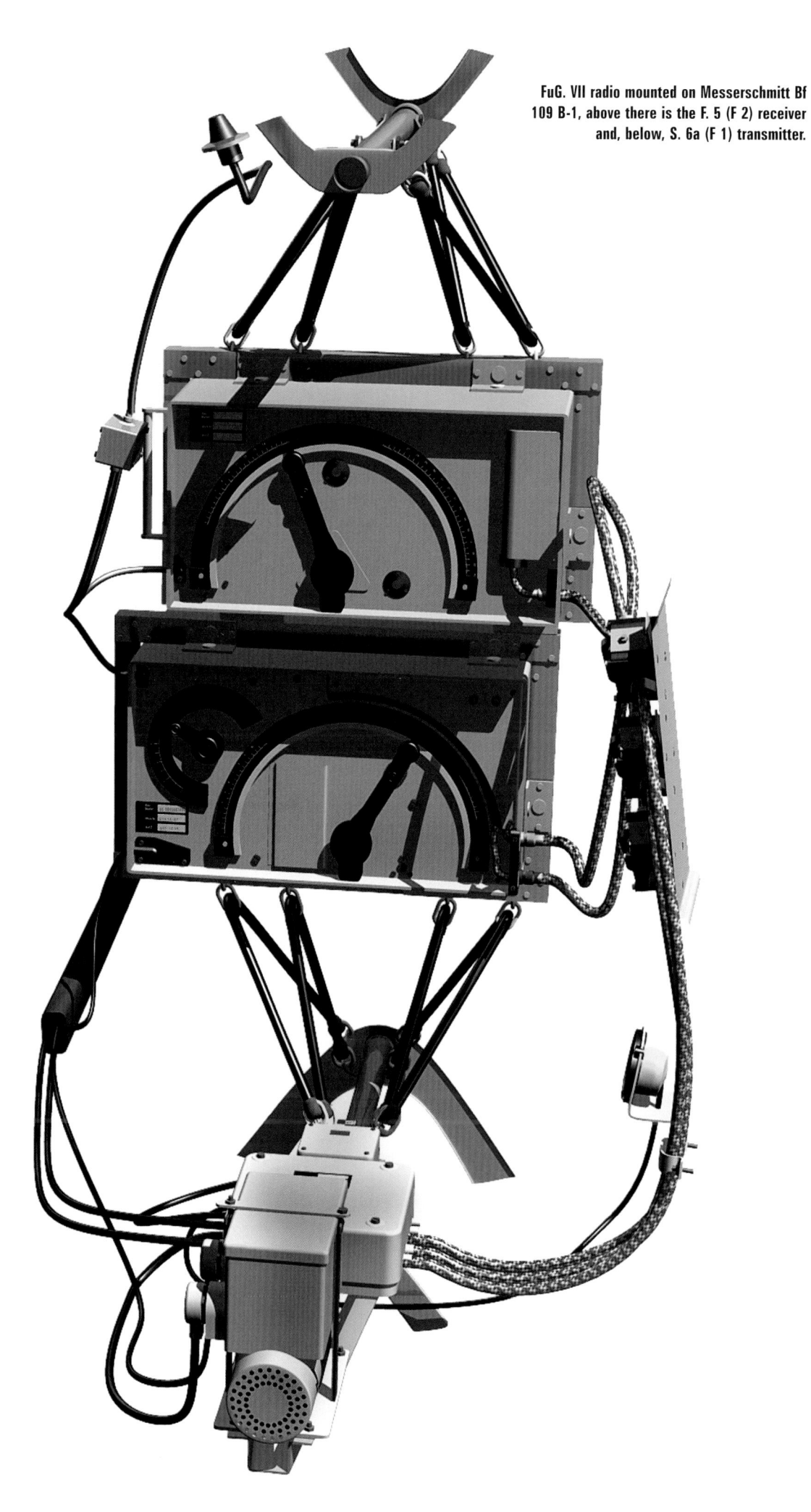

FuG. VII radio mounted on Messerschmitt Bf 109 B-1, above there is the F. 5 (F 2) receiver and, below, S. 6a (F 1) transmitter.

Another view of a Messerschmitt Bf 109 B-1 radio equipment.

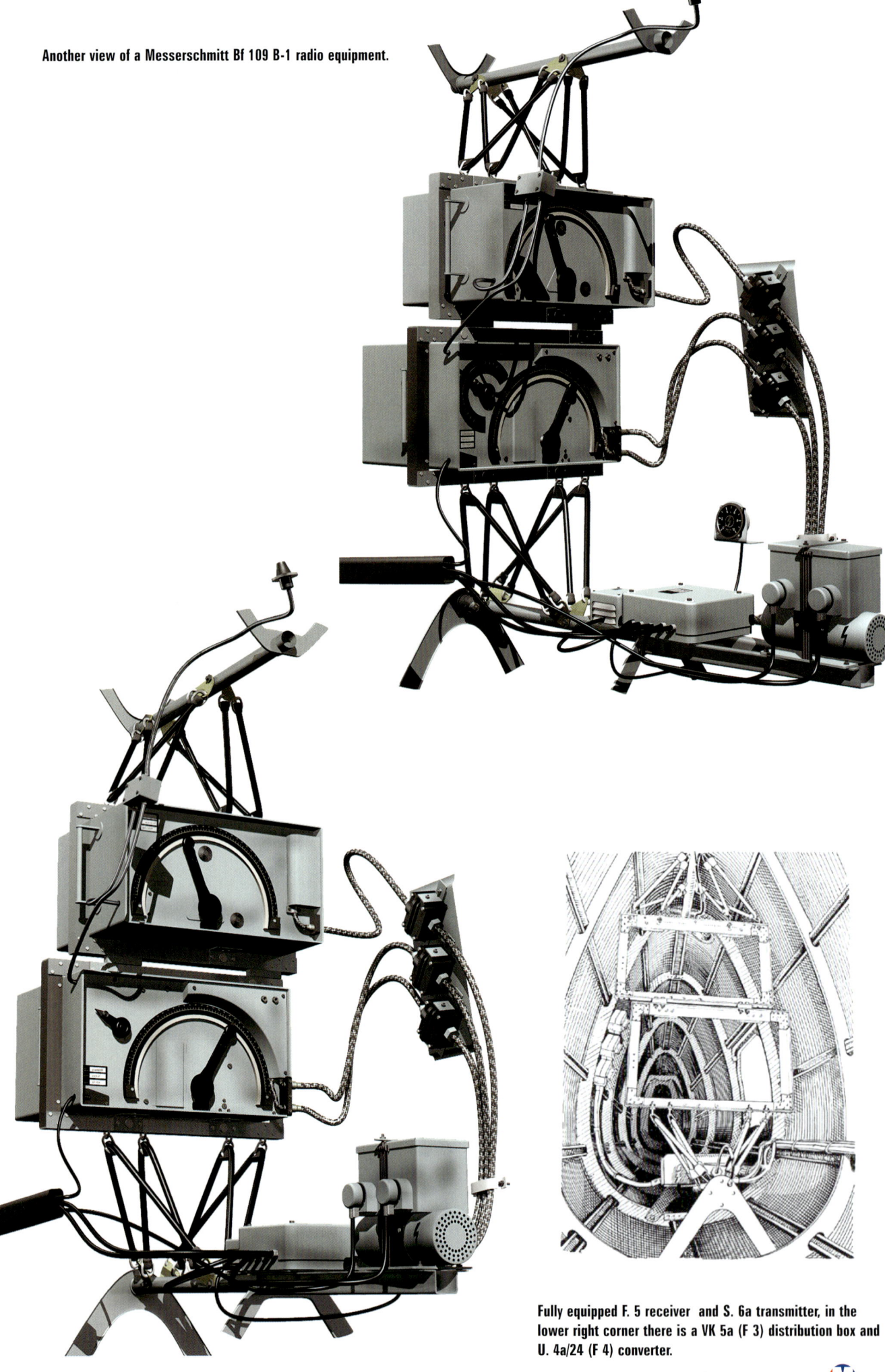

Fully equipped F. 5 receiver and S. 6a transmitter, in the lower right corner there is a VK 5a (F 3) distribution box and U. 4a/24 (F 4) converter.

Close-ups of a F. 5 (F 2) receiver and S. 6a (F 1) transmitter

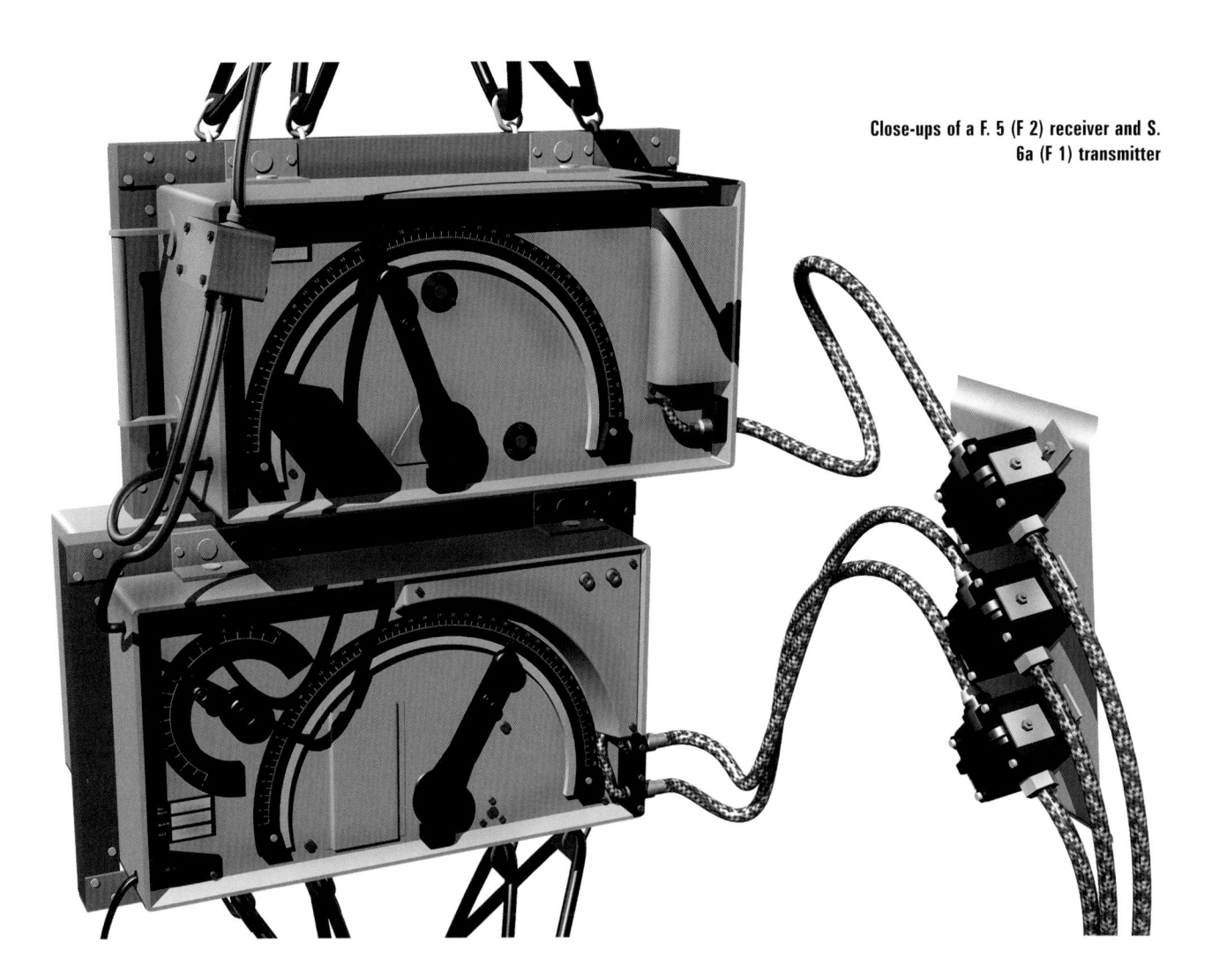

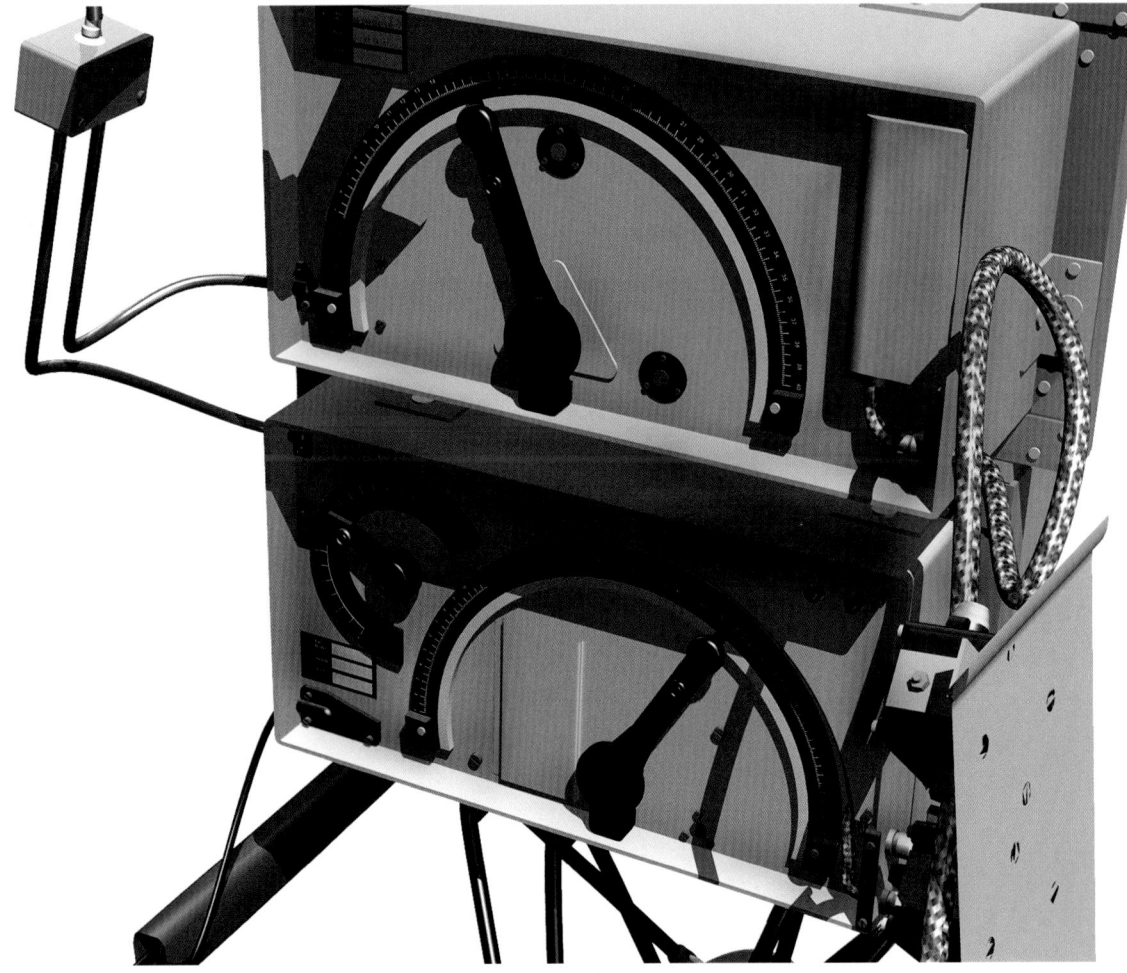

Messerschmitt Bf 109 Early Versions — 141

FuG. VII radio mounted in Messerschmitt's Bf 109 B-1 fuselage.

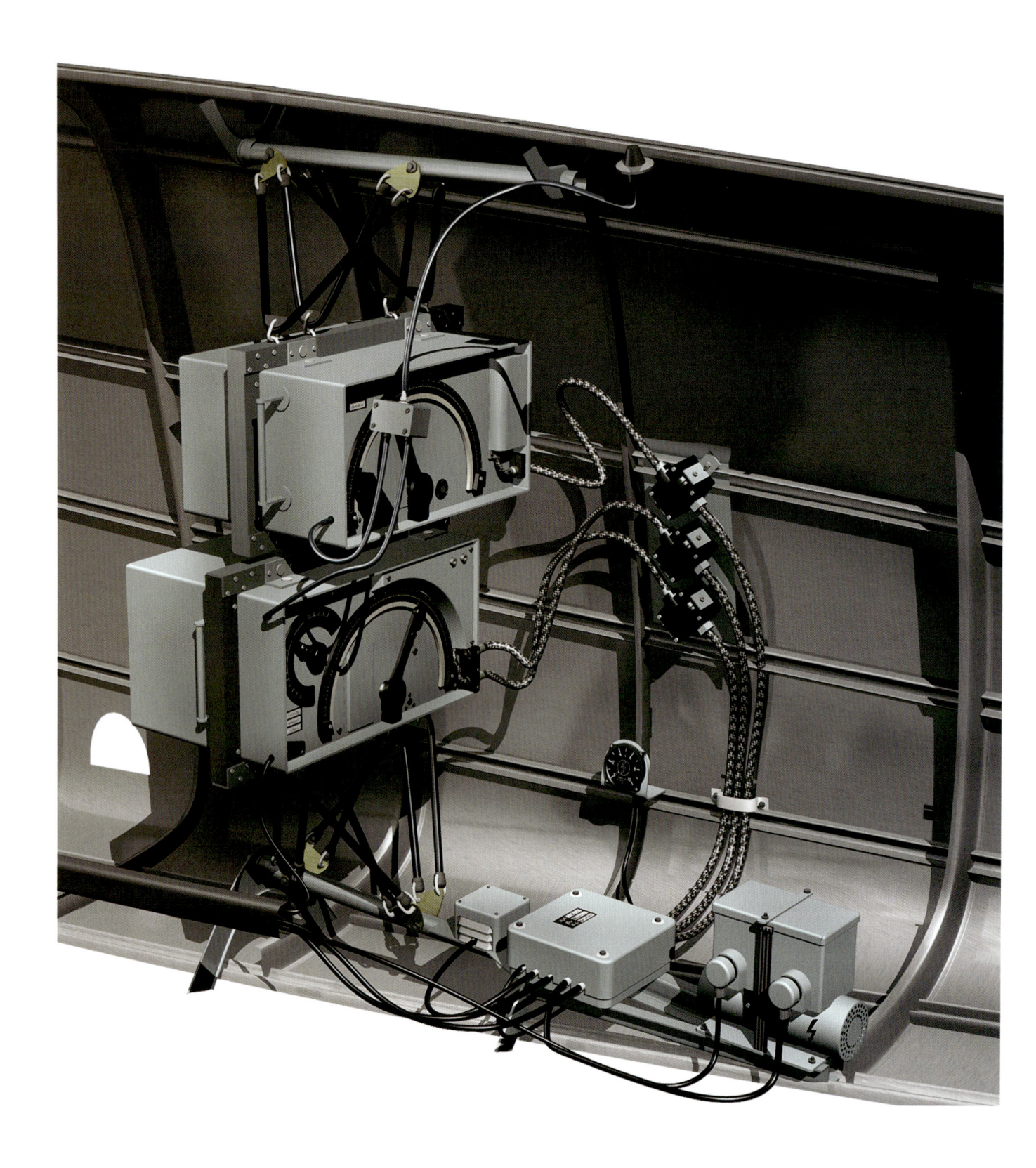

Access to the FuG. VII radio was possible through rectangle-shaped hatch on the left fuselage board. It was closed with the screwed cover.

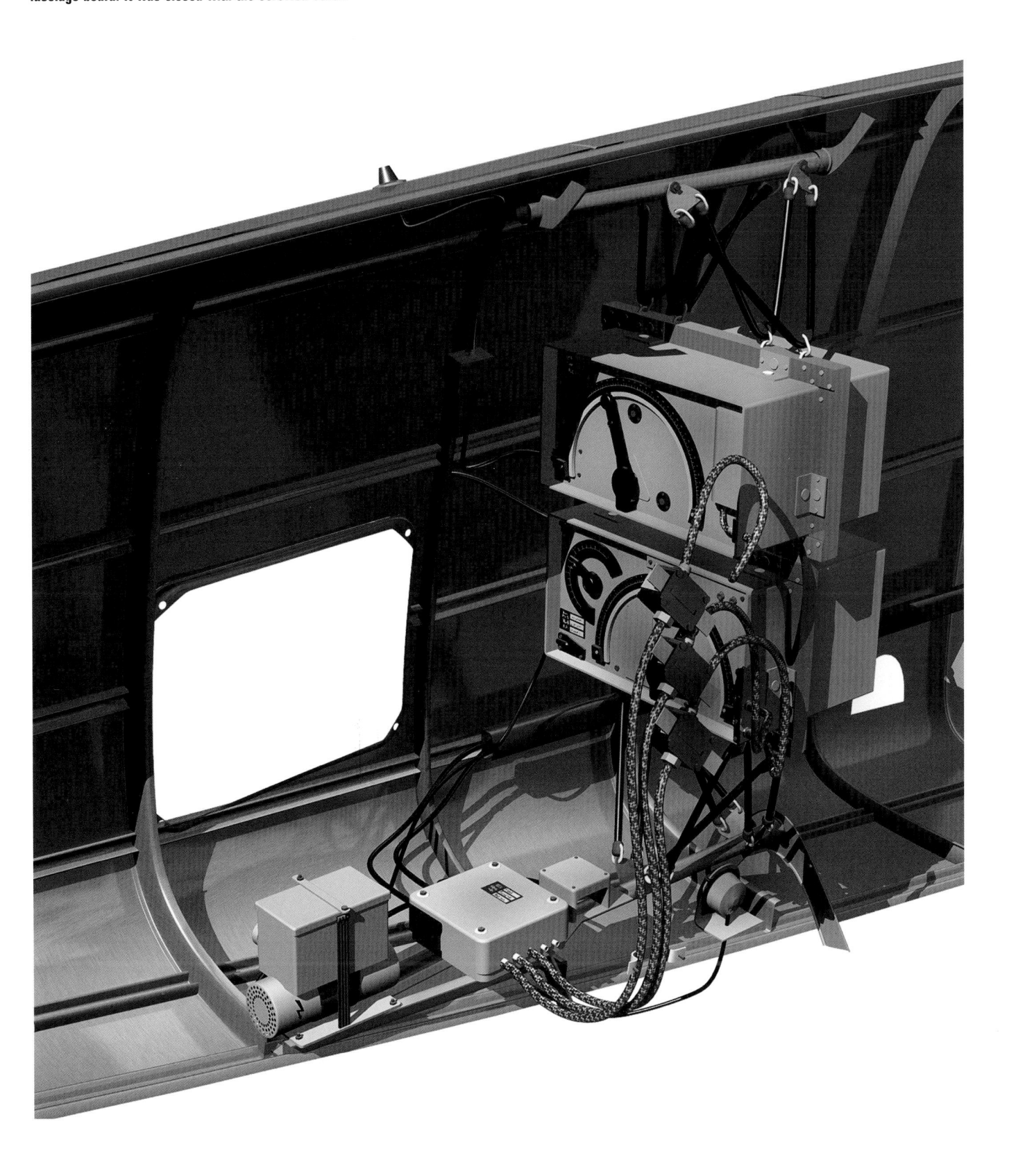

Tail view of FuG. VII radio mounted on the fuselage.

FuG. VII radio mounted in Messerschmitt Bf 109 B-1 fuselage.

Messerschmitt Bf 109 A cockpit.

Messerschmitt Bf 109 A cockpit, on the left board there is a throttle lever and trimmer and flaps regulation knobs.

Messerschmitt Bf 109 A cockpit, on the right board there is an oxygen installation main valve (with oxygen manometer); primer fuel pump lever is nearby.

Messerschmitt Bf 109 A cockpit close-up.

Messerschmitt Bf 109 B-1 cockpit.

Messerschmitt Bf 109 B-1 cockpit, left side view.

Messerschmitt Bf 109 B-1 cockpit, right side view.

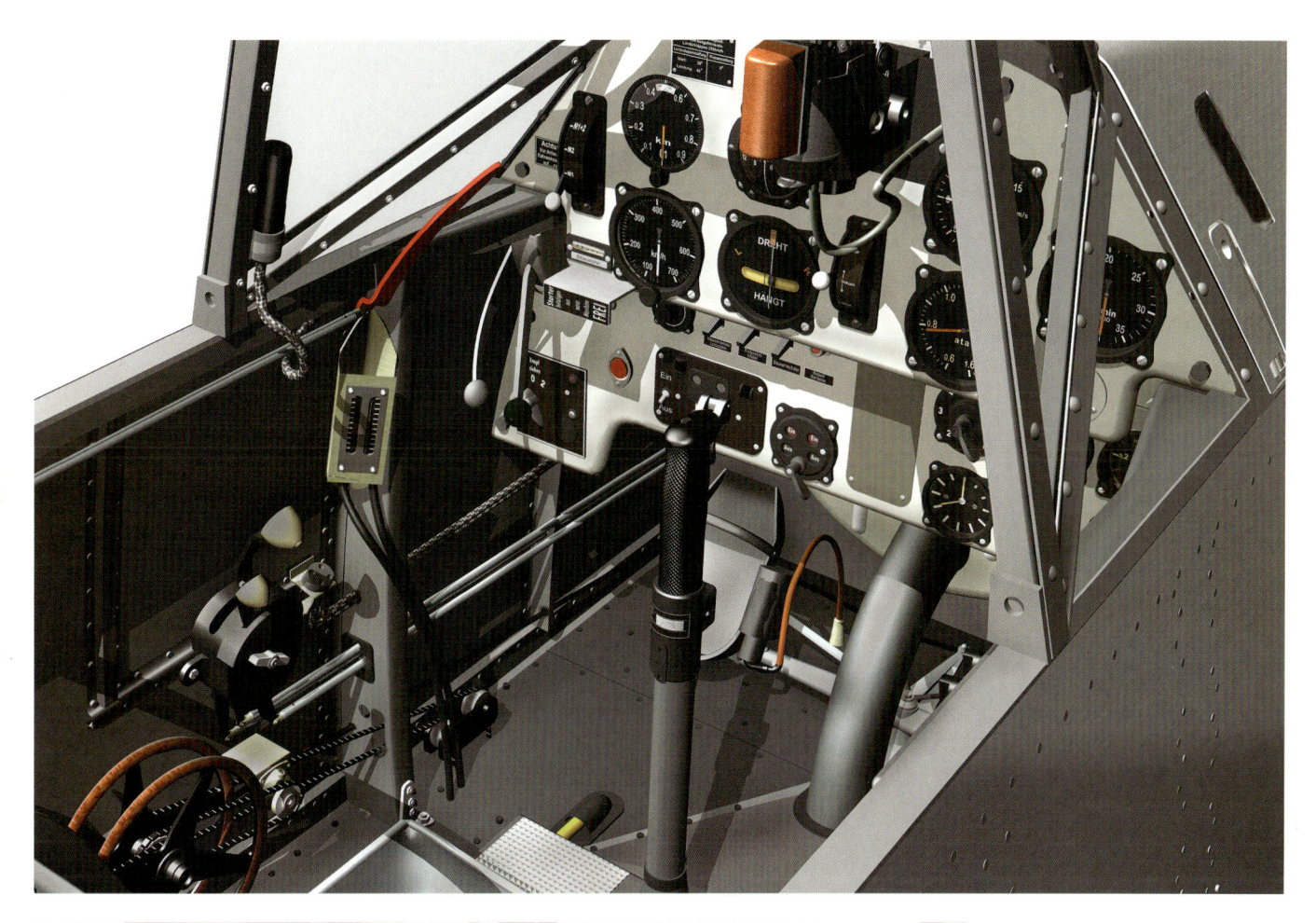

Messerschmitt Bf 109 B-1 cockpit close-up.

Messerschmitt Bf 109 D-1 cockpit.

Messerschmitt Bf 109 D-1 cockpit, left side view.

Messerschmitt Bf 109 D-1 cockpit, right side view.

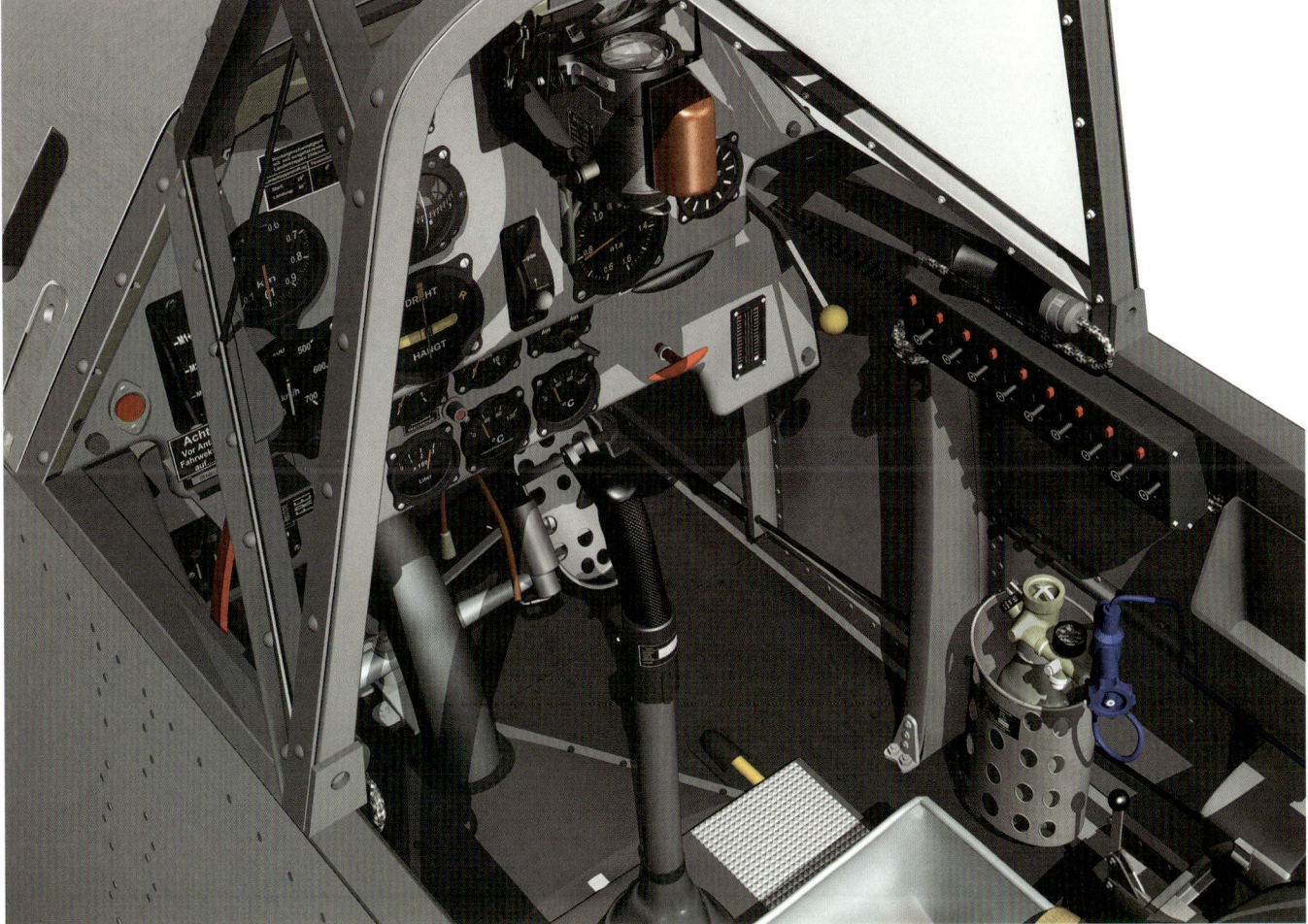

Messerschmitt Bf 109 D-1 cockpit close-up.

Instrument panels (from top):
Messerschmitt Bf 109 A,
Messerschmitt Bf 109 B-1 and
Messerschmitt Bf 109 D-1.

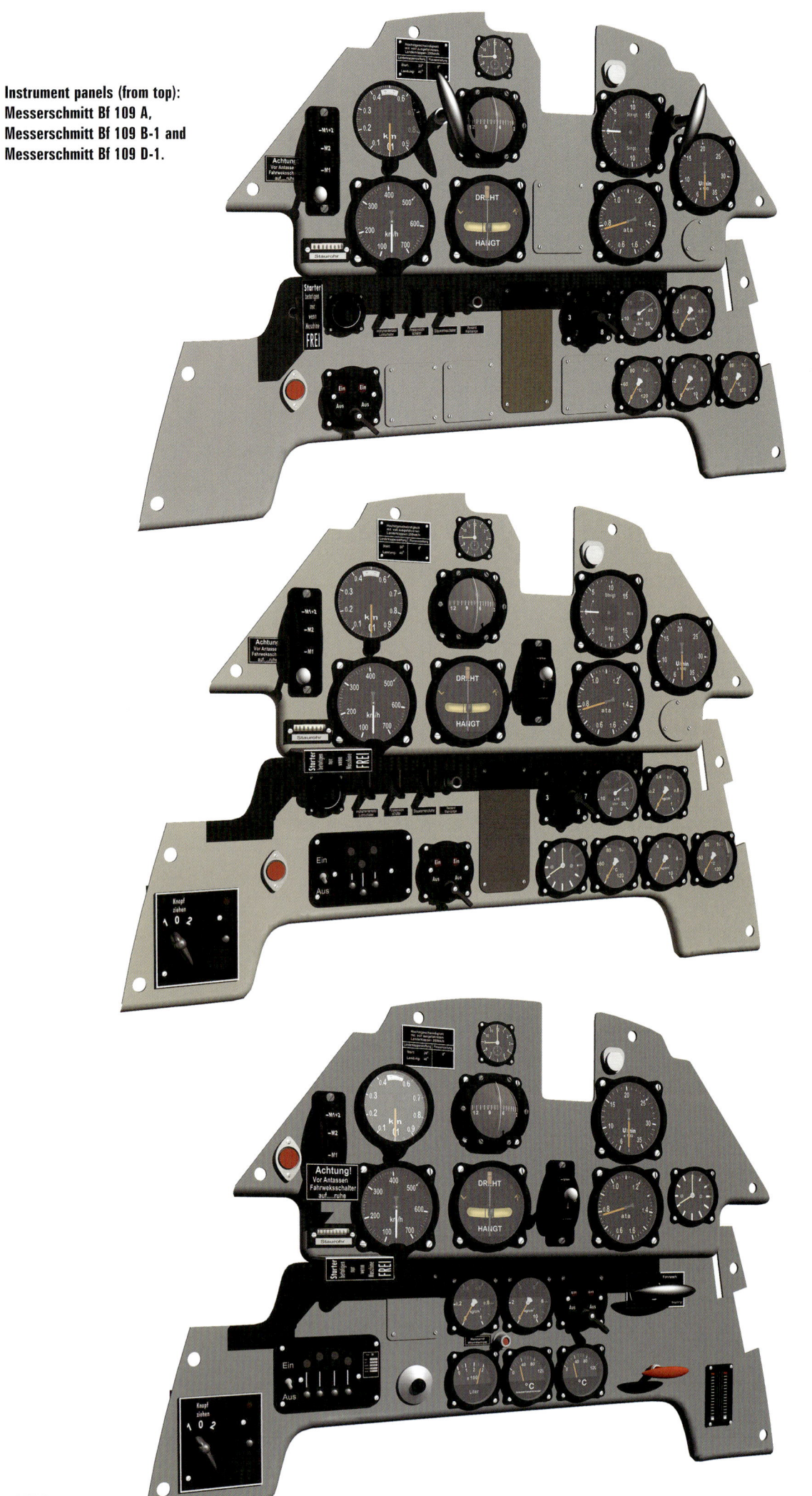

Revi C/12 C reflector sight.

Messerschmitt Bf 109 Early Versions

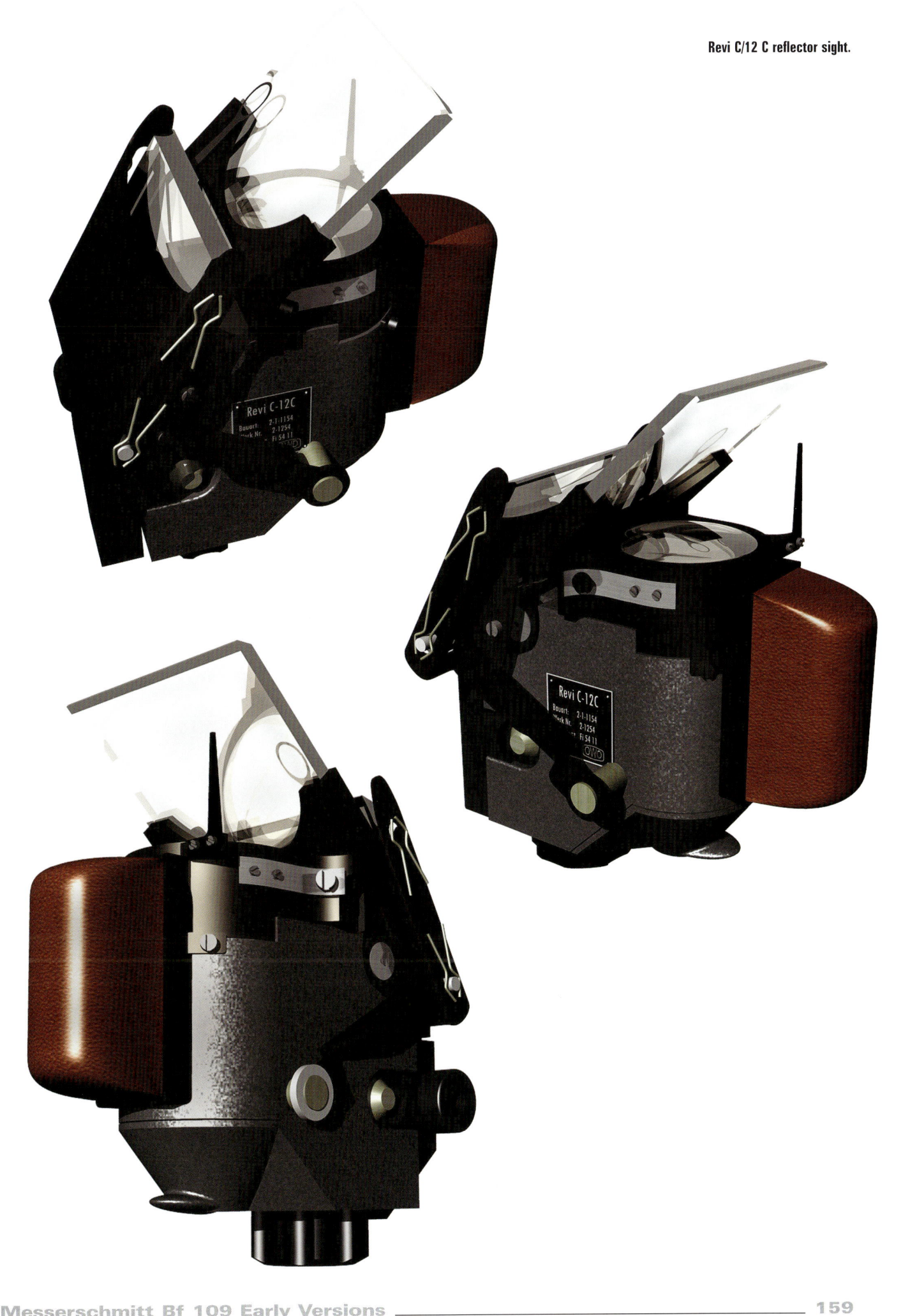

Messerschmitt Bf 109 A-D canopy.

Messerschmitt Bf 109 D-1 floor with pilot's seat, rudder-bar and control stick.

Messerschmitt Bf 109 Early Versions — 161

Fuselage MG 17 cal. 7.92 mm machine guns mounted on Messerschmitt Bf 109 D-1, right side view.

Fuselage MG 17 cal. 7.92 mm machine guns mounted on Messerschmitt Bf 109 D-1, left side view, from pilot's perspective.

Fuselage MG 17 cal. 7.92 mm machine guns mounted on Messerschmitt Bf 109 D-1, left side view; under machine guns there are ammo boxes containing 500 rounds of ammunition.

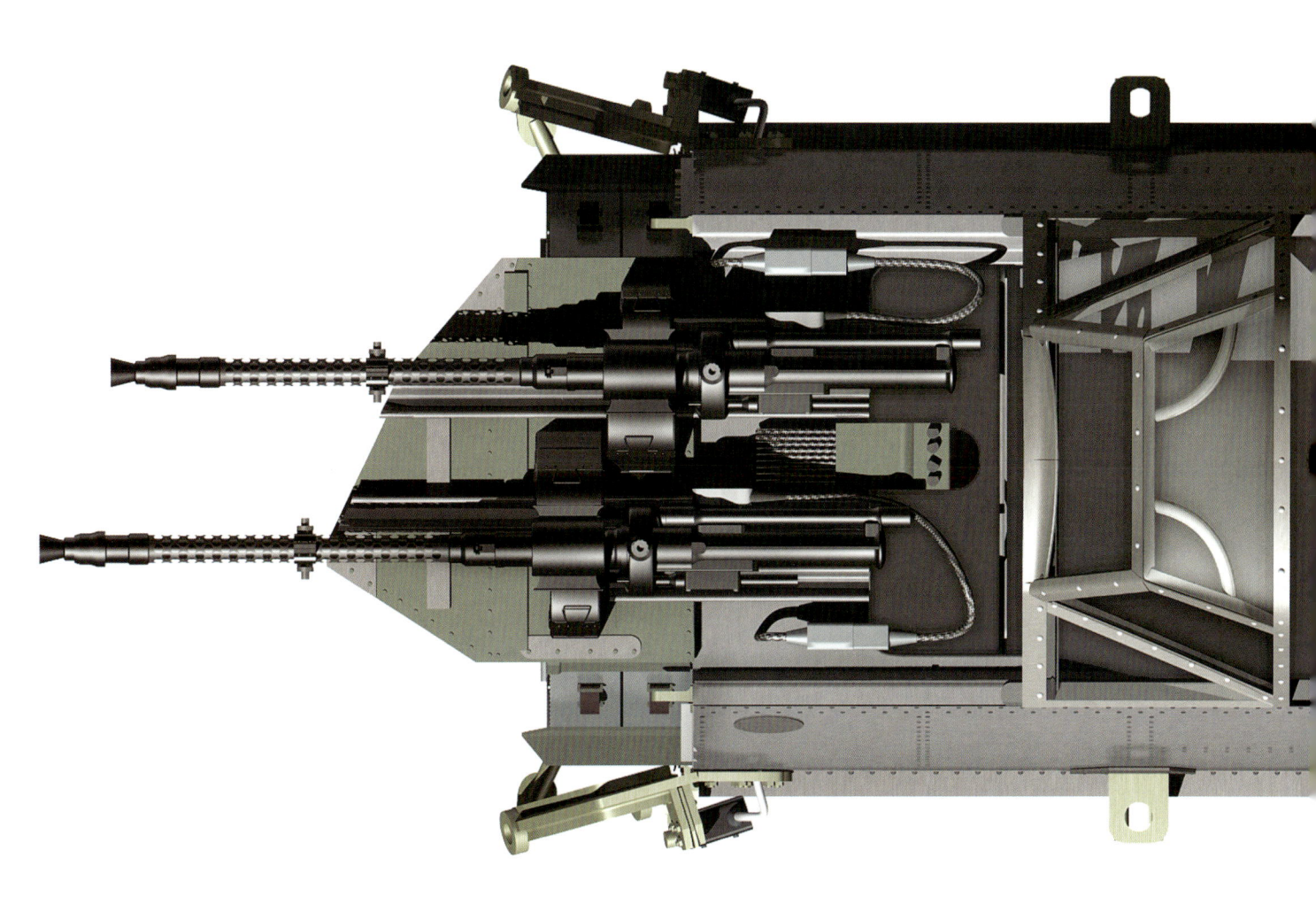

Close-up of fuselage MG 17 cal. 7.92 mm machine guns mounted on Messerschmitt Bf 109 D-1.

Messerschmitt Bf 109 Early Versions 165

Armament view of Messerschmitt Bf 109 D-1: two MG 17 cal. 7.92 mm machine guns and same caliber machine gun mounted on the wing – it was loaded from ammunition belt hidden inside the wing.

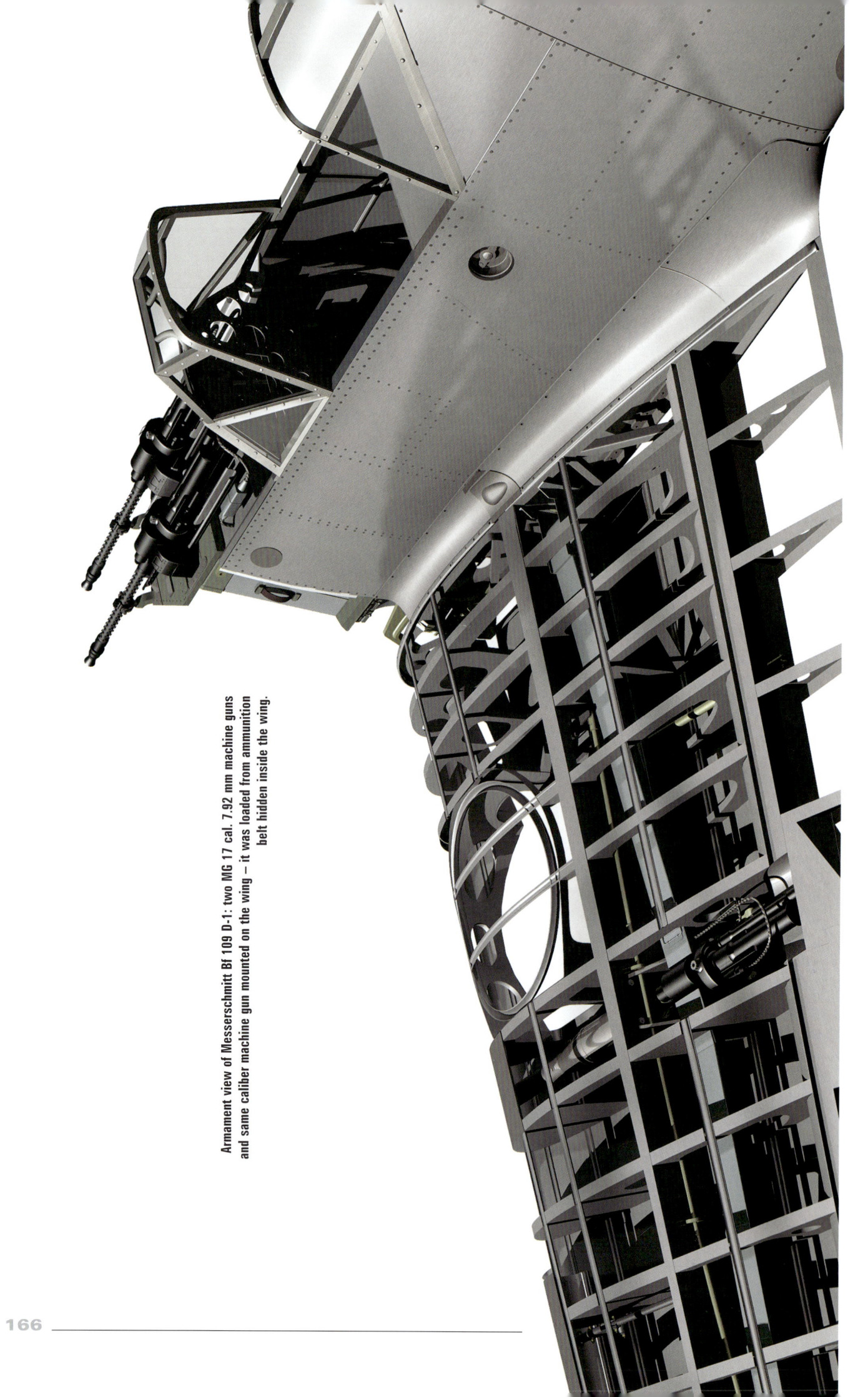

Armament view of a Messerschmitt Bf 109 D-1, two MG 17 cal. 7.92 mm machine guns and wing machine gun with 1000 rounds of ammunition.

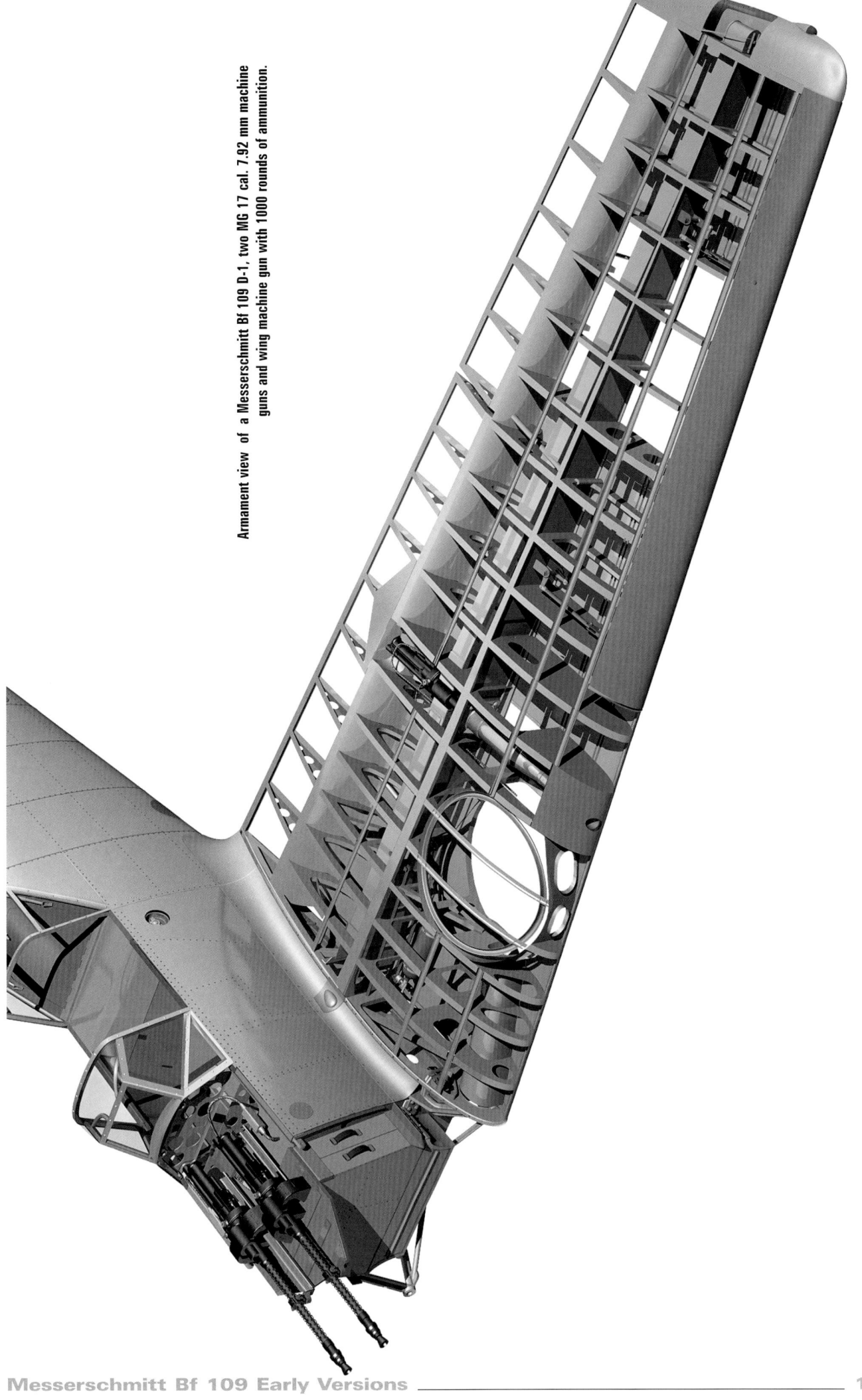

Armament of a Messerschmitt Bf 109 C-3 were two MG FF cal. 20 mm cannons instead of MG 17 cal. 7.92 mm machine guns.

Wing machine gun MG 17 cal. 7.92 mm with ammunition belt guides for 1000 rounds.

Messerschmitt Bf 109 Early Versions

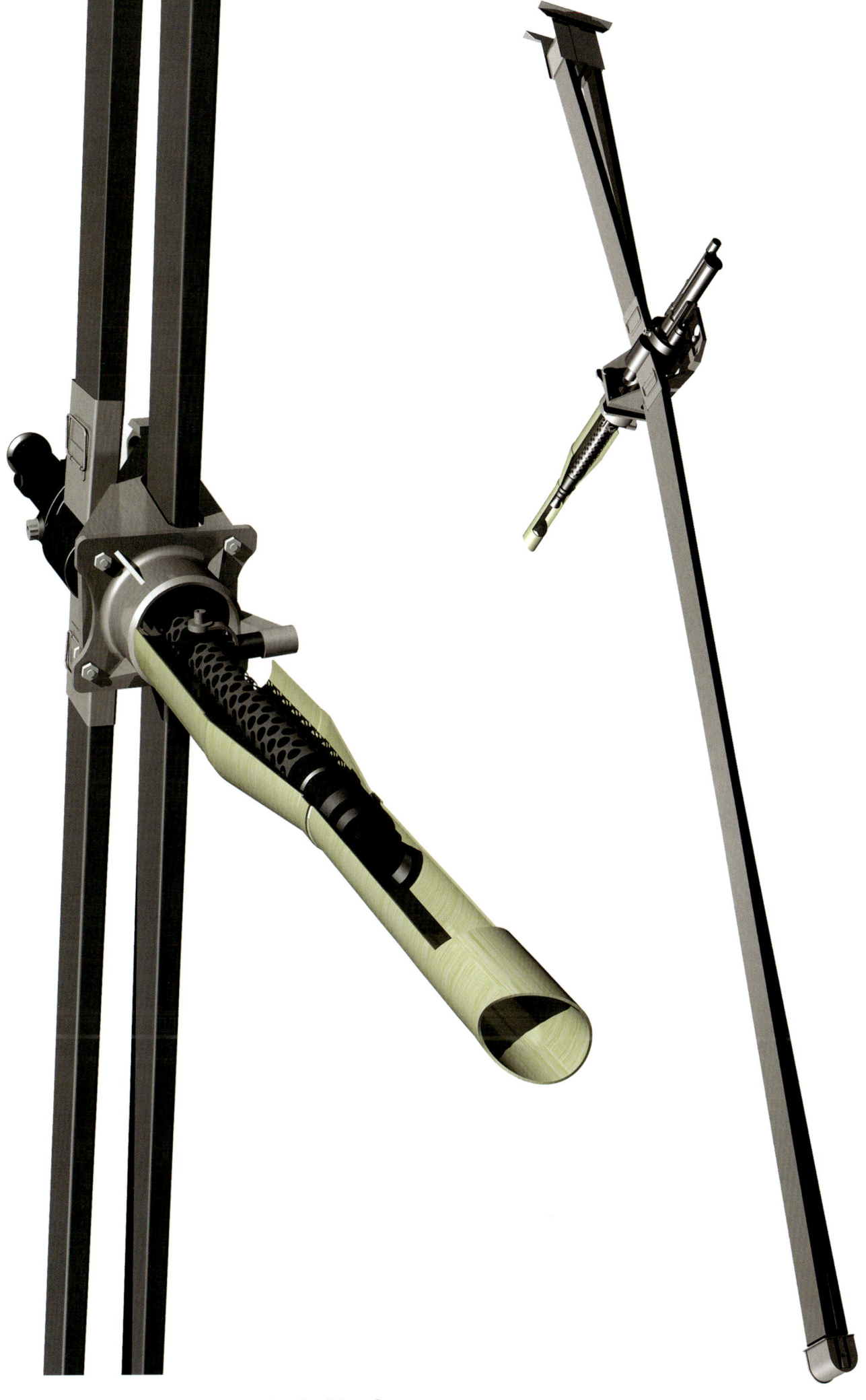

169

Cross-section of a Messerschmitt Bf 109 D-1 fuselage.

Close-up of a Messerschmitt Bf 109 D-1 fuselage cross-section with windscreen and wing fitting.

Messerschmitt Bf 109 Early Versions

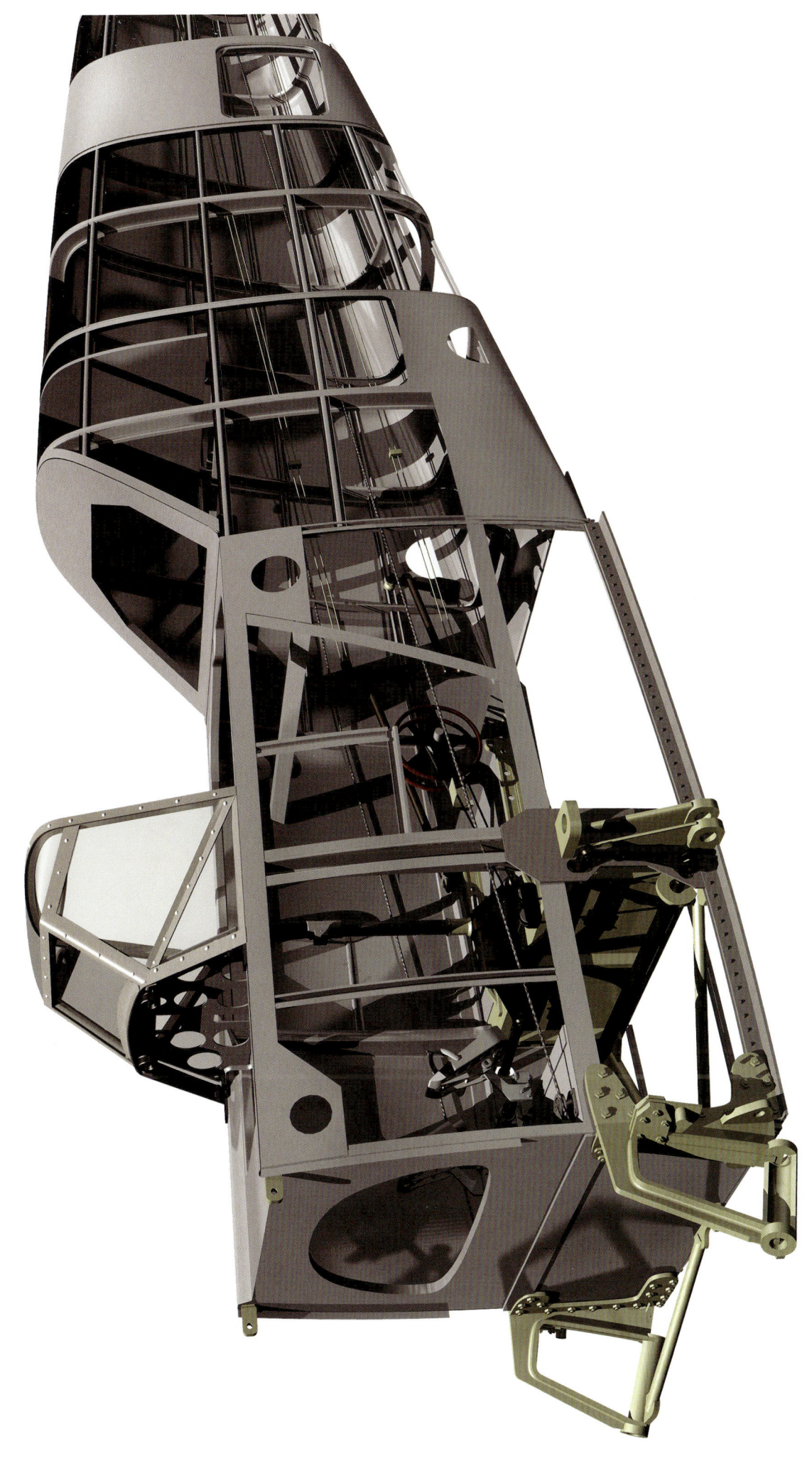

Cross-section of central part of Messerschmitt Bf 109 D-1 fuselage (with cockpit).

Cross-section of Messerschmitt Bf 109 D-1 fuselage, note main fuel tank under the cockpit.

Messerschmitt Bf 109 Early Versions

Cross-section of a Messerschmitt Bf 109 D-1 with main undercarriage.

Cross-section of a Messerschmitt Bf 109 D-1 fuselage, tail view.

Visualization 3D Asen Atanasov

Close-up of a Messerschmitt Bf 109 D-1 fuselage cross-section.

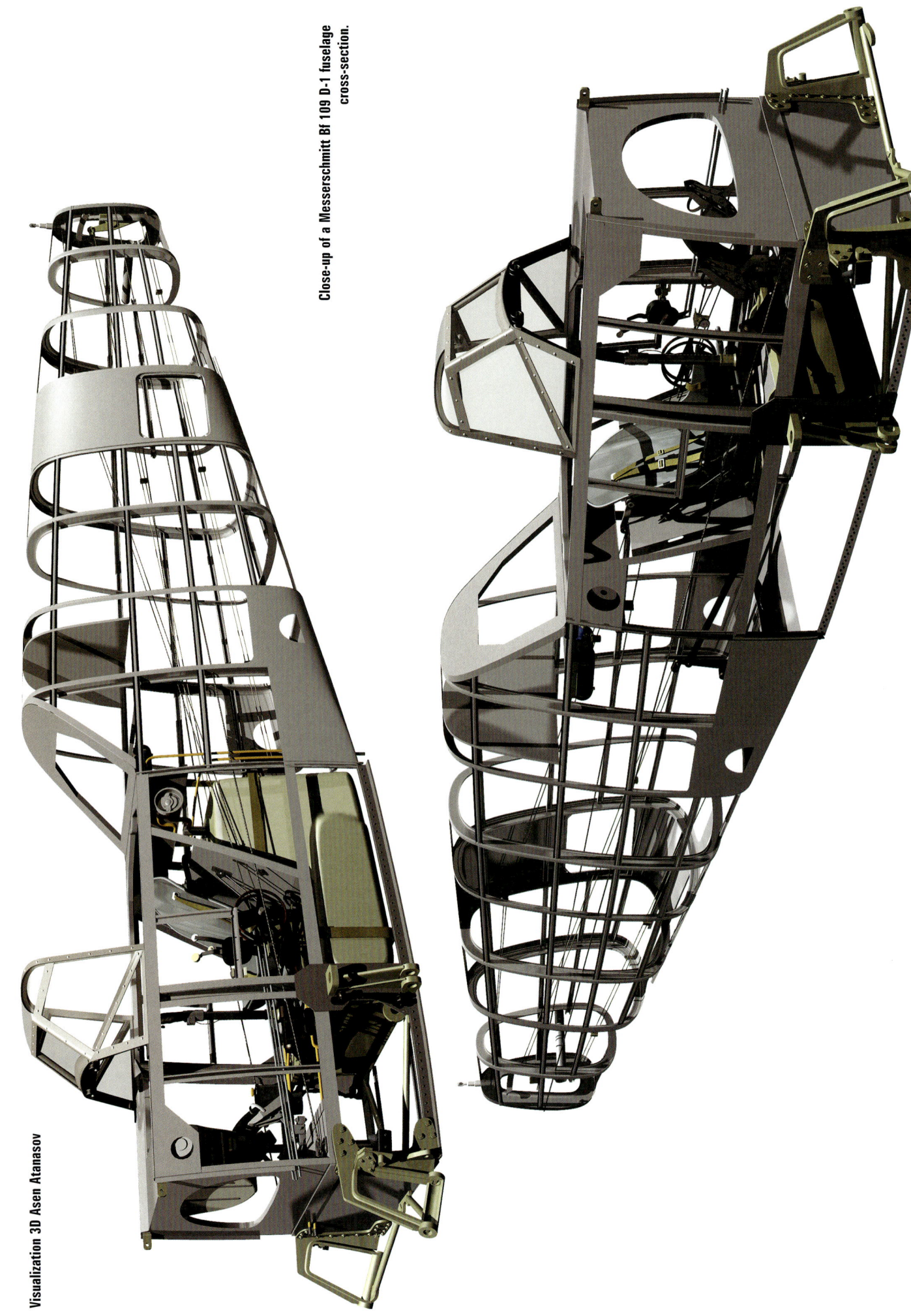

Painted by Janusz Światłoń

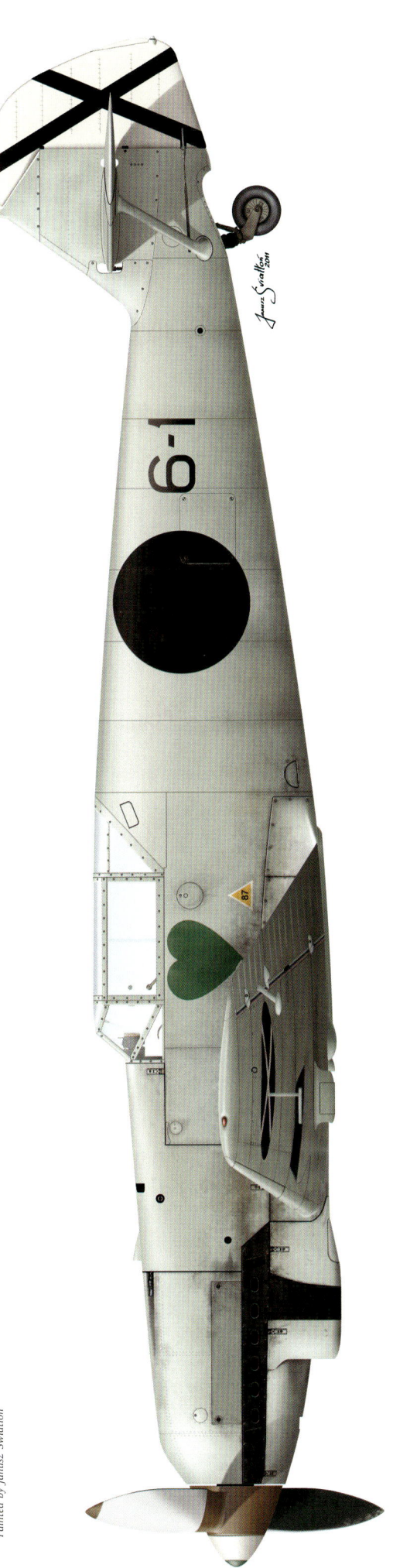

Messerschmitt Bf 109 V3, W.Nr. 760, 6-1 from VJ/88. The aircraft was flown by Obr. Hannes Trautloft of the Condor Legion. Tablada airfield, Spain, January 1937. The aircraft features natural duralumin finish with a thin clear coat of preservative paint giving the airframe its distinctive greenish hue. Front surfaces of the propeller blades painted silver; rear surfaces sprayed with anti-reflective paint (RLM 70?). The blades' mid-section and tips in natural, dark wood finish. The same color predominates on the propeller spinner, except a white ring around its front section. The tip of the spinner is painted green. The green heart motif painted under the cockpit.

Messerschmitt Bf 109 V7, W.Nr. 881, D-IJHA flown by Dipl.Ing. Carl Francke. Zürich-Dübendorf, Switzerland, late July 1937. The aircraft features an overall silver-grey finish (highly polished L40/52 paint). The registration is painted in black on both sides of the fuselage and on the wing's upper and lower surfaces. The black numeral "1" is painted on a white rectangle. Black "V7" is painted just forward of the windshield framing on the port side of the fuselage.

Painted by Janusz Światłoń

Messerschmitt Bf 109 D-1, 6•86, 1.J/88, pilot: Hptm. Siebelt Reents of the Condor Legion. Spain, September 1938. Upper and side surfaces painted RLM 63 Hellgrau; lower surfaces feature a coat of RLM 65 Hellblau. The unit's badge is painted on the left side of the fuselage. Large national markings painted on the wings, wingtips painted white.

Messerschmitt Bf 109 D-1, Stab I./ZG 2, pilot: Hptm. Johannes Gentzen. Groß Stein airfield, Germany, September 1939. The paint scheme is a combination of RLM 70 Schwarzgrün, RLM 71 Dunkelgrün and RLM 65 Hellblau. The unit's badge painted against silver background under the windshield. Vertical stabilizer features two white bars. The chevron is white with a black outline.

Painted by Janusz Świątoń

Messerschmitt Bf 109 D-1, W.Nr. 2079, 11.(N)/JG 2, Trondheim-Vaernes, Norway, May 1940. Upper surfaces painted RLM 71 Dunkelgrün and RLM 02 Grau. RLM 65 Hellblau was used on lower and side surfaces. "N 9" painted in black with a thin, white outline. Also black is the serial number painted on the fin.

Messerschmitt Bf 109 B-1, 6•36, 1.J/88, pilot. Hptm. Harro Harder. Condor Legion airfield at Santander, Spain, September 7, 1937. The aircraft features a standard Luftwaffe splinter camouflage scheme consisting of RLM 70 Schwarzgrün and RLM 71 Dunkelgrün on the upper and side surfaces. Lower surfaces feature overall RLM 65 Hellblau finish. The wingtips are painted white. The propeller blades in natural metal finish with dark (RLM 70?) rear surfaces. Three white victory bars are painted on the fighter's fin.

Messerschmitt Bf 109 D-1, 6•79, 3.J/88. The aircraft was flown by Hptm. Werner Mölders during his service with the Condor Legion. Spain, November 1938. Upper and side surfaces painted RLM 63 Hellgrau, while lower surfaces feature the RLM 65 Hellblau finish. The propeller spinner is red, wingtips are painted white. Also white are the victory bars on the vertical stabilizer and the inscription "Luchs".

Messerschmitt Bf 109 A, 6•6, 2.J/88, pilot: Uffz. Herbert Ihlefeld. Condor Legion airfield at Escratión, Spain, June 2, 1938. The aircraft features a natural metal finish with a thin, clear coat of preservative paint giving the airframe the distinctive greenish hue. The propeller blades in natural metal finish with dark (RLM 70?) rear surfaces. Wingtips are painted white. The unit's badge appears only on the left side of the fuselage.

Painted by Janusz Światłoń

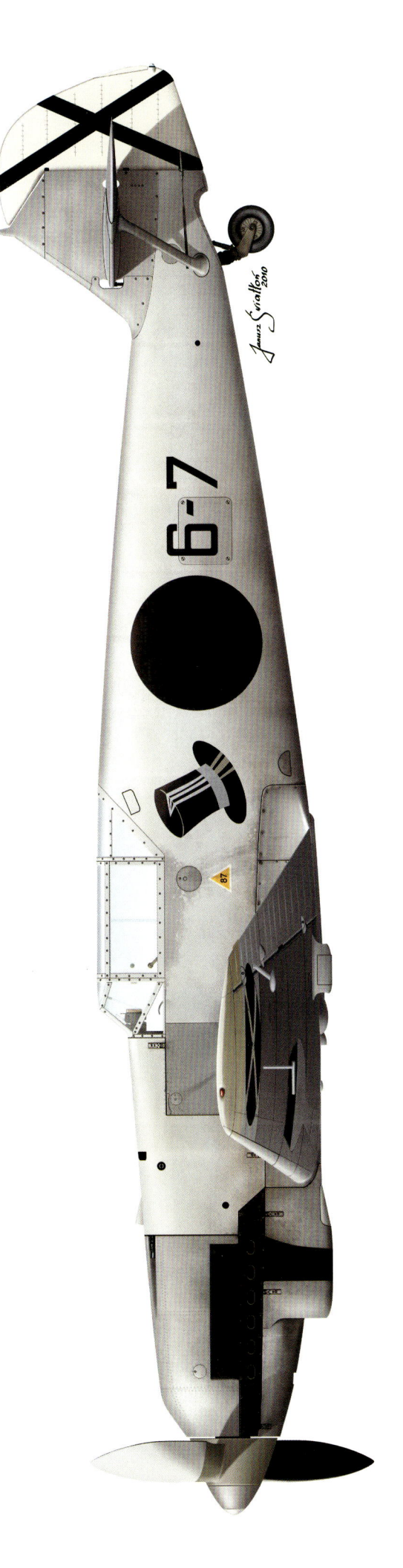

Messerschmitt Bf 109 A; ,Black 6-7', flown by Fw. Norbert Flegel of 2. J/88, Legion Condor, La Albericia airfield, Santander, Spain, August-September 1937. The plane was left in natural metal finish like all Bf 109s initially delivered to Spain. Its fuselage seams were most likely puttied. This machine carried standard identification markings of the Legion Condor, which consisted of black roundels painted on the fuselage and wings (here supplemented with white St. Andrew's crosses), and a white rudder with both sides marked with black St. Andrew's crosses. It also had white wingtips. The black code 6-7 was applied to the fuselage aft black roundel. It denoted the type of the aircraft (6) and its subsequent number (7). The top hat emblem of 2. J/88 was carried on the portside of the fuselage only. The aircraft survived a take-off accident and after the repair was later flown by Werner Mölders and Rolf Pingel.

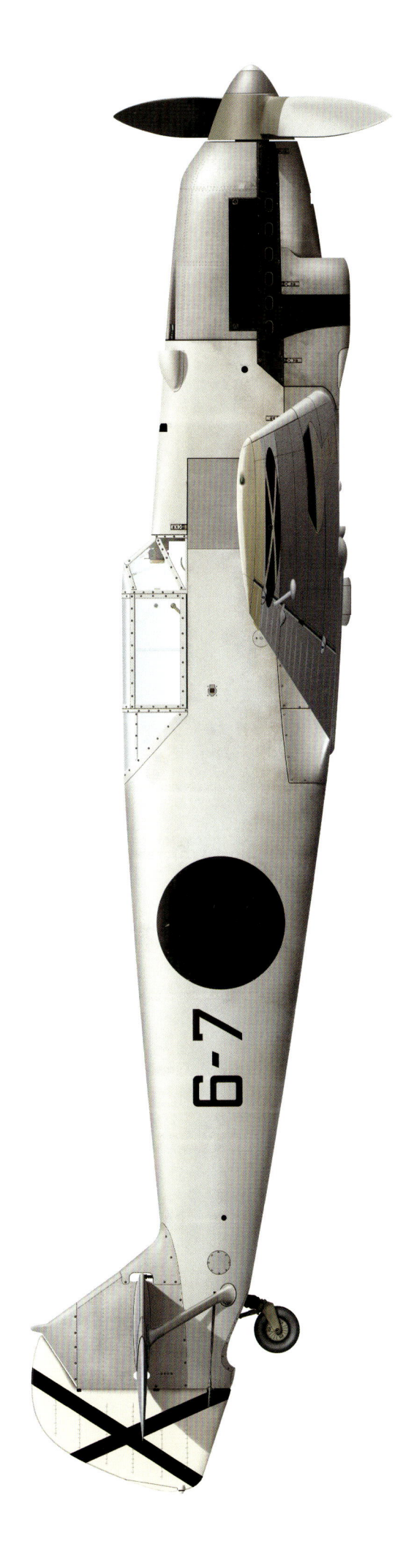

Painted by Janusz Światłoń

Messerschmitt Bf 109 D-1; W.Nr. 2302, ,White J-307' probably of Überwachungsgeschwader, Dübendorf, Switzerland, June 1945. Swiss Bf 109 D-1s were delivered in a RLM 70/65 scheme with a hard demarcation line between the colours. They had Swiss-produced armament and therefore a different fairing was installed on the fuselage in front of the windscreen, the access panels to the wings' gun bays were also modified., J-307' is presented here with distinctive neutrality markings, which were applied from mid-September 1944. Red and white bands were added to the already existing broad red bands with white Helvetic crosses on the fuselage and wings. The engine cowling, wing tips and horizontal tail tips were painted white. The rudder was red and sported a small white cross. The stencils were bilingual: German and French. W.Nr. 2302 was disposed on 28 December 1949.

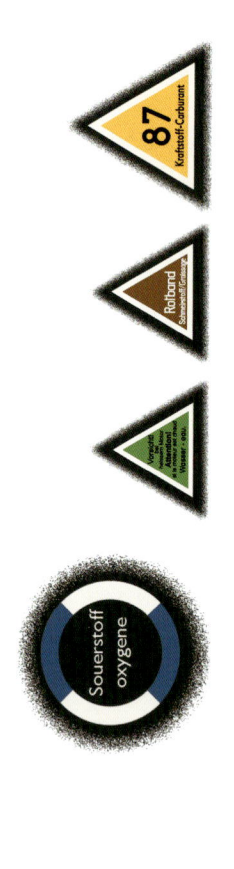

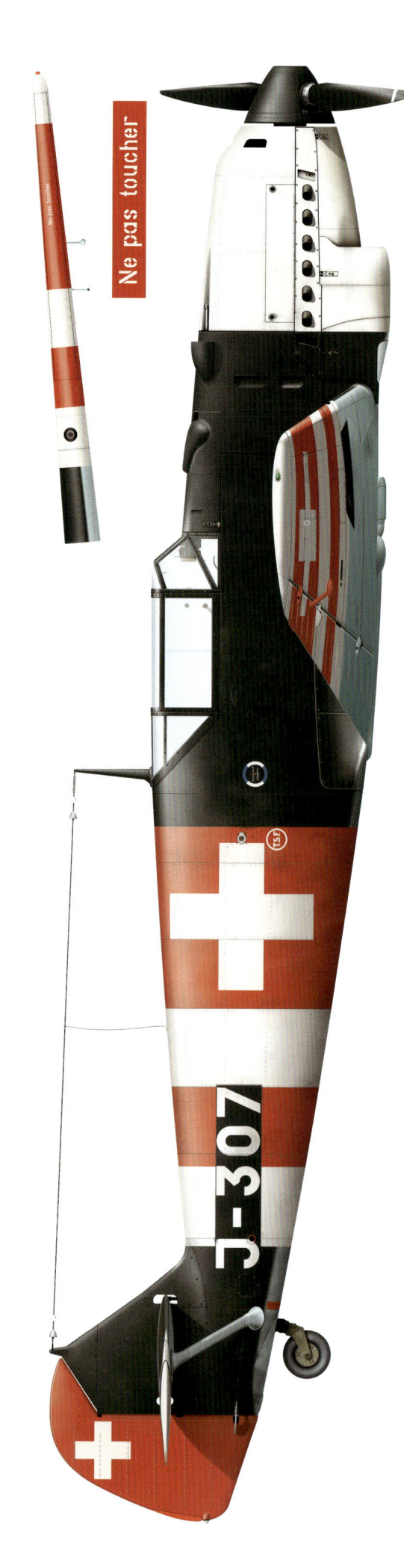

Painted by Janusz Światłoń

Painted by Janusz Światłoń

Painted by Janusz Światoń

Messerschmitt Bf 109 B-1; Black 6•34', flown by Obrit. Erich Woitke of 1. J/88, Legion Condor, Alfamén airfield, Spain, February 1938. 'Black 6•34' was most likely left in its original pattern of RLM 70/71 on the uppersurfaces with RLM 65 underside. The black roundels on the fuselage were supplemented with little white diagonal crosses - a marking of 1. Staffel. Otherwise, the identification markings are typical for the aircraft used in Spain. At some point the fuselage marking convention was changed and here included the type number (6), black roundel and then the individual aircraft number (34). The plane is presented without 4 white victory markings, which were probably painted on the fin during the later period.

Messerschmitt Bf 109 D-1, 'White N+5', flown by Lt. Joachim Böhner of 10.(N)/ZG 26, Hage, Germany, early January 1940. This plane was just repainted in the so-called '40er-Anstrich'. A splinter pattern of RLM 71 and 02 was applied to the uppersurfaces, the fuselage sides and underneath were painted RLM 65. The emblem of the Staffel, a black cat, was carried on the portside of the fuselage only. The Staffel was redesignated 10.(N)/JG 26 on 5 January 1940.

Messerschmitt Bf 109 D-1 of Stab I./JG 131, Jesau, Germany, Spring 1938. This aircraft had RLM 70 and 71 uppersurfaces with RLM 65 beneath. The 'Jesau Kreuz' badge of the Gruppe was painted below the cockpit on both sides of the fuselage. Please note the white ring on the spinner, which indicates that the plane belonged to the Gruppe HQ flight, and the highly unusual markings in the form of black chevron and lightning, both outlined in white. The size of the crosses and position of the swastika are typical for this period.

Painted by Janusz Światłoń

Messerschmitt Bf 109 C-1, <+I from Stab I./JG 20 (later Stab III./JG 51), Berlin-Döberitz, Germany, August 1939. The aircraft features standard Luftwaffe splinter camouflage scheme consisting of RLM 70 Schwarzgrün and RLM 71 Dunkelgrün patches on the upper and lower airframe surfaces. Lower surfaces painted with a coat of RLM 65 Hellblau.

Messerschmitt Bf 109 B-1, 3+- from 5./JG 132 "Richthofen", Jüterbog-Damm airfield, August 1937. The fighter sports standard Luftwaffe splinter camouflage of RLM 70 Schwarzgrün and RLM 71 Dunkelgrün applied to the upper and side airframe surfaces. Lower surfaces painted RLM 65 Hellblau.

Painted by Janusz Światłoń

Messerschmitt Bf 109 D-1 marked 'Red 11' of 2./JG 71; Fürstenfeldbruck, September 1939. The aircraft is finished in RLM 70 Schwarzgrün, RLM 71 Dunkelgrün and RLM 65 Hellblau, the greens are in low contrast. Of interest are white stripe in the rear part of the spinner and the unit's emblem painted under cockpit.

Visualization 3D Bolek Rykowski

Messerschmitt Bf 109 D-1 marked 'White 2' flown by the Staffelkapitän of 1./ZG 2 Oblt. Waldemar von Roon; Groß-Stein, Upper Silesia, September 1939. The aircraft is finished in RLM 70 Schwarzgrün, RLM 71 Dunkelgrün and RLM 65 Hellblau, the greens are in low contrast. Of special interest is the black-white-black fuselage band. Front end of spinner is white. The 'Schwarze Hand' on the engine cowling is the Staffel emblem, and the 'Bernburger Jäger' under cockpit is the Gruppe badge.

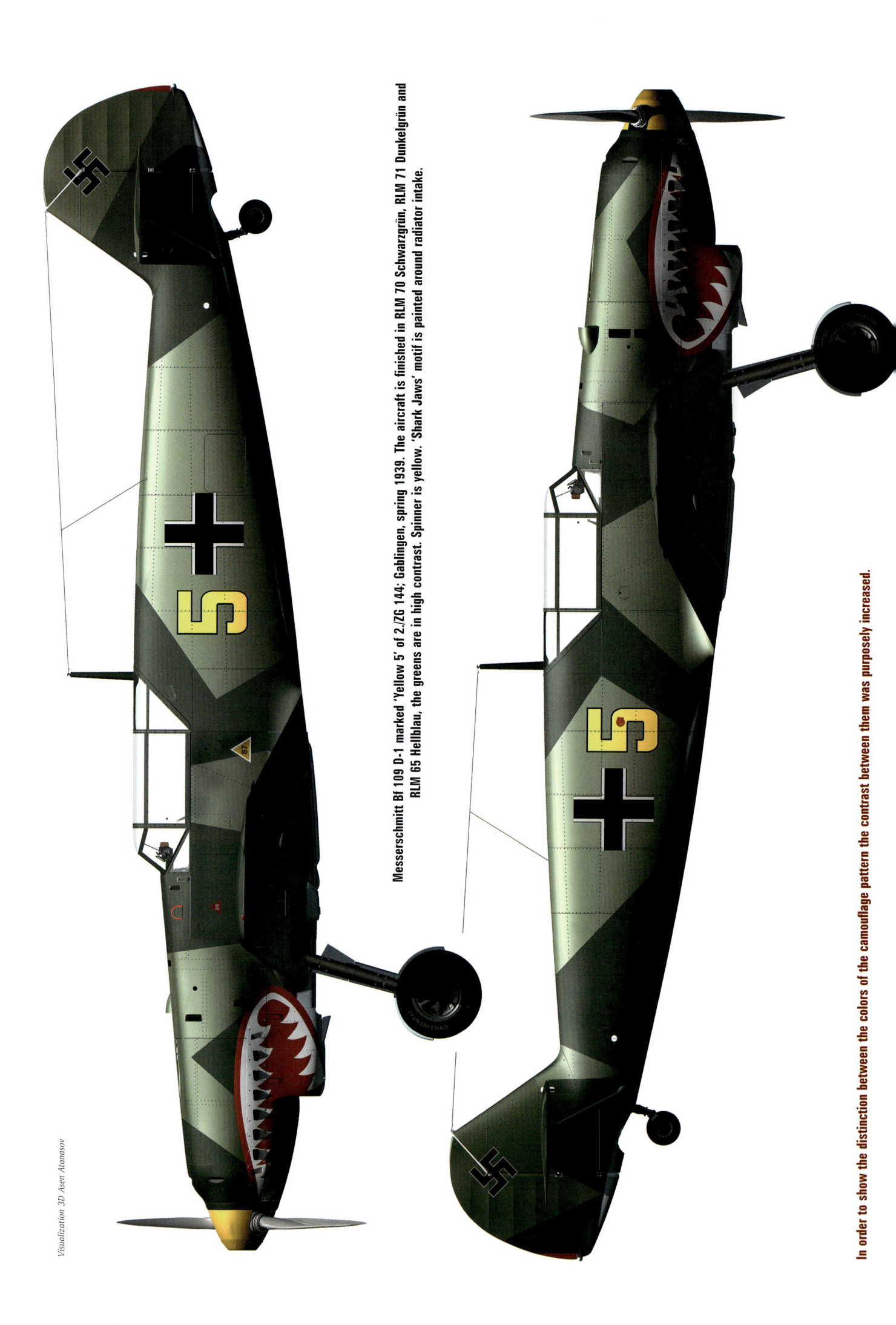

Messerschmitt Bf 109 D-1 marked 'Yellow 5' of 2./ZG 144; Gablingen, spring 1939. The aircraft is finished in RLM 70 Schwarzgrün, RLM 71 Dunkelgrün and RLM 65 Hellblau, the greens are in high contrast. Spinner is yellow. 'Shark Jaws' motif is painted around radiator intake.

Visualization 3D Asen Atanasov

In order to show the distinction between the colors of the camouflage pattern the contrast between them was purposely increased.

RLM 65 (FS 35414)

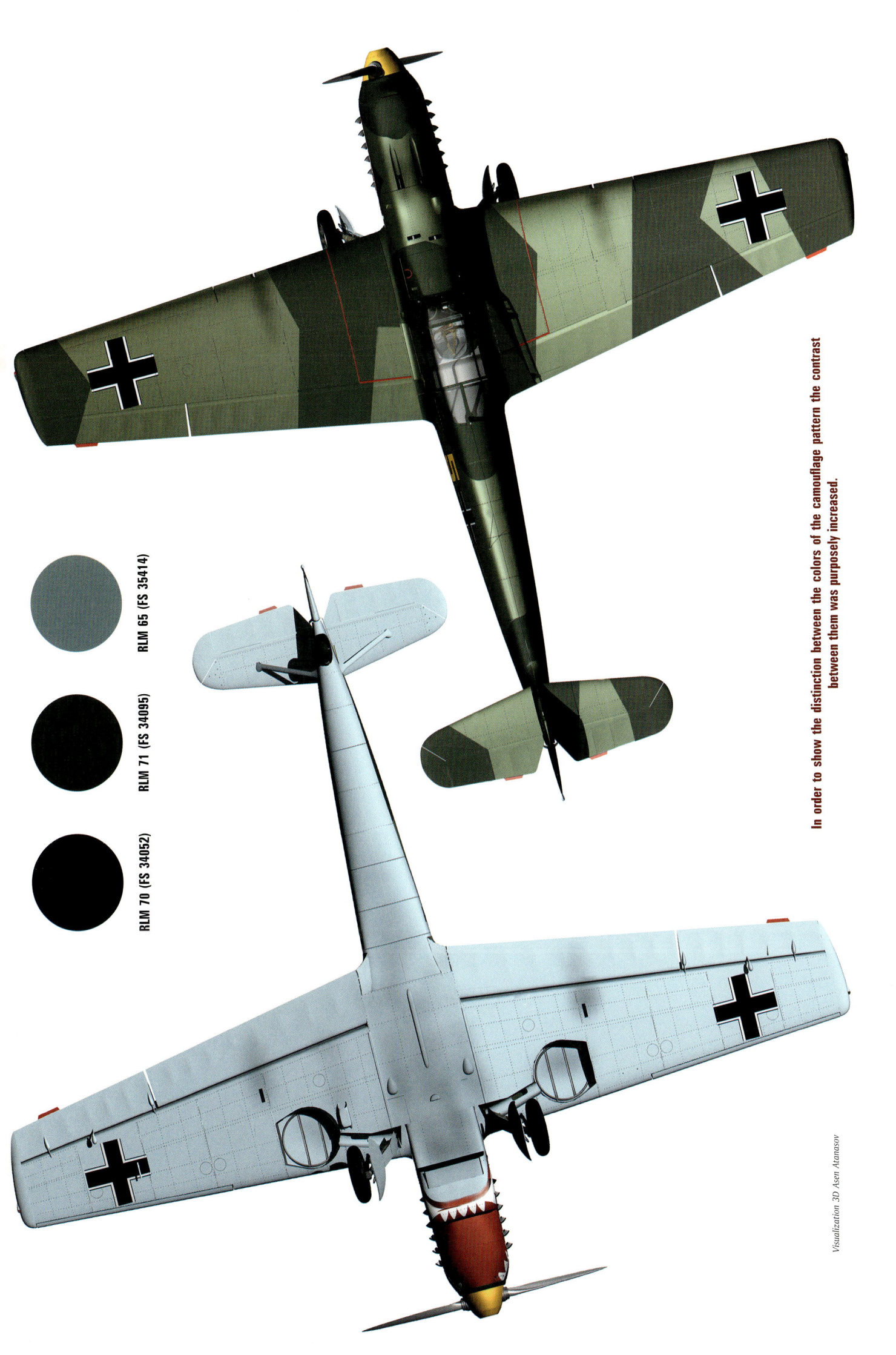

RLM 71 (FS 34095)

RLM 70 (FS 34052)

In order to show the distinction between the colors of the camouflage pattern the contrast between them was purposely increased.

Visualization 3D Asen Atanasov

Messerschmitt Bf 109 D-1 marked 'Yellow 5' of 2./ZG 144; Gablingen, spring 1939. The aircraft is finished in RLM 70 Schwarzgrün, RLM 71 Dunkelgrün and RLM 65 Hellblau, the greens are in high contrast. Spinner is yellow. 'Shark Jaws' motif is painted around radiator intake.

Visualization 3D Asen Atanasov

In order to show the distinction between the colors of the camouflage pattern the contrast between them was purposely increased.

In order to show the distinction between the colors of the camouflage pattern the contrast between them was purposely increased.

Visualization 3D Asen Atanasov

Coming soon

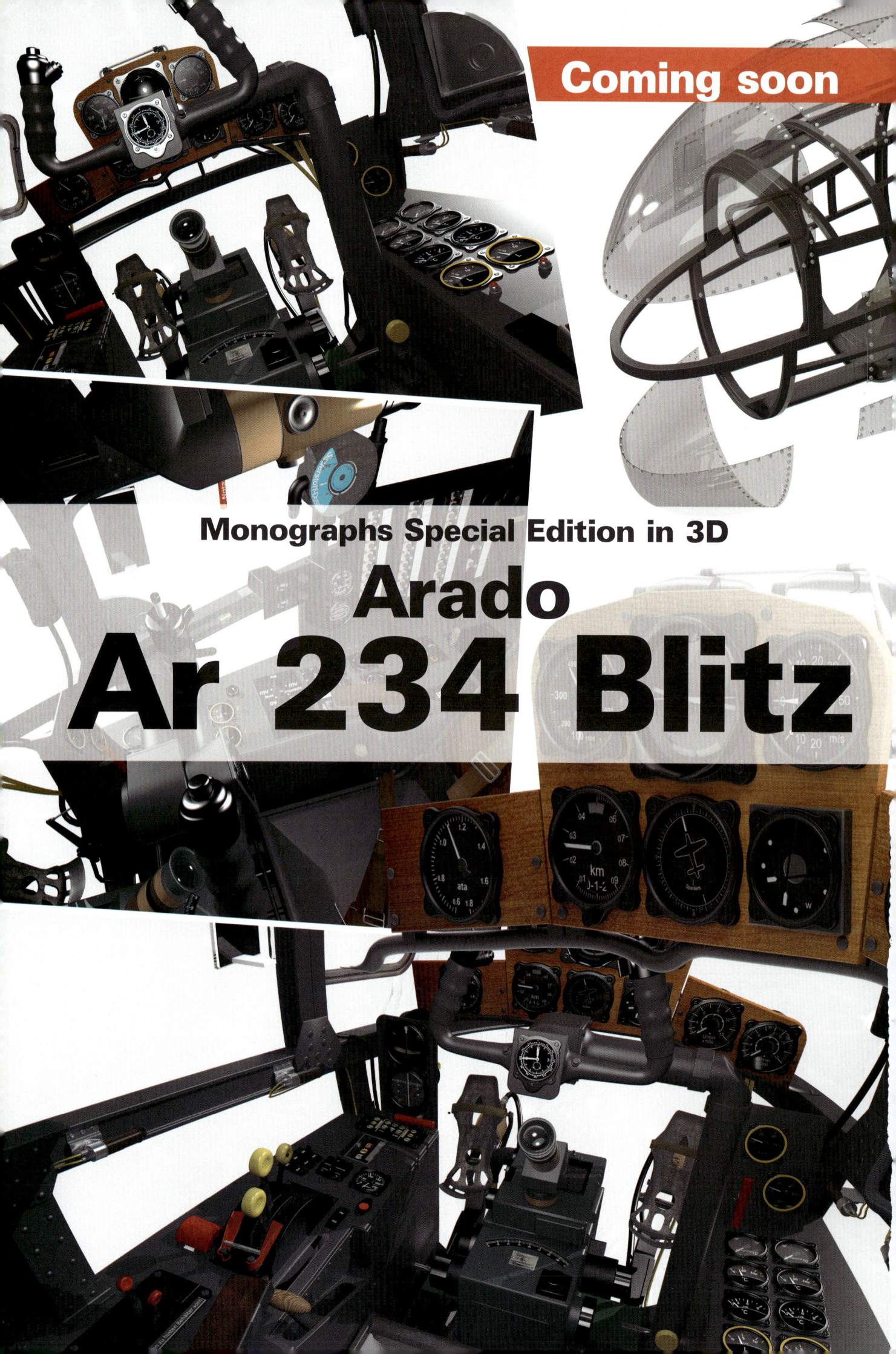

Monographs Special Edition in 3D

Arado
Ar 234 Blitz